Hiking Whatcom County

Fourth Edition

Ken Wilcox

110 Hikes & Walks

Along the coast, in town, in the lowlands & foothills,
around Mount Baker & in the North Cascades

Plus Parks, Viewpoints, Water Access & Campgrounds

Northwest Wild Books
Bellingham, Washington

Hiking Whatcom County
4th Edition

© Copyright 1986, 1990, 1996, 2000 & 2003 by Ken Wilcox.

ISBN: 0-9617879-8-8
Northwest Wild Books
Bellingham, Washington

Photography and maps by the author, except page 200, by David Longdon. Designed & published by Northwest Wild Books. No old-growth trees were harmed by the printing of this book. Manufactured in the U.S.A.

Front cover: Iceberg Lake and Herman Saddle; Glacier Lilies on the Boundary Way Trail; Nooksack Falls; and Marine Park in Blaine.

Back cover: Mount Baker from Table Mountain; tiger lilies at Welcome Pass; Shadow of the Sentinels Trail; and Diablo Lake.

Hiking guides from Northwest Wild Books...
> Hiking Snohomish County (1998)
> Hiking the San Juan Islands (includes Whidbey Island; 2001)
> Hiking Whatcom County, 4th Edition (2003)
> Hiking Skagit County (Summer 2003)
See www.nwwildbooks.com for more.

We welcome your comments, corrections, kudos, criticisms and/or suggestions regarding current and future editions of these titles. Write us at NW Wild Books, P.O. Box 4003, Bellingham, WA 98227, or email: info@nwwildbooks.com.

Foreword

AMAZING BUT TRUE, it's been nearly 16 years since the scruffy first edition of *Hiking Whatcom County* was published in 1987. What began as a trim collection of 44 favorites expanded to 62 walks and hikes by the third edition in 1996. A couple of new trails were added with a reprint in 2000, and now, with the release of the fourth edition, the listings have expanded considerably to more than 100.

That is not to say that there are now many more trails to hike in the wilds of Whatcom (there are some great new ones), but instead reveals a desire to make this a much more comprehensive guide than in the past. It also makes this book more consistent with two other recent guides to Snohomish County and the San Juan Islands, as well as a forthcoming guide to Skagit County (also due out in 2003). For areas beyond Snohomish County, and for the Washington Cascades generally, Harvey Manning's work remains the prime source for the modern Northwest trailster.

In this major upgrade of *Hiking Whatcom County* all the previous listings have been updated, and nearly every trail was hiked anew. Each new listing is current as of late 2002. All the maps and most of the photos are new, and details have been added for many hikes, such as improved driving directions, hiking distances, elevation gains, views, features of interest, potential campsites, water availability, best times to visit, and the like. To further enrich the hiking experience, tidbits of natural or cultural history have been added where space allows.

Two trips from the previous edition were dropped: a former beach access at Birch Point (it was fenced off by the owners), and the Chilliwack River Trail, accessed from Canada, which suffered from major blowdown and trail damage a few years ago—although some of the more ambitious 'shwackers among us could probably still manage it (see *Other Hikes* for directions to the Chilliwack River trailhead).

On a more philosophical note (there is hidden meaning between these covers), there is something inherently nice about walking on trails. I don't know what it is, but it seems to have something to do with being sumptuously immersed in nature—the trees, rocks, birds, bugs, slugs, fresh air and streams that babble on forever. It's not at all like running or biking or driving a car. Hiking, even briskly, tends to slow us down considerably, keeping us young and smiling—and probably a lot less stressed. In fact, I have never encountered an unfriendly or unhappy camper on the trail—with the possible exception of a cranky kid once or twice. If only we could encourage everyone to experience trails and wilderness on occasion... not all at once, of course.

Around Whatcom County, unmitigated nature is powerful stuff. The most memorable hikes are really encounters with wildness: the sight of a startled black bear sprinting to avoid your approach, a thunderous calving of ice on the Deming Glacier, the whistle of a marmot in the fog at Morovits Meadows, the first crop of avalanche lilies blooming in the late-spring snow, the lonely hoot of an owl in an old-growth forest, the wondrous stench of spawned-out salmon in Chuckanut Creek, Nooksack Falls at flood stage after a fall storm, a raven making off with your lunch...

The contrast of these experiences with the more familiar realities of working and shopping in America is striking, to say the least. Over-population, climate change, extinction of species, diminishing water resources, pollution, human greed, and the non-sustainable exploitation of the Earth's resources underscore an urgent challenge to us all: to protect what remains of the wildness we inherited from those who preceded us. This isn't a matter of being green and fashionable, or ranting an old environmental tune. It's becoming perilously clear that protecting and restoring wild places are among the most critically important things we can do as enlightened people.

In the earlier editions, I wrote: "At last, some say a new environmental ethic is emerging, that people care more about this remarkable blue planet. We don't want to give up our cars or our habits of excess consumption, but at least we care (ditto heads and anti-enviro fanatics notwithstanding). If true, this new ethic, a positive long-term shift in fundamental societal values, may help us zero in on the harder personal and community choices still waiting to be made..."

While some of us really do care, many of our fellow *homo sapiens* are still buying trophy homes and gas-guzzling SUVs, while most of our leaders, including the most anti-environmental dingbat president America has ever known (I'm trying to be generous), seem far more interested in big-money politics than in the fundamental stuff of life.

Yet the reasons for optimism continue to expand, especially here in Whatcom County. It helps that people really do seem to love this place.

Efforts to protect wildlife, to expand our designated wilderness areas, to restore salmon streams, to create new parks and trails, to demand access to renewable energy, and to make our communities more livable and sustainable are all grounds for optimism. So if you're not already involved, find a cause and get to it.

On the trail, the choices we make ring clear. On the trail, "worries drop off like leaves" John Muir once said. Time slows down. Reality stares us down and we begin to get our priorities straight, whatever they may be.

Well, all the worries aside, hiking is also just plain fun. As always, I hope this book is most useful in that regard.

Happy trails,

Ken Wilcox
March, 2003

Acknowledgments
One can never issue enough thank-yous to those who assist with or inspire the work of writing a book. Advice, assistance and support which helped make this book a reality came from many great friends and hiking buddies, like Keith K., Bud H., Kiko A., Peter M., and most especially Susan K. whose encouragement and companionship reach far beyond this little guidebook.

Others who helped me along the way, on and off the trail, include Joan C., Bob and Lynne M., Betty P., Chuck, Dee and friends at Village Books, Mike R., Jean K., Wendy S., Helga W., Steve W., Jim O., Ed H., Lynne P., Lorraine B., Jerry H., Stuart Z., Gordon S. and Sara R. Agency trail staff are always a pleasure to work with, among them Tim W., Susan W. and Chuck M. with Bellingham Parks, Roger D., Lynne G. and Steve L. with Whatcom County Parks, and Lief H., Kevin K. and the front desk folks at the Mount Baker District office and Glacier Public Service Center of the U.S. Forest Service. Special thanks to David Longdon for use of his Sourdough Mountain photo (*Hike #98*), and to Fiona C. and others at the Bellingham Herald for their kind coverage.

DISCLAIMER
This guidebook is intended for use by competent hikers who accept the inherent and sometimes unpredictable hazards associated with the activity. Read the introductory material and be sure of your ability to safely hike any of the trails listed before venturing out.
The user assumes all risks!

Contents

Walks & Hikes   👣 = Easiest / 👣 👣 👣 👣 = Most Difficult

The Coast—

Urban Areas—

The Chuckanuts—

Lowlands & Foothills—

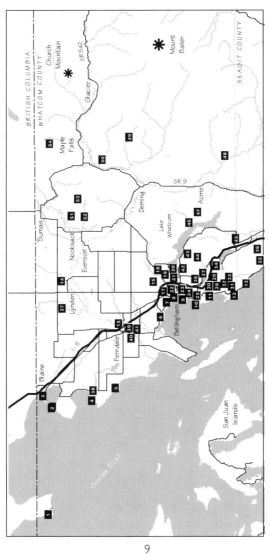

Whatcom County - West

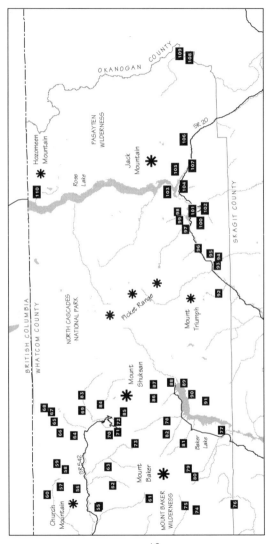

Whatcom County - East

Mount Baker Area—

The North Cascades—

A few author recommendations:

Best for visitors & newcomers...
    Easy: 3, 7, 8, 12, 22, 24, 25, 26, 39, 46, 49, 70,77, 95, 104
    Moderate: 20, 31, 36, 45, 101
    More Difficult: 29, 30, 35, 49, 58, 61, 62, 66, 67, 68, 70, 73, 79, 85, 91, 99, 108
    Most Difficult: 56, 80, 83, 92, 98, 105, 106

Best by season...
    Spring: 2, 3, 13, 14, 20, 22, 26, 30, 31, 34, 35, 36, 38, 39, 45, 46, 50, 52, 55, 77, 88, 89, 94, 95, 96, 99, 101, 104, 107, 110
    Summer: All hikes are good in summer!
    Fall: 19, 20, 22, 23, 26, 28, 29, 30, 31, 33, 35, 36, 44, 45, 46, 49, 52, 55, 56, 58, 61, 62, 67, 68, 70, 71, 79, 83, 84, 85, 91, 93, 99, 101, 107, 108, 109, 110
    Winter: All lowland hikes plus: 55, 77, 89, 93, 94, 101,

Best by area...
    The Coast: 2, 3, 5, 7, 8, 9, 11, 12, 13
    Urban Areas: 14, 19, 20, 22, 23, 24, 26
    Chuckanuts: 29, 30, 31, 32, 33, 35, 36
    Lowlands & Foothills: 39, 43, 45, 46, 49
    Mount Baker: 56, 58, 61, 62, 66, 67, 68, 70, 73, 77, 79, 80
    North Cascades: 83, 85, 88, 89, 91, 92, 95, 98, 99, 101, 104, 105, 108, 109

Best for kids...
    Easy: 1, 2, 3, 5, 7, 9, 12, 13, 14, 17, 24, 25, 26, 28, 39, 40, 46, 51, 54, 55, 70, 71, 77, 93, 94, 95, 96, 102, 104, 107, 109
    Moderate: 4, 20, 21, 23, 31, 36, 43, 45, 88, 89, 97, 101
    More Difficult (for older, stronger kids): 30, 35, 49, 58, 62, 63, 66, 68, 69, 70, 71, 73, 74, 79, 85, 91, 99, 103, 108, 109, 110

Old-growth Douglas Fir, Shadow of the Sentinels Trail.

Introduction

The surprising diversity of nature in Whatcom County, Washington, is indeed a delight to explore on foot. Numerous parks and hundreds of miles of trails provide access to storm-sculpted rocky shorelines, rain-shadow beaches, lowland fields and flowers, lakes, streams, verdant forests, waterfalls, and the breathtaking alpine meadows, glaciers and towering peaks of the North Cascades, making this one of the most enjoyable regions to walk in Northwest America.

This guidebook offers a comprehensive selection of the region's trails, from the easiest walks to the most strenuous hikes in each part of the county. An emphasis has been given to trails in the lowlands and the Mount Baker area that aren't well described elsewhere; however, much more is included. Although the overall focus of this guide is on day hikes, many routes do offer attractive overnight backpacking possibilities. Listings of parks, campgrounds, viewpoints, and water access areas around the county are also included.

While many hikers may be content to wander aimlessly and soak up the views, a much richer experience can be expected for those who make the effort to inform themselves of some of the cultural and natural history of a particular place, or who learn to identify the rocks and minerals or the more common plant and animal species and their signs and sounds, or who take the time to read or hear what others have experienced about a place (or about themselves) in their brush with the wild. A few resources to help accomplish this are suggested, although sometimes it's enough to hit the trail simply to escape the common annoyances of the work-a-day world.

Read on for a short background on this place called Whatcom County, including a brief overview of present and future trails in the region, an environmental and historical synopsis of the county, a bit more on the weather, and suggestions for further reading.

Those who are new to hiking and who could use some extra guidance, turn to page 33, "**What to Know Before You Go**." Then see "**How to Use This Book**" on page 46 for an explanation of the trail listings.

Trails in Whatcom County

When Highways Were Trails

Before any of the white guys with furs, shovels, axes and dollar-sign eyes arrived here in the mid-1800s, native people had been calling this land home for at least 8,000 years—an era when land transportation consisted only of trails and feet. To live, play, gather, hunt, fish, trade, explore and marvel at the Creator's impressive work, ancestors of the Lummi, Nooksack, Skagit and other tribes blazed trails along the coast, up the rivers, and into the mountains in many directions. A few trails today still generally follow some of the old routes, like the way up Ruth Creek to Hannegan Pass, and along the Nooksack River and its Middle Fork to the Koma Kulshan volcano—Mount Baker, as most of us know it today. The Nooksacks and Skagits ventured into the high country around Mount Baker and the North Cascades to collect berries, bulbs and botanicals, to hunt mountain goats, deer and elk, to trade with others, to revere the spirits, and for some at least, to bask in the beauty of it all. The rivers and mountains remain important to these cultures today.

The non-native newcomers quickly utilized these routes and added to them, including a gold-seekers route along the Nooksack River through Sumas and Chilliwack to the interior of British Columbia, called the Whatcom Trail. Portions of this historic gold-rush trail can still be found at Manning Park in British Columbia, although Whatcom County has more or less forgotten its early significance. In *Nooksack Tales and Trails* (1949), historian, P. R. Jeffcott, described the 1858 completion of the Whatcom Trail this way:

> *Then, like a sudden thunderbolt, the long awaited news burst on the city of tents on Bellingham Bay... The Northern Light came out with an extra issue, proclaiming the good news: THE TRAIL THROUGH! NO HUMBUG THIS TIME!*
>
> *[Then] the firing of the 100 guns from the hill, and the reverberating answers from Sehome across the Bay. All afternoon, at regular intervals, the thundering kept up, until every native on the semi-circle of Bellingham Bay was aware that the great day had come--that the Trail was at last open.*

Headed up by Army Captain, Walter de Lacy, the Whatcom Trail was designed to make old Whatcom (now Bellingham) the prime jumping-off place for an emerging post-California gold rush on the Fraser and Thompson Rivers and beyond. The year the trail was completed, the gold rush attracted as many as 30,000 men, most of them Americans, and this new American route avoided the need to secure a permit in Victoria in order to take a boat up the Fraser River. If you were careful, you might also scoot in and out of Canada without paying the miners tax. The little town on Bellingham Bay was headed for the big time—or so it seemed.

The trail was extremely rough and entailed several weeks' travel for some parties to reach the placer mines of interior B.C., a distance we now drive in a few hours. A crude ferry ride negotiated the Nooksack River at The Crossing near Everson, while the Sumas River and other streams were crossed on giant fallen logs, hewn flat on the upper side to accommodate the hopeful travelers and their pack horses. The trail met the Chilliwack River, crossed the divide, and descended Little Beaver Creek to the Skagit River (now Ross Lake), then ran north to the Dewdney Trail linking Hope, B.C. to Princeton.

To the surprise of local business promoters and at least one flamboyant, no-humbug news editor, the Whatcom Trail proved too difficult and cumbersome for even the most starry-eyed, B.C.-bound prospector. Thus the Whatcom Trail never achieved its maker's dream. After the initial rush, only a few more gold-seekers, trappers and hunters used the route. Most of the trail was abandoned as steamship travel increased along the coast and up the Fraser River, and as other approaches materialized, from Semiahmoo Bay to Fort Langley, from Harrison Lake north, and from the Columbia River east of the mountains.

Many of those arriving at Bellingham Bay paused long enough, however, to fix their eyes on the rich resources of timber and coal closer at hand. More trails and then roads began to penetrate the vast wilderness. The Telegraph Trail headed north along the bay to Canada and Alaska and its intended continental crossing to Siberia. This too was largely abandoned after the Atlantic Ocean was spanned by a cable in 1866. By the 1870s, the Telegraph Road had been constructed up the Nooksack River to The Crossing at Everson. In 1883, the only other road to speak of was the Military Road to Fort Bellingham. Prospector trails ascended various tributaries of the Nooksack to the high meadowlands, though few significant strikes were ever made. Wherever a scant gold find inspired a serious mining effort, a more substantial trail was developed, and a few of those still exist today: in the Twin Lakes area, at Yellow Aster Meadows, Goat Mountain, Swift Creek, Ruby and Canyon Creeks (on the upper Skagit), and elsewhere.

In 1891, the legendary Joe Morovits homesteaded near Baker Lake and began his own quest for gold, singlehandedly constructing more than 40 miles of trails in the process. In 1908, a climbing party of 50 Mountaineers built a trail to Boulder Ridge on the east flank of Mount Baker; 39 reached the summit. A year later, the Mazamas of Oregon talked the Forest Service into extending the Deming Trail up the Nooksack's Middle Fork to ease access for their own expedition; 38 of them also made the summit.

The area's first forest rangers began to build trails around the turn of the century in order to patrol the new Washington Forest

Mount Larrabee (right) and the Border Peaks.

Reserve and to guard against fires and poaching. An extensive trail network on these federal lands persisted throughout the region until commercial logging destroyed most of it in the second half of the 20th century.

While the Chuckanut Mountains south of Bellingham were being railroad logged in the early 1920s, the Heather Meadows area northeast of Mount Baker was becoming a major focus of recreational development, as the Mount Baker Club and others successfully promoted the area for tourism. Those efforts brought construction of the predecessor of today's highway, as well as the elegant Mount Baker Lodge (later destroyed by fire) and many new trails, including the loops around Heather and Bagley Lakes and Table Mountain. In the 1930s, FDR's Civilian Conservation Corps, the celebrated CCC, put men to work on roads, trails, bridges, campgrounds, telephone lines, and fire lookouts. To our own good fortune, much of their outstanding work is still with us. (For more local history, see **www.whatcommuseum.org/history/** and **www.nps.gov/noca/history.htm**.)

Whatcom Trails Today

In the lowlands and foothills, many trails would ultimately be displaced by new roads, railroads, clearcut logging, private development and "no trespassing" signs, leaving very little still intact of the once extensive and informal trail system on public and private lands. Wide-scale logging in the foothills then in the North Cascades obliterated much more. With the creation of North Cascades National Park and Pasayten Wilderness in 1968, and the Mount Baker and Noisy-Diobsud Wilderness Areas in 1984, a substantial portion of the existing trails inventory was secure, at least in the most remote mountainous areas.

By 1990, the trails outlook for National Forest lands in the region improved considerably as the public finally succeeded in transforming federal land management policies away from the rapid liquidation of the people's forests and more toward environmental protection and low-impact recreation. Unfortunately, the Washington Department of Natural Resources (DNR) has resisted this trend and still maintains an outdated timber bias in its land management policies on our publicly-owned *state* lands. As a result, existing and potential trail opportunities on Blanchard Mountain, Sumas Mountain and in the Lake Whatcom Watershed may be at particular risk— not to mention the trees. While some logging is justfied, substantial portions of these areas simply should not be clearcut (see **www.ecosystem.org/** for more). Some private timberland owners have been kind enough to allow trail access in many areas, but they too appear to be as hungry as ever for smaller and smaller logs.

Also in 1990, the trails outlook for Bellingham brightened significantly when voters approved a multi-million dollar levy to acquire trails and open space in what's since become a nationally recognized urban greenway system. The popular levy was extended by voters in 1997. A similar county-wide measure has been discussed and is clearly needed, but more people will need to speak up soon to make it happen.

Other important initiatives in the region include the prospect of a 74-mile Bay-to-Baker Trail from Little Squalicum Beach to Shuksan Arm at the Mount Baker Ski Area. Although the project is advancing very slowly, portions of the route are in development in Bellingham and Everson (*see Hike #16*). A $120,000 grant for a five-mile portion of the Bay-to-Baker near Glacier was obtained in the early 1990s and more than 200 kids from the Nooksack Valley School District helped remove brush along the route. Yet the project was stalled by a handful of nay-sayers, even though the trail would clearly benefit both the economy and quality of life in the foothills. (Area residents who want this section completed should contact the county council or park department.)

A multi-agency master plan was completed in 1996 for an 80-plus-mile trail system on Chuckanut and Blanchard Mountains. This effort has been a bit more successful. The Hemlock and Raptor Ridge Trails envisioned in the plan have been completed (*see Hike #30*). Other new trails in the Chuckanuts would improve links between Bellingham, Larrabee State Park, Chuckanut Ridge, Pine and Cedar Lakes, Lost Lake, Lake Samish, Lizard and Lily Lakes, and Oyster Dome. One other master plan for an ambitious 50-mile multi-use trail generally along the coast from the Samish flats to White Rock B.C., referred to here as the Salish Coast Trail, was completed in

2000 (*see Hike #6*). Despite a $1.2 million federal grant received for the project, progress on development has been slow.

Other significant trail developments have occurred in the county in recent years, including a looped trail system at Squires Lake near I–5 on the Skagit County line (*Hike #45*). The Whatcom Land Trust was a key mover in this project, as well as the Canyon Lake Creek Community Forest (*Hike #49*) where several miles of new trails and converted logging roads now access both the lake and adjacent old-growth forest. The land trust and the county have also worked to acquire several miles of riverfront on the South Fork of the Nooksack River near Acme, where future trail development will accommodate access to the river, forest and the historic Nesset homestead.

Even with all this effort, there are still huge gaps in the regional trails system, albeit no shortage of good ideas. Various trail plans and the recreation chapter of the county's Comprehensive Plan identify numerous possibilities for new trails, including many loops and linkages, as well as routes interconnecting smaller communities, the Bellingham area trail network, and all major parks in the county. An extended trail along the Nooksack River remains a key component of the regional vision. Plans for new trails on the north end of Sumas Mountain (*Hike #52*) could bear fruit soon. Still simmering is the desire for at least some minimal form of trail access to Portage Island and the mountainous southern half of Lummi Island.

Hikers, equestrians and bicyclists have participated in developing these and other ideas for more trails in the region, and have identified a special need in rural areas where public trails of any real length are extremely lacking. Studies and surveys at the state and local level suggest that the majority of county residents not only use trails, but would support the acquisition of more trails, parks and shoreline areas, even if it means raising taxes or restricting development. Parks and trails truly deserve strong funding support, though the some anti-tax nuts think we should keep cutting their budgets. Washington State Parks, one of the most popular park systems in the nation, was recently generating about $80 million a year in tax revenues on an annual budget of less than $50 million. If they are producing tax revenue, why cut them back?

More people also participate in walking and hiking than any other outdoor recreational activity. In 2002, the Washington Interagency Committee for Outdoor Recreation found that walking and hiking are the leading outdoor recreation activities enjoyed by the state's citizens. The agency estimated that while about 13% of the population plays golf, 12% swims and 9% jogs, 56% of all citizens (all ages) walks or hikes for recreation (see **www.iac.wa.gov/**).

In recent years, Lynden, Blaine, Everson, and Birch Bay have all shown strong support for trails and have seen significant improvements on the ground, like the Jim Kaemingk Sr. Trail along Fishtrap Creek in Lynden (*Hike #14*), the short but promising Riverwalk in Ferndale (*Hike #15*), and the scenic trail along Semiahmoo Bay in Blaine (*Hike #3*). Blaine envisions a "necklace" of trails around Drayton Harbor, while Ferndale hopes to extend the RiverWalk upstream (Lynden or bust!) and downstream to Pioneer Park and beyond. A bicycle/pedestrian bridge over the river at Hovander would nicely link Ferndale to the park and to the Salish Coast (Millennium) Trail. Lynden also appears interested in the Nooksack Trail and has considered a link to the river from the Jim Kaemingk Sr. Trail, from town to Berthusen Park, plus another path along Bertrand Creek (much will depend on volunteers and donated easements). Dikes in Ferndale, Lynden and Everson all offer great potential to fill in some of the gaps in the regional trail system. Sumas and Nooksack have been somewhat less ambitious in their plans. The Lummi and Nooksack Tribes have indicated interest in new trails as well.

Bellingham, of course, leads the pack in trail development, thanks to a dedicated parks and recreation staff and the public's willingness to commit its tax dollars to the cause. Greenways-funded projects have included trails at Connelly Creek, along South Bay from downtown to Fairhaven, extensions along Padden and Whatcom Creeks, and a slew of neighborhood routes.

Over the next several years, city parks staff expect to see new trail links developed between Big Rock and Northridge Parks; from Salmon Park to Whatcom Creek; from Boulevard Park to the old Taylor Street Dock (via a new over-water pedestrian pier); from Bug Lake to Sunset Pond; plus a new section of the Whatcom Creek Trail from Racine Street to I-5. Longer-term goals call for links between Lake Padden and Salmon Park via Yew Street Hill; from Northridge

Park to the Bay-to-Baker Trail; an extension of the Bay-to-Baker Trail to Dewey Valley; links through the downtown area and along the North shore of Bellingham Bay for the Salish Coast Trail; completion of the Whatcom Creek Trail through downtown; plus links to trails on Galbraith and possibly King Mountains. Trails are likely as well on newly acquired park lands around the city, and on some conservation lands in the Lake Whatcom watershed.

In the county, a funding initiative similar to the Greenways program, perhaps coordinated with the smaller cities, could raise several million dollars that, matched with grants, could be applied toward trails and the purchase of critical corridors and easements while still available and affordable. With these and other resources, including a veritable army of volunteers, we could begin to develop and maintain a respectable system of trails in the smaller communities and around the county and help enhance the livability of our region. Lacking resources, County parks staff can only do so much.

On state lands, progress on trail development has been limited. A new link at Larrabee State Park connects the main park area with the Clayton Beach Trail. New links identified in the Chuckanut Mountain Trails Master Plan, particularly between Chuckanut Ridge and Lost Lake, may be developed soon through volunteer efforts. Trails on DNR-managed state lands, most notably Blanchard and Sumas Mountains, should be improved and extended somewhat to provide more complete systems with improved access. On Sumas Mountain, a link to Lost Lake and another to the Ostrom Conservation Site are most needed. At Blanchard, several short links and a major new connection between Lizard Lake and the other Lost Lake (within Larrabee State Park) are high priorities.

In the high country around Mount Baker, various trail projects have been completed over the past decade, including new trails at Heather Meadows (*see Hike #70*); a new Yellow Aster Butte Trail (*Hike #66*) that replaced the old Keep Kool Trail; completion of the 14-mile trail along Baker Lake (*Hike #89*); and the Boyd Creek salmon interpretive trail. Major trail upgrades have occurred at Table Mountain, Church Mountain, Anderson-Watson Lakes, Park Butte and elsewhere. Thanks to Congress' inability to adequately fund the Forest Service's relatively minuscule trails program, the agency expects to make only limited headway in trail development over the next several years. A small portion of the Bay-to-Baker Trail below the Mount Baker Ski Area may be the only new trail of significance to appear in the near future in the Mount Baker area. Development of this multi-use route, mostly along old logging roads, is partly driven by the need to provide a link in the Salmon Ridge Nordic Ski Area between the existing upper and lower trails. Heavy maintenance or reconstruction of existing trails is also expected over the near-term for Goat Mountain, Hannegan Pass, Lake Ann, Boulder Ridge, Shannon Ridge and Elbow Lake. Budget cuts have put most other projects on hold—to the delight of the anti-tax fanatics.

On lands administered by North Cascades National Park, the more significant additions in the past decade include the Happy Creek boardwalk interpretive trail (*Hike #104*) near Ross Dam, the Thunder Knob Trail (*Hike #101*) near Diablo Dam, and several short paths near the visitor center at Newhalem (*Hikes #93 and 94*). Significant maintenance and reconstruction has occurred on many trails, although funding is always a constraint, especially for new construction. Nevertheless, the park should give consideration to developing a couple of significant new day-hiking opportunities in or above the Skagit River Gorge, perhaps to one of many fine vistas that exist within the Ross Lake National Recreation Area, also administered by the agency. While new trails in designated wilderness should generally be discouraged, a number of less sensitive, yet still outstanding destinations could be explored. In the meantime, no major new trails are expected in the park in the foreseeable future, other than the shorter, interpretive variety which are always good for an up-close appreciation of nature. What's needed, however, are a couple of new links to dramatic vistas where people can experience the greater majesty of the range. A handful of minor trail extensions would help also. Overall, given how well the staff at North Cascades National Park stewards the existing trail network, the future should remain bright for first-class hiking in the North Cascades.

With our support, all of these agencies should be able to maintain the best of their traditions by continuing to provide visitors and residents of Whatcom County with some of the finest hiking opportunities available anywhere in the Northwest.

About Whatcom County

On a line north to south, Whatcom County spans barely 25 miles, though its western coastline touches over 130 miles of saltwater. The land stretches 115 miles west to east from the Point Roberts peninsula to Harts Pass at the crest of the Cascades Range. Three-fourths of the land area is rugged mountain wilderness, as rugged and remote as anywhere in the lower 48 states. Nearly all 170,000-plus inhabitants live in the western lowlands within 15 miles of Georgia Strait (or "Northern Puget Sound" or the "Salish Sea," as some people call these waters). The lowlands consist of 200,000 acres of glacial outwash called Whatcom Basin. A mile-thick sheet of ice more than once covered the region, finally receding northward just a few thousand years ago. Great meltwater streams, predecessors of the Fraser and Nooksack Rivers, dumped their sediments here to form this huge rolling delta.

South and east of Whatcom Basin, the lowlands rise several thousand feet into foothills: 300,000 acres of little mountains heavily forested with second and third generation timber. Sumas and Vedder Mountains lift the horizon to the northeast, while a unique series of foothills straddling the Whatcom/Skagit County line extends all the way from the jaggy peaks of the North Cascades to saltwater at Chuckanut Mountain—the only place along the Cascade Range where its foothills touch the marine shore. The 50-million year-old sandstone of the Chuckanut Formation forms much of the region's bedrock and provides Larrabee State Park with its dramatic rocky coast.

Nestled among the hills are four major lakes, all with developed public park facilities: Lake Padden, Silver Lake (camping), Lake Samish, and the largest, Lake Whatcom (5,000 acres). The higher elevations are found on Lookout, Stewart, Blue and Sumas Mountains; all are under 3,500 feet above sea level. Just south of Bellingham, the Chuckanut's Blanchard Mountain rises to 2,400 feet—a considerable height so close to saltwater. The Nooksack River, with its three forks and extensive tributary system drains a respectable watershed encompassing most of the western half of Whatcom County, including the north and west flanks of Mount Baker.

Mount Baker, Boulder Glacier and Sherman Crater.

Beyond the foothills lies the sprawling glacial-carved wilderness of the North Cascades. These federally managed lands comprise about two-thirds of the county's 1.4 million acres. Well over a half-million acres of magnificent wildlands are protected for future generations as national park and national wilderness, including the spectacular alpine country surrounding Mount Baker. This great landmark dominates the horizon as far away as Seattle and Victoria. Edmond Coleman first reached its summit in August, 1868, and now as many as 5,000 climbers attempt the ascent each year.

Mount Baker may be an icy, 10,781-foot napping volcano, but it demanded some real attention in the 1970s when it began blowing off a considerable amount of steam. Melting glacier ice formed a small lake in the crater and there was concern that if the melting continued, catastrophic flooding could endanger communities along the Skagit River. It was at least as active several times before that in the mid-1800s, and though it quieted down after a few months, geologists suggest that the 30,000 year-old volcano is likely to erupt again in a much bigger way, though no one can say when.

In the rest of the North Cascades, the geology is as complex as the scenery is dramatic, a "mountain mosaic" of diverse rocks and mysterious origins, as described by geologists Tabor and Haugerud in *Geology of the North Cascades* (2000). Evidence suggests that broken pieces of ancient continents have been carried here from great distances through the process of plate tectonics. The scenario seems almost unfathomable until it's recognized that movement along the San Andreas fault in California is bringing Los Angeles an inch and a half closer to San Francisco each year (or about 12 feet per century). At that rate L.A. should be zipping past Seattle in another 25 million years. See Babcock and Carson's *Hiking Washington's Geology* (2000) for more great insights on the region.

In the North Cascades, local relief from valley bottom to alpine summit often exceeds one vertical mile. The greatest elevation difference, more than 10,000 feet, occurs between Baker Lake and Mount Baker. Other high peaks often exceed 8,000 feet in elevation. Glaciers have carved deep recesses into major valleys and the sides of mountains, helping to create an earthly drama of ice, peaks, lakes, meadows and forests worthy of a national park, a national recreation area, and four wilderness areas. At least another 100,000 acres of unprotected roadless areas deserve protection as wilderness (see **www.wildwashington.org** for more).

Heavy winter snowpack above 3,000 feet produces tumultuous runoff in the spring and early summer, creating an endless symphony of waterfalls and cascades for every traveler to enjoy. Three large reservoirs, Ross, Diablo and Baker Lakes, capture much of this moisture, occupying roughly 20,000 acres in the Skagit and Baker River valleys. Another 200 lakes, most above 3,000 feet, can also be found.

Bountiful rain and snow, as well as abundant summer sun, obviously influence the diversity of life that inhabits our region. The Northwest coastal forest of the foothills and lowlands, at least where it hasn't been cut, is dominated by douglas fir, western hemlock and western red cedar thriving in a lush bed of ferns, berries, vine maples and numerous forest wildflowers. Predominant hardwoods include red alder, birch, big-leaf maple and cottonwood. Wildlife populations are equally diverse, ranging from delicate and elusive amphibians, small and medium furry mammals up to large black bears, elk, deer, cougar and mountain goats. Bird species residing in or passing through the county number in the hundreds.

Much of this flora and fauna extends into the North Cascades, but then changes significantly with elevation, rainfall and habitat. Forests of the mid- and upper-elevations include many species not present in the lowlands, like Alaska-cedar, silver fir, subalpine fir and mountain hemlock. Treeless alpine meadows are common above 5,500 feet. Englemann spruce and western larch are common east of the Cascades crest where timberline can exceed 7,500 feet. Along with the wildlife species noted above, wolves and grizzlies are likely residents of the North Cascades, but they are so rare that almost no one ever sees them. Both are listed as threatened or endangered species by state and federal agencies. Other listed species in the region include northern spotted owl, peregrine falcon, bald eagle, marbled murrelet, Canada lynx and western gray squirrel. A few animals that are not yet listed but may be soon are the common loon, northern goshawk, pileated woodpecker, Vaux's swift, Pacific fisher and Townsend's big-eared bat.

There are many excellent guides to birds, wildlife, wildflowers and related natural history currently available in bookstores and libraries, including such favorites as Mathews' *Cascade-Olympic Natural History* (1999), Pojar and MacKinnon's *Plants of the Pacific Northwest Coast* (1994), Sibley's *Sibley Guide to Birds* (2000) and many more equally impressive works. Smaller pocket guides are available too and are more easily carried along on a hike. It shouldn't take long for just about any serious hiker to be able to identify much of what's out there.

The Human Landscape

In a short time, geologically speaking, this land was densely forested, glaciated, reforested, and occupied (or perhaps reoccupied) by native American tribes, including the Lummi, Nooksack and Skagit people. Only a century and a half ago, white settlers arrived at Bellingham Bay to chase gold, harvest old-growth timber, and mine sizeable deposits of coal, at the same time forcing the natives to confine themselves to bits of land west, north and east of Bellingham.

Despite the moist marine climate, the remoteness, and recurring economic ups and downs, these hardy American and European pioneers ("intruders" would be less polite) adapted well to the challenge. The Nooksack River was made navigable, forestry and agricultural communities rapidly emerged upstream, the wooded floodplains were converted to farmland, salmon canneries were built, and secondary industries sprung up to bind them all together. (Remarkable and detailed histories of the region are preserved on many dusty pages found on the shelves of local libraries.)

Now, much of these tamed pastoral lowlands have been converted to urban and rural development, or are devoted to agriculture, supporting one of the larger raspberry and milk-producing counties in the nation. That which isn't farmed or developed into cities, towns and rural homesteads is almost entirely forested or otherwise managed for timber production. Agriculture, fishing, oil refining, aluminum production, mall shopping, tourism, higher education (Western Washington University), and a somewhat frazzled wood products industry, are among the fatter jacks of the local economy. This economy is becoming more diversified as new people and businesses immigrate to the area, attracted in large part by the high quality of life that still exists here.

That cherished *quality of life*—pastoral countryside, forested open space, quiet lakes and beaches, small town ambiance, clean water, unclogged streets and lonely trails—isn't quite what it used to be. Southern California-style growth and development (who said it couldn't happen here?) has been clogging the landscape north and east of Bellingham and elsewhere for some time now. Strangely enough, a few developers, land speculators, politicians, and leaders of the local property rights crusade left many folks wondering, not about what poor planning can do to the rural lifestyle, but about their supposed right to make Whatcom County a growth and development free-for-all. Fortunately, the number of people endlessly shouting about their property rights seems to be declining.

Now, in the early years of the 21st century, a significant and generally friendly rural human population inhabits the lower slopes of the foothills and adjacent valley bottoms. Some of the smaller communities are remnants of bustling mill towns and marketing centers of a colorful past. Much of the foothills, however, is owned in large blocks by the state and by private timber companies and is managed primarily for timber production. Hundreds of miles of trails and logging roads wind through this shadowy landscape offering potential access to hikers, hunters, and off-road vehicles. In some areas, logging clearcuts, old and new, have had an obvious impact on views and the environment—the price we pay, perhaps, for big houses, telephone poles and paper on which to print books. Nevertheless, great views, wildlife, lakes, waterfalls and other sights are hidden here. While large areas are generally accessible to the public and some outstanding portions of this great forest have been preserved as parks, many areas are not open to the public, so please don't trespass.

CLIMATE & SEASON

As many newcomers are quick to discover, the alluring summer greenscapes of Northwest Washington present a rather incomplete picture of what it's like the rest of the year to live in this land of more-wet-than-not. Summer months may be warm and cozy, and usually over with way too quickly. But the rest is decidedly wet—or pleasantly glum once you get used to it. In Whatcom County, we make it a point to enjoy the best of *both* seasons: "summer" and "glum"—the latter generally referring to that dreary gray fusion of fall, winter and spring, interspersed with an occasional sunny glitch.

Odds are that the innocent summer visitor who decides in August to relocate here will last about a year or two, maybe three, before yanking up roots and beating feet to somewhere else. But for those who do manage to outlast the averages, including those who were just born here (a distinct genetic advantage), and those who are only visiting, the rewards of living in the natural wonderland of the Northwest are considerable—hammered as it is by the exploiters, developers, and our hoards of planet-spoiling automobiles, not to mention the sprawl, clearcut forests, pollution, extinction, ignorance, corporate greed, weak-kneed politicians, right-wing wackoism, and perverse human decadence, of which we have our share. We *could* just blame it on the weather.

Weather is perhaps of greatest concern to those heading for the high country—precipitous ground with a lot of precipitation. Except for a few low-elevation trails along the Nooksack, Skagit and Baker Rivers, most hiking areas in the mountains are buried in deep snow six months of the year. As much as 150 inches of water, including about 30 to 50 feet of snow, falls on Mount Baker annually. The Mount Baker Ski Area watched a world-record snowfall develop in the winter of 1998-99 when more than 95 feet of snow fell, producing a snowpack over 25 feet deep! Mount Baker's phenomenal precipitation dwarfs the 35-40 inches that fall in Bellingham (mostly rain) and the 60 or more inches in the foothills. At Baker Lake, the average is over 100 inches, while to the east, from Ross Lake to the Cascade crest (the eastern county line), only 50 to 75 inches fall, almost entirely in the form of snow. The extreme eastern portion of the county is drier, but virtually unknown among most of the population. It is a high and wide-open mountain wilderness landscape, a big-sky country flanked by forests of pine and fir. It is also four hours away by car from Bellingham (*see Hikes #108 and #109*).

A warm Pacific High usually dominates the summer weather over much of northwest Washington, while moist marine and dry arctic air masses compete to influence the weather during the rest of the year. The lowlands experience a mild (but moist) climate and remain reasonably accessible throughout the seasons. In the light breeze, springtime jaunts are ideal here while the Cascades are still snowed in. That means hiking doesn't have to be limited to sunny days, as some might suppose. Beach walks are great any time, but beware of rising and falling tides, especially during stormy periods. The casual hiker, properly clothed and shod, will find a November sunset stroll along a windy shore can be just as enjoyable as an April day hike up Chuckanut Mountain, or a cool October outing into the colorful Nooksack Cirque.

But in summer the flowering alpine meadows high in the North Cascades are especially inviting and difficult to surpass in their superb and inspiring beauty. July through September, and sometimes June and October, are the best months for good weather in the North Cascades. In heavy snow years, higher trails may not even start to open up until July. Wildflowers and snowfields have all but disappeared by September, and fall colors often peak by early October.

Maiden hair fern.

Weather is often unpredictable, so good rain gear is essential in the mountains. Many days of cold rain and/or gusty winds can be expected anywhere anytime with or without any warning. Thunderstorms are not unusual, so avoid ridge tops, taller trees and open water if you think lightning may strike in the vicinity. Snow is possible any day of the year above 5,000 feet. HYPOTHERMIA, therefore, IS A MOST SERIOUS CONCERN, having claimed the lives of more than a few unprepared victims. In the lower elevations, if you're dressed for the weather, hiking season lasts all year.

What To Know Before You Go

Preparation

A rewarding trip is usually one with good prep: proper dress, adequate food and water, and a few other basic safety items in the knapsack. Unsolicited advise: tell someone where you're going and when you'll return. Know your limits under the conditions around you. Sharpen your senses before and during your walk. Go at a comfortable pace and make it an enjoyable outing for yourself and your companions. Travel in a small group—three to six is ideal. Anticipate problems that might arise and prepare for them. Is the weather unstable? When does it get dark? When does the tide come in? Will there be snow on the trail?

The shortest walks require little more preparation than what's needed to check the mail at the end of the lane. Some hikes require much more foresight, especially in remote areas. Overnight trips are another matter altogether. This guide is not intended to prepare you for overnight backpacking, though many of the hikes listed offer great overnight potential. Consult libraries, sporting goods stores, outdoor clubs and knowledgeable persons about furthering your skills in backcountry wilderness adventure. Numerous books are available that address clothing, equipment, navigation skills, camping, weather, ice axe use, hazards and other elements you may or may not be familiar with. Remember that trail conditions change due to any number of factors, so the trail descriptions in this book are not cast in concrete. Carry along a bucket of common sense.

Clothing & Equipment

For convenience, a suggested clothing and equipment list is included below. Volumes have been written on the selection and use of gear for a variety of hiking environments. Outdoor shops are excellent sources of information. Dressing comfortably means wearing loose-fitting layers that can be added or removed as necessary. Just being fashionable won't do. Under typical Northwest skies, the best combination in the mountains often includes a fast-drying synthetic layer against the skin, a light wool shirt or sweater, wool or synthetic durable pants (avoid cotton), a heavy wool sweater or pile jacket, a wind and water-resistant shell, top and bottom, gloves or mittens, and a wool hat or balaclava. Feet need special attention and a boot that fits is mandatory. Sturdy, water-resistant lug-soled boots are recommended for mountain trails and on snow. Thick socks over thin help absorb friction away from your skin.

Wet clothes, especially denim and other cotton fabrics, can lead to a rapid and dangerous loss of body heat. Add layers, gloves, a hat and parka in colder weather. Nights in the mountains, even in summer, are usually cold. A wool hat that pulls down over the ears makes a great thermostat. Put it on before you start shivering and remove it before you sweat or overheat. Fashionable sunglasses with UV protection, and sun cream (SPF 15 or better) are appropriate for bright days, cloudy days in the snow, and hot tub parties.

For short day trips, a large waist or fanny pack may be useful to carry food and drink, a nature guide, camera, windbreaker, etc. A backpack or rucksack will be required for mountain trips. Some of the higher trails can still be snow-covered in summer, so an ice axe and the ability to use it may be necessary for safety. Contact outdoor shops or clubs to learn proper ice-axe technique. In remote areas, care must be taken to avoid getting caught in darkness or bad weather without the essentials in your pack. Study the following list and notice what other experienced hikers carry with them. For those who may be hiking by wheelchair (let's hear it for accessible trails), modify the list as needed.

Short walks:

Food, water, proper clothing, footwear, camera, binoculars, guidebook, sunglasses, sun cream.

Short hikes:

Same as above, and sturdy lug-soled boots, small pack, extra clothing (sweater, raingear), pocket knife, whistle, flashlight, batteries, first aid kit. Some now carry a GPS unit and/or cell phone (cell phones are less reliable in the mountains).

Longer dayhikes:

Same as above, and extra food and water, more clothes and raingear, map and compass (learn to use them), matches, fire starter, foam pad, toilet paper, insect repellent, emergency shelter.

Backcountry Sanitation

Cleaning yourself or your food containers and cook pots should always occur well away from water sources. Use common sense if you need to make a nature call. Get well off the trail and a good distance—100 feet or more—from streams or water bodies. Dig a shallow hole into the humus soil layer then cover it up well with soil, rocks and sticks. If it's safe (damp and raining), burn your toilet paper; otherwise pack it out in a special bag with your trash or recyclables. Leaves or snow work well if you forget the TP. Whenever possible, take care of these little duties before you hit the trail.

Conditioning

The better shape you're in, the more enjoyable the hiking. And the best way to get in shape may be (surprise!) to go for a hike. If you hike often, each trip better prepares you for the next, each becoming more and more effortless as your condition improves. Most trips require only average physical condition. To cover more miles while avoiding burnout, maintain a comfortable pace. Check with your doctor if there's any doubt about your health or ability to make the trip. If you're not in the greatest shape, start with shorter walks and slowly work up to more strenuous hikes. Don't push yourself to the point that you are gasping for air or listening to your pulse pound in your head. This is supposed to fun. Take plenty of breaks, relax and enjoy the natural surroundings. Think, ponder, contemplate. Discover meaning in your hiking partner's sniffle.

Some Rules & Precautions

In the Cascades, check on park or forest regulations, trail conditions and other details before arriving at the trailhead. Just because a hike is listed in this or any other book doesn't mean that it will be totally safe when you visit. Conditions can change dramatically over a short period of time. Prepare well, and turn back if trail conditions or the weather are seriously deteriorating, or if you suddenly find you are in over your head.

On federal park and forest lands, a few rules need to be noted: keep the party size small, never more than twelve; practice "no trace" hiking and camping; don't trample or destroy vegetation by camping on it or short-cutting trails; pack out your garbage; control your pet (pets are not allowed in certain areas, like the national park); avoid camping or building fires outside of designated areas; carry a small backpack stove for cooking. Northwest Forest Passes (*see p. 41*) and free backcountry permits are required at many trailheads.

Some knowledge of first aid is highly recommended and essential when traveling in remote places. Carry plenty of water. Stream or lake water must always be purified, or you run an increasing risk of catching the giardia bug and other serious health maladies. Beware of changing conditions and unseen hazards. Creek crossings can be dangerous during high runoff periods. Notice that streams often fall during the night and rise in the afternoon. In early season especially, avoid all steep open snow slopes, due to avalanche danger. If you're unsure, don't chance it. Stay on the trail and don't lose it. At junctions or in places where the trail fades, look back for a moment so the scene is familiar on the return. *If you do get lost, calling out, whistling, staying put, and marking your location so it's visible from the air may be your best options. Keep dry and out of the wind, and exercise if needed to stay warm. And know that the vast majority of lost hikers make it out just fine the next day.*

On logging roads, watch out for large trucks hauling their heavy loads of timber off the mountain and give them the right-of-way. Washouts, rocks, water and windfall are common on these roads from fall through spring so keep a sharp eye out to avoid disaster. Be cautious during hunting season (generally in the fall). Wear bright orange when large mammals are in season, or don't go.

Wildlife Encounters

If a large mammal like a bear or cougar decides, unlikely as it is, that maybe *you* might be in season, consider the following. Grizzly bears are extremely rare in the North Cascades. In the unlikely event you see one, savor it for a moment then back away slowly. Some say it's unwise to look them in the eye and far worse to run. Running from black bears or cougars also may only encourage them to turn on their predator instincts and come after you (some say play dead if it's a grizzly—a highly unlikely encounter in the North Cascades). Don't panic or scream. Occasionally, a problem black bear can spoil your day by going after you or your food because careless others have taught them to associate humans with food. Be wise. Cook well away from your tent, and always hang your food, garbage, toothpaste, etc. at least ten feet off the ground when camping overnight. Fortunately, problem bears are uncommon in the Cascades, thanks to bear-proof garbage cans and bear-wise campers. If a black bear seems to come after you (also very rare), drop a bandana or hat to distract it and continue to move away.

With cougars, use firm language, hold your ground and make yourself look big. If attacked, fight back aggressively. Climbing a tree is probably moot since both black bears and cougars climb way better than we do. The best defense against these animals may be to not approach them in the first place. Don't threaten their young or get between a mother and her offspring. If you stumble on a partly eaten carcass, move on. Be heard and seen when hiking in the woods or backcountry. With such a low risk of an encounter in the North Cascades, bells and the like are normally dispensed with as more of nuisance than they're worth. Avoid hiking alone, especially if you're a smaller person without a pack. Keep kids and pets close by. And report unusual wildlife sightings or encounters, or any grizzly or gray wolf sighting to an area wildlife biologist or ranger. Wolves, by the way, are very rare in the Cascades and will generally go out of their way to avoid you. The vicious attacks portrayed in the movies are far from the reality of gray wolf encounters, even in Alaska.

Other Dangers

If the worst happens (it rarely, rarely does) and you are confronted by a wacko, thieving, trouble-making *human* on the trail, try to stay cool. Cooperate if it will avoid violence to you or your party. If not, attract someone's attention, scream, run, or fight back as good-old common sense dictates. Give up your valuables if that's what it takes to protect your safety. To reduce the risk, don't travel alone. Trust your instincts when you encounter someone who makes you uneasy. Avoid them or leave. Remember details and descriptions if this is something that should be reported to the police. Report any criminal activity to the proper authorities, and/or call 911 if there's an emergency. Fortunately, violent crime seldom occurs on the trail (I have neither experienced a violent offense on the trail nor ever known anyone who has in 25 years of hiking). Common sense would suggest that walking alone at night on a deserted unlit city street or trail would be one of the riskier scenarios. Hiking with a group during daylight hours, of course, would be a better choice.

Criminal activity, fires, accidents and lost hikers should be reported to local emergency officials, or just call 911. Search and rescue activities are coordinated through the county sheriff. *Call the Sheriff or 911 if you need help with an injured party or to report an overdue hiker*. Forest fires can be reported to 911 or to DNR at (800) 562-6010, or to the local ranger. For non-emergency related inquiries, contact the local land management agency.

Bugs

If big and threatening wild animals—whether two-legged or four legged—haven't frightened you out of the woods altogether, consider, then, the most hideous and terrifying wild beings of them all: bugs. Actually, bugs aren't that bad, rather it's their bites and stings that can spoil an otherwise perfect outing in the hills. For more sensitive folks (you probably know who you are), stings can be downright dangerous and may require immediate care (check with your doctor ahead of time if think you might have a reaction). However, for most of us, bug bites are just part of the package. The worst tend to be yellow jackets. They nest in rotten stumps and logs or holes in the ground, and once disturbed, they are amazingly quick to react. Sooner or later, just about everyone who hikes regularly will encounter them, although if you stay on the trail when you're below timberline, the odds of stepping on a nest are almost nil. Mosquitos and no-see-ums are also a pain, but usually only early morning and early evening, although there are exceptions. To ward them off, find a high breezy place to relax, use a little jungle juice (citronella seems less intense than DEET, but might have to be applied more often), cover yourself with clothing or mosquito netting, light up a cigar (the smoke deters them—don't inhale, of course), or try moving a few hundred yards (and away from moist areas).

Deer flies and black flies (black flies tilt steeply to bite) can be worse than mosquitos and are often intense even in the heat of the day. Similar techniques may allow you to escape their wrath. Horse flies are the big ones that whip around as if on a string. They can bite well, but fortunately, there aren't usually a lot of them buzzing around you at the same time. From May through early August, expect a lot of bugs in the mountains in good weather, and plan accordingly. Happily, their numbers tend to drop off later in summer and in cool, breezy or wet weather.

Hantavirus

One other pesky life form to be aware of is the *hantavirus*, a rare but deadly malady carried mostly by a few deer mice. When someone comes into contact with an infected rodent, say, by cleaning, disturbing, or sleeping near one or its nest, it's possible to inhale tiny airborne bits of mouse urine, saliva or feces which could then cause the occurrence of *hantavirus pulmonary syndrome*. As of late 2001, almost two dozen cases had been confirmed statewide, including two in Snohomish County and one in the San Juan Islands. Of 288 cases nationally, about 38 percent were fatal. Fever, chills, muscle aches, and other flu-like symptoms develop within one to four weeks of contact, then rapidly turn into severe respiratory distress. Deer mice, the principal carriers, are about six to seven inches long to the tip of the tail and have a cute white belly.

Prevention is the key. Avoid the mice and their nests, as well as crude cabins, shelters, or other enclosed areas that may be infested or which are not well ventilated, and consider sleeping in a tent rather than on bare ground. Keep food and utensils sealed and protected from rodents. While the odds of contracting the illness are very remote in Washington, reducing the risk to a minimum isn't a bad idea. All in all, there are far more friendly and benign critters in the wild to be appreciated than there are creatures to be feared. So, be wise—not paranoid—and enjoy the wilderness.

Be a Conservationist

Finally, take the time to learn about the natural environment before and while you're in the middle of it. Bring your natural history guide to the wildflowers rather than the other way around. Exercise respect for other walkers, wildlife, and the environment.

Include a few minutes of trail work on every outing, whether it's just kicking a few limbs off the trail or cleaning out a small ditch or culvert to prevent erosion.

At home, take time on occasion to learn about local efforts to protect our vanishing wild places and make time to speak up for trails and wilderness. Before you and I arrived on the scene, others were doing that for us.

Here's a quick summary of some of the land conservation efforts underway in the county:

On federal lands, volunteers with Mount Baker Wild! are working to win wilderness designation for more than 100,000 acres of roadless areas in the Mount Baker region, including spectacular alpine meadows, lakes, salmon streams, high peaks and glaciers, plus much of the old-growth forest that was excluded from the 1984 bill designating the Mount Baker and Noisy–Diobsud Wilderness Areas. Some hikers may be surprised to know that such familiar wild places as Church Mountain, Shuksan Lake, portions of Skyline and Cougar Divides, Baker River, Noisy Creek, Sauk Mountain (in Skagit County), and the west slopes of the Twin Sisters Range are not currently protected as park or wilderness (for more, check out the Wild Washington campaign at **www.wildwashington.org**.)

On state lands, the local Mount Baker Group of the Sierra Club (**www.mtbakergroup.org**) and the Northwest Ecosystem Alliance (**www.ecosystem.org**) are working to protect Blanchard Mountain and other public lands of greatest importance to the public. DNR is not doing nearly enough to preserve and protect the best of our scenic, recreational and environmentally sensitive lands, including the most promising of our maturing second-growth forests at Blanchard, Sumas Mountain and in the Lake Whatcom watershed. The best of these lands should be allowed to recover as old growth. The state legislature should act to protect the best of what's left.

State Parks could use some advocates for additional funding from the legislature. Budget shortfalls have forced the agency to close some parks and institute day-use parking fees for others. Yet a recent study found that, as the fourth most popular park system in the nation, our state parks generate far more tax revenue from visitors than what it costs to run the entire agency. By slashing the budget, it would seem that the state is only thwarting the revenue potential of an otherwise outstanding park system.

In the county, many local groups are working to protect habitat and open space in rural areas and the foothills. The Whatcom Land Trust (**www.whatcomlandtrust.org**) is also very active in land conservation. In Bellingham, the Greenways program (**www.cob.org/ parks/greenways/**) and the city's watershed acquisition program have made great headway in acquiring park land, open space and trail corridors, thanks in large part to broad community support.

A Note on Multiuse Trails

Many of the trails described in this guide are open to nonmotorized multiple use. So it should probably be emphasized that this book is not intended to invite mountain bikers into all the areas described (this is not intended as an anti-bike statement). As a rule, bikes are best suited to old road grades and more durable multiuse trails designated for such use. Mountain biking is a fine activity (I ride one myself), but not when it's to the detriment of a footpath or those who tread more softly upon it. Our local mountain biking club, Whatcom Independent Mountain Pedalers (WHIMPS), has done an excellent job building awareness around trail issues like these, while also organizing a heck of a lot of trail work in our region. Equestrians, often organized through the Backcountry Horsemen of Washington, are also very active in trail construction and maintenance, and the work of both groups directly benefits hikers. Trail running has assumed some increased popularity of late, and runners should be (and generally are) sensitive to other trail users, especially on steep terrain, blind corners, and on routes that are popular for birding and wildlife watching. Avid hikers should plan to participate in at least one or more trail maintenance work parties each year. Contact any of the land management agencies for details on how and where you can help.

Northwest Forest Pass & State Park Fees

A Northwest Forest Pass (formerly "Fee Demo Trail Park Pass") is now required in both the National Forest and National Park. For information or to purchase a pass contact North Cascades National

Park or Mount Baker Ranger District in Sedro Woolley at (360) 856-5700. Passes are also available at the Glacier Public Service Center, Marblemount Ranger Station, Newhalem Visitor Center, and at many local businesses that cater to trail users.

Beginning in July, 1997, the US Forest Service instituted a trailhead parking permit system to raise money for much-needed trail and trailhead maintenance on federal lands. Permits were required year-round for nearly all trailheads on the Mount Baker-Snoqualmie National Forest. Since no entrance fee is collected for North Cascades National Park, that agency joined the program. A day pass is $5 and an annual pass $30 (subject to change). Discounts are available for seniors and the less able-bodied among us. Trail maintenance volunteers can earn a pass through their labor. A pass purchased for our region is good at other Northwest Forests as well. Of the money raised, about 80 percent goes to trail and trailhead maintenance. (See also **www.fs.fed.us/r6/mbs/passes/**.)

Are these fees fair? Many trail enhancements we have seen in the past few years were paid for by trail pass dollars and one could presume they may not have happened otherwise. At the same time, there is debate about what we, as taxpayers, ought to expect from our government in the way of basic public services, and what ought to be paid for through user fees. These lands belong to us all. As co-owners, we all have equal access and an equal responsibility to ensure future generations have the same opportunity to enjoy them. We should not have to pay to enjoy what is already ours. Instead of cutting maintenance budgets to make ends meet, shouldn't Congress and the President be insisting that all public facilities are well taken care of first? So while many folks probably don't mind shucking out a few dollars for a nominal fee, many others do, especially if you happen to be strapped financially. But if the money raised is simply replacing what Congress should be providing anyway, that's not necessarily a good thing. Some have suggested that the pass is a strategic move toward the private commercialization of our public lands—a very serious concern that needs to be watched.

Obviously, there are merits to both sides of the argument, even if the program seems to have become an excuse for axe-happy politicians to duck their responsibility to properly fund public facilities.

As the money gets siphoned off for other non-trail-related expenses, public support for the program will surely plummet. That said, the Forest Service in our neck of the woods has done a good job involving people in the debate, listening to and incorporating ideas. We'll see where it all leads. In the meantime, it remains the most reliable source there is for much needed trail improvements.

As noted earlier, the Washington State Parks and Recreation Commission instituted a highly controversial fee system in January 2003 (**www.parks.wa.gov/**). All state parks began requiring a $5.00 daily parking fee ($50.00 for an annual pass). Bicycle or walk-in users pay no fee. Camping fees increased as well. Yet our state parks already generate tens of million of dollars in tax revenue every year—far more than the cost of operating the entire park system (1/4 of 1% of the state budget). They benefit every citizen of the state. Free access to these areas should be a fundamental benefit of paying our taxes, though some in the legislature seem to think otherwise.

Most Washington Department of Fish and Wildlife sites now require an annual Vehicle Use Permit ($10) for parking (**www.wa.gov/wdfw/**), a much more reasonable fee.

Private Property

Veteran hikers in the county may notice that some lowland trails are not included in the book. Some may traverse private lands whose owners might not wish to advertise their use by the general public. Liability for injures, vandalism and fires are common concerns (although landowners are well protected from liability by state law; *RCW 4.24.200 & 4.24.210*). A few careless people appear to be responsible for most public access problems being experienced. Check with other hikers or area residents to locate these semi-secret places.

A lot of good hiking country is under private timber company ownership where access is sometimes a little easier. You can generally avoid trouble with these folks by obeying all signs, closed gates, fences, seasonal fire closures or other indications that your presence is not welcome. Always assume that camping and campfires are not permitted outside of designated sites. Obtain permission where necessary. *Descriptions in this guide should not be construed as permission to violate private property rights*.

Your Valuables

As for your own private property—your personal valuables—don't leave them in your car at trailheads. Way too many brainless thieves have a habit of showing up at the oddest hours to break a window and make off with your goods. Report all thefts or vandalism to the authorities.

Beach Access

It is often assumed that any old beach is open to the public. That is generally true in Oregon and Hawaii and other coastal states, but it's not so cut and dried in Washington. Regrettably, the State of Washington sold off its best tidelands around our inland sea to private interests over much of the last century. Not only was it an absurd thing to do, it left us with major difficulties in finding good access to more than a fraction of the county's spectacular shoreline. The practice was banned about 25 years ago, but the damage was done. However, there is still a legal argument—and the author agrees—that the public never gave up its right (i.e. the *public trust*) to use tidelands to access public waters, whether for commerce or recreation or whatever, even though the mud and the crud may belong to an adjacent landowner. That said, private property still deserves some respect.

Private or otherwise, the vast majority of tideland owners are not snobs and couldn't care less whether you and I go for a harmless stroll along a remote beach. However, they are not inclined to advertise these places to the general public due, in part, to the problems caused by a few individuals who abuse the privilege. Obnoxious behavior, litter and vandalism are primary concerns, especially where waterfront homes are located close to the shore. Fortunately, remote areas are more interesting to visit and responsible hikers will encounter few problems with anxious landowners. On all beaches, public and private, use common sense: don't take or leave anything; don't start fires; be quiet; avoid large groups; respect wildlife and the marine environment; smile; be courteous to residents; stay off the stairs and pathways leading up to their yards; and avoid walking on railroad tracks.

Beach walks may be good year-round, except during stormy periods. The suggested walks and hikes in coastal areas (Hikes *#1 through #13*) include those with public access, although both public and private tideland ownership may occur. Nevertheless, these areas have been used regularly by the public in the past. While it would take a title company and a survey crew to know for sure which areas are private, there are substantial public tidelands present. It is the user's responsibility to obtain prior authorization if necessary. Plan your visit during lower tide levels (check the tide tables), and be aware of rising tides which can surprise, strand, and/or drown you if you're not careful. **Walk these and all other areas at your own risk!**

More Hiking Information

Hiking Whatcom County is the only guide with broad coverage for the entire county, from the saltwater shore to the crest of the Cascades. However, several other guidebooks are available which provide comprehensive coverage of trails in the North Cascades, most notably *100 Hikes in Washington's the North Cascades National Park Region* (Spring, Manning; The Mountaineers, 2000), and several smaller guides to the Mount Baker area and the National Park published by the Northwest Interpretive Association (**www.nwpubliclands.com**/). The Spring/Manning classic and other titles are available at most book stores and outdoor shops in the region. Local outdoor clubs sponsor guided hikes throughout the year, usually free of charge. These are listed at the end of the book along with emergency contacts and various land management agencies. Libraries are another excellent source of how-to and where-to hiking information.

USGS and Green Trails™ topographic maps, as well as topographic mapping software for your computer, also deserve mention here as requisite tools for the mountains. These are all generally available at book stores and outdoor shops. In the cyber world, the Washington Trails Association maintains an excellent Web site (**www.wta.org**/) that is loaded with information, including literally thousands of trail reports filed by users and management agencies, details on volunteer opportunities, and other trail resources and information.

How To Use This Book

To make best use of this guidebook, first read the **Introduction** and **What to Know Before You Go**, then decide on a walk or a hike. Check the **Trail Location Maps** up front for possibilities, read the trail descriptions, then check other maps in the back of the book for possible side trips to parks, viewpoints, water access, or campgrounds in the vicinity.

Trails have been divvied up, somewhat arbitrarily, into easy, moderate, more difficult and most difficult hikes, as noted by the "W" symbols in the table of contents. The easier hikes or "walks" generally require less than an hour or two round trip, are usually 0.5 to 3.0 miles long, and are often close to level or at least very short. The rest are more strenuous but vary greatly in length, steepness and overall difficulty. Of course, what may seem to one person to be an easy stroll may be a real workout for the next.

The Listings

In the write-up for each hike, round-trip distances to one or more destinations are provided, along with the approximate time needed, elevation gain, best months to visit (varies year to year, of course), and directions from I-5 or the nearest town or highway, including mile-post (MP) notations to the nearest one-tenth of a mile. The estimated times are loosely gauged for walking speeds of one to two miles per hour. Three miles per hour is brisk, and four is almost a trot and difficult to maintain over much distance. Additional time is added where elevation gain is more significant. Read the trail description to see what the times and distances given refer to.

Trips are organized into six geographical areas: The Coast, Urban Areas, Chuckanuts, Lowlands & Foothills, Mount Baker Area, and the rest of The North Cascades. Admittedly, some hikes don't fit clearly in one category or another. For consistency, trails outside the Chuckanuts that generally stay below 3,000 feet above sea level are listed under Lowlands & Foothills. While these areas can be snowed-in part of the year, they can also be snow-free in the dead of winter if the weather's been mild. A special emphasis has been given to walks and hikes which are not adequately described in other guide-

Old-growth forest, Baker Lake Trail.

books, especially between the coast and foothills. A number of other potential trips are mentioned at the end of the numbered trail listings. These are not described in detail for a variety of reasons, such as private property concerns, poor maintenance or difficult navigation. A determined adventurer will soon cultivate the detective skills needed to locate these and other worthwhile trails.

All maps in this book are intended for general reference only, not for navigation. Far better full-sized topographical maps to all areas are available at many outdoor shops. USGS and Green Trails™ maps (and some topographical mapping software) are excellent choices and may be indispensable for most hikes in the North Cascades.

Listings of public parks briefly describe the location and facilities available, and may include short walks not listed elsewhere in the guide. Viewpoints and water access are accessible by car, bike, or a short walk and are self-explanatory. A list of public campgrounds is provided for those who might want to combine one or more dayhikes with a comfortable evening in the woods.

THE COAST

—See note on beach walks, page 44—

Mount Baker from Lighthouse Marine Park.

THE COAST—
1.   **Lighthouse Point & Boundary Bay**

Distance: 1 - 2 miles round trip   Time: Allow 1 - 2 hours
Season: Year-round

Several short beach walks and a visit to Lighthouse Marine Park easily justify a day trip to Point Roberts—even if it means slogging through two border crossings on the way in and out of Canada. Being a little detached from the rest of us, six-square-mile Point Bob (as some like to call it) is perhaps better known by our northern neighbors than by mainland Whatcom Countians. When the 49th parallel was established as the international boundary here in 1846, the Point was left dangling below the line—an oddity that would eventually sprout several large pubs where a Canadian could enjoy a legal beer on Sunday. Suds and fish-canning have since given way to a somewhat more diverse local economy, while a semi-rural ambience invites at least several short saunters.

Head north into British Columbia from the I-5 Blaine border crossing, follow Highway 99 about 18 miles to Highway 17, then go west five more miles to Tsawwassen. Turn left at the 56th St. light which leads to the border crossing in about two miles (roughly an hour's drive from Bellingham). For Lighthouse Marine Park continue straight on Tyee Dr. and jog right at the marina; the park is 0.5 mile ahead. Once at the park, walk the beach or climb the view tower to see the Gulf and San Juan Islands, Vancouver Island, B.C. ferries on Georgia Strait, and maybe gray or orca whales, both of whom are known to approach close to the beach. Gray whales migrate to and from Alaskan waters in spring and fall, while summer months are best for orca sightings. Winter is a great time for water birds: gulls, terns, jaegers, loons and ducks. Enjoy a stroll along the beach. Picnic shelters and campsites are available.

Next, drive or bike around the Point to visit two or three other beaches. Either head north two miles on Marine Dr. to find Monument Park at the border—an undeveloped eight-acre county park on the left with a rough steep trail to the beach. The park commemorates the westernmost point of the U.S. along the 49th Parallel. Then head east to Tyee Dr. follow it and turn east on Johnson,

Benson or APA Roads. In 1.5 miles turn left (north) on Boundary Bay Rd. (becomes Goodman Rd.) to find Maple Beach at Point Roberts' northeast corner. Kudos to the Whalen family for donating these tidelands to the Whatcom Land Trust and Whatcom County Parks. Public tidelands extend about a half-mile southward. The flats can be quite extensive at lower tides. In summer, as the tide returns, the warm sand heats the water to a comfy wading temperature.

The premier marine bluff in the county, Lily Point, is found at the southeast corner of Point Roberts, almost two miles south of Maple Beach. The area is private and more difficult to access, though used informally by area residents for many years (don't trespass; *see p. 44*). Gorgeous, eroding "feeder" bluffs 200 feet high provide the sediments that build and maintain the beaches down-drift of the bluffs. If you go, frequent sloughs and slides suggest giving the bluff a wide berth—above and below. A grove of big-leaf maple trees, diverse wildlife, and the area's archaeological importance are appealing, although proposed development above the bluff makes public access uncertain. The area would clearly qualify for a park or nature reserve and should be a high priority for acquisition, conservation and public enjoyment.

The Coast—
2. Semiahmoo Spit

Distance: 1 - 3 miles round trip   Time: Allow 1 - 2 hours
Season: Year-round

With so much of the marine tidelands in Whatcom County under private ownership, it's hard to find a good public beach of any length to walk. The unique spit at Semiahmoo Park is therefore a real treasure. A resort development at the north end of this 1.3-mile long back-to-back beach system (an accretion shoreform) attracts throngs of visitors in summer. Visit the park in the off-season and you might have most of the spit to yourself. Spring, fall and winter are good for birding. In summer, when the MV Plover, a wonderfully restored 17-passenger foot ferry, is running between the north tip of the spit to Blaine Harbor, it's well worth combining this walk with a stroll (or bike ride) along Semiahmoo Bay (*Hike #3*). You can check the ferry schedule on the Web at www.mvplover.org.

To reach the spit, take I-5 exit #274 to Portal Way, then immediately turn left (west) on Blaine Rd. In 0.7 mile go right on Drayton Harbor Rd.; follow signs to Semiahmoo, about five miles from I-5. From the park, walk either beach or a paved path along the spit to the resort. The west beach can be followed southward to a point where fallen trees and drift logs make the going difficult. The views are great across Drayton Harbor toward Mount Baker, and across Semiahmoo Bay to the city of White Rock, B.C. Some of the old buildings left over from the days of the historic Alaska Packers Association fish cannery were converted to interpretive facilities, a library and gift shop, although plans are afoot to relocate some of these facilities to the north end of the spit. The trail on the spit is part of the planned Salish Coast Trail (*Hike #6*) which would also include a leg around the east side of Drayton Harbor.

MV Plover.

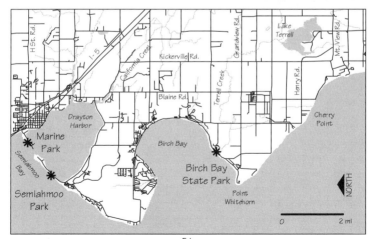

51

Blaine's Marine Park on Semiahmoo Bay.

THE COAST—
3. Semiahmoo Bay

Distance: 1 - 2 miles round trip   Time: Allow 1 - 2 hours
Season: Year-round

Easily the best walk in Blaine can be found at Marine Park, north of the boat harbor, west of downtown, and a whistle away from Canada. A scenic loop trail parallels Semiahmoo Bay and Marine Dr. and offers great views, picnic sites, an amphitheater, intriguing orca and salmon sculptures, a totem pole, and at the west end of the harbor area, a nicely improved public fishing pier. The historic foot-ferry, MV Plover, makes frequent summer runs from the boat harbor to Semiahmoo Spit (*see Hike #2*). The bay and tidal flats present excellent birding opportunities, including eagles, herons, gulls, terns, and numerous species of ducks and shorebirds—the perfect place to learn to identify many native birds. This is the place to see yellowlegs and godwits probing the mud while a determined merlin pursues a shimmering flock of dunlin. Benches and picnic shelters provide great viewing platforms.

From northbound I-5, take exit 276, the last exit before entering Canada, and head west under the freeway, then turn right on Marine Dr. Find the trail just ahead on the right. Park anywhere and wander the paths along the bay, west toward the public fishing pier, or south along the boat harbor. Many of the trails are barrier-free (mostly smooth, packed gravel). Organized groups have begun to visit the area regularly—which may help explain why Blaine is taking an interest in promoting wildlife conservation as a significant driver of the local economy.

THE COAST—
4. **Birch Bay & Point Whitehorn**

Distance: 1 - 6 miles round trip   Time: Allow 1 - 5 hours
Season: Year-round

One of the nicer beach walks in the county, this trip is also good for birds—over 300 species have been counted at Birch Bay State Park. In winter and spring, take the bird book and binoculars and watch for bay and shore birds, including brant geese, American widgeons, scoters, harlequins, long-tailed ducks, loons, dunlin and many more. Huge flocks hang around in spring when the herring are spawning. Harbor seals might be seen basking on rocks close to shore. The San Juan Islands, Gulf Islands and Vancouver Island dominate the west horizon. Most of the tidelands are public, but keep off the occasional paths and stairways leading up to private homes. For easier going, begin the hike while the tide is receding.

From I-5 exit #270, Birch Bay-Lynden Rd., head west four miles, turning left at the water slides, then left again onto Birch Bay Dr. (*map, p. 51*). Reach the State Park in two miles (camping is available). Begin anywhere along the beach and wander north through the park, or southward toward Point Whitehorn in the distance. Northwest Coast Salish Indians—principally the Lummi and Semiahmoo tribes—occupied this region for many generations as

*Point
Whitehorn.*

evidenced by deposits of discarded seashells, or *middens*. As you head south, the beach changes from sand and fine gravel to pebbles and cobbles. Large boulders released from the high eroding bluffs are relics of the ice age and a melting continental glacier that dumped the material here as recently as 15,000 years ago. As the beach gradually bends 90 degrees to the left, Lummi Island becomes visible to the south-southeast. This is Point Whitehorn, about a 40-minute walk (just over a mile) from the south end of the park, and a good place to turn around. For a longer beach hike, one can continue southeast (at low tide) about two miles more toward the big pier at the Cherry Point Refinery. In the past, one could continue to Gulf Rd., but security issues at the pier may now impede this option.

THE COAST—
5. Cherry Point Beach
Distance: 1 - 4 miles round trip   Time: Allow 1 - 3 hours
Season: Year-round

The Cherry Point beach may be in the center of a heavy industrial area of refineries and an aluminum smelter, but most of the heavy-duty facilities are well back from the shore, leaving a pleasantly walkable coast for the public to enjoy. The easier walk is to the south-

Cherry Point.

east where it's possible to wander about a mile to near the big pier. One can also stumble northward a mile on a coarse cobble beach leading toward the large pier at the Cherry Point Refinery. This option parallels a unique berm and backwater marsh in the first 0.2 mile, then crosses a small creek (on logs or by wading) to easier ground ahead. The area has been and will continue to be a focus of controversy as developers press for more heavy industrial development in the vicinity. Near-shore spawning habitat once supported some of largest concentrations of herring in Washington—an important food-fish for salmon. We can only hope that any new development will be sensitive to the marine environment, the herring, and other valuable wildlife and recreational resources that exist here.

To reach the beach from I-5, take Slater Rd. six miles west to Lake Terrell Rd.; turn right. Go two miles to Mountain View Rd. and turn left (one could also follow Main St. through Ferndale to reach this point). Heading west, follow Rainbow Rd. rightward, then at the Kickerville Rd. junction keep heading west on Henry Rd. a longish mile to Gulf Rd.; turn left to find the beach 0.5 mile ahead (*map, p. 51*). Someday, a spur of the Salish Coast Trail (SCT) may also lead to this the beach. Weaving the SCT through the Cherry Point industrial area will be a bit of a challenge and will depend somewhat on the willingness of the refineries to accommodate limited trail access in perimeter areas (albeit well back from their operations).

THE COAST—
6. North Bay & Salish Coast Trail
Distance: 0.6 mile (or more) round trip   Time: Allow 1 hour (or more)
Season: Year-round

In the early 1970s, bicycling advocates put together preliminary plans for a Pacific Coast bicycle route from California to Canada, including a section through Whatcom County. The idea was picked up locally in the 1980s and was noted in 1989 in the Whatcom County parks and recreation plan as the "Coastal Bike Route." But without funding or staff, the plan seemed relegated to perennial shelfdom. Enter the Trillium Corporation, a local developer who owned land along the route and found the idea appealing enough to convene a meeting of local agency staff and interested others. Ultimately, Bellingham, Whatcom County, the Port of Bellingham and the Whatcom Council of Governments jointly developed a brand new plan for what was renamed the "Coast Millennium Trail" (yours truly served as project planner). Since the "Millennium" thing seems to

Salish Coast Trail on Marine Drive.

have faded somewhat, the author is meekly suggesting "Salish Coast Trail" as an alternate. The many tribes of our region's inland sea are known as Coast Salish (Salish meaning "people"). The name is intended to honor the tribes and the integral relationship between people and the coast that has existed here for thousands of years.

Whatever you choose to call it, the route would consist of trails, beaches, road shoulders and bikelanes from at least the south end of the Chuckanuts to White Rock, B.C., and would incorporate existing facilities like the Interurban Trail (*Hike #28*), South Bay Trail (*Hike #9*), the Port's short trail along Marine Dr. (*see below*), as well as paths at Hovander Park (*Hike #40*), Birch Bay, Semiahmoo (*Hike #2*), and Blaine (*Hike #3*). Recent award of a $1.2 million federal grant should help turn an old idea into a new reality. *(See www.wcog.org/projects/ for current plans and maps.)*

So while you're waiting for the complete trail to materialize over the coming years, check out the sections noted above, or try the short "North Bay Trail" on the bluff above the north shore of Bellingham Bay near the airport. From downtown Bellingham, follow Holly St., which becomes Eldridge Ave., which becomes Marine Dr., and continue a mile past Bennett Dr. to the signed trailhead on

the left. The trail is short (0.3 mile) but the view of the bay (near the parking area) is great and inspires enthusiasm for making sure the coastal trail actually gets built—and not, once again, reshelved. To extend the hike, walk the shoulder of Marine Dr. back toward Bellingham for 0.5 mile and turn southwest on Locust Ave. Head down the hill 0.1 mile and under a squat railroad bridge to find an unmarked path on the right (do not park here). This leads 0.1 mile on path and stairs down to the beach which can be followed a mile southeast to Little Squalicum Beach (*see Hike #7*).

57

Little Squalicum Beach in winter.

THE COAST—
7. Little Squalicum Beach

Distance: 1 - 6 miles round trip   Time: Allow 1 - 4 hours
Season: Year-round

This attractive gravely beach just north of Bellingham is littered with small relics of historic industry on Bellingham Bay. Old bricks and odd, rusty contrivances add interest to a surprisingly scenic saunter. The beach is adjacent to the Little Squalicum ravine which allegedly will become a park someday. There are two easy ways to reach the beach. The quickest is to follow Roeder Ave. northwesterly out of downtown to where the main road bends right under a railroad bridge and becomes Squalicum Pkwy.; but stay left here on Roeder to find a small parking area and beach access just beyond Mount Baker Plywood. Or, for a slightly longer approach, begin at the Bay-to-Baker Trail (*Hike #16*) off W. Illinois St. From the downtown area, follow W. Holly St. and Eldridge Ave. to Nequalicum Ave.; turn right, then left on Nome St., then left again on Illinois (*map, p. 73*). A boulder marks the trail at the end of the street. It's a 0.4-mile walk to the beach.

From this upper access, pass under the Eldridge Ave. overpass and a large railroad trestle at the water's edge at Little Squalicum Beach—at one time one of Bellingham's best swimming beaches. Pollution from industry and residential septic systems put an end to that, though improved enforcement of regulations could lead to a reopening of Whatcom County's own Waikiki. For now, head northwest under a pier which, with any luck, could become the west terminus of the Bay-To-Baker Trail. Follow the beach to a pipeline where the walk ends if the tide is up. The next section passes below the old Columbia Cement plant. Beyond, the hike becomes a little wilder and more interesting. Watch for eagles in perch trees above the shore. About 0.9 mile from the pier, near a cluster of old pilings, a short and somewhat hidden trail leads up the bank to Locust Ave. west of Marine Dr., a third potential access to the beach (a lack of parking makes this less useful as a trailhead). Depending on conditions, one may be able to continue the beach walk northwesterly for one to two miles, passing the old Fort Bellingham site before encountering organic debris on the flats, impeding further progress. This is the delta of the Nooksack River—one of the largest, relatively intact estuarine ecosystems in the Puget Sound region. Please note that there is no practical exit to Marine Dr. beyond Locust.

Tʜᴇ Cᴏᴀsᴛ—
8. Squalicum Harbor

Distance: 1 - 4 miles round trip   Time: Allow 1 - 2 hours
Season: Year-round

Bellingham's central boat harbor, Squalicum, is virtually surrounded by about two miles of paved paths and walkways that offer a pleasant stroll in all but the most blustery conditions. The harbor is easy to find off Roeder Ave. northwest of downtown Bellingham. Park your car or bike in the big lot immediately north-

Squalicum Harbor at Zuanich Point Park.

west of the Harbor Center, or at Zuanich Point Park off Coho Way (go left at the stop sign), a short distance beyond the Harbor Center (*map, p. 73*). Wander either direction on the wide path around the harbor and along adjacent walkways. Zuanich Point Park was named for long-time Port Commissioner, Pete Zuanich, who saved up the stipends he received for public service, ultimately donating $20,000 toward the park. An impressive sculpture commemorates fishermen and women lost at sea.

The opposite end of the walk passes Tom Glenn Common, a public waterfront plaza next to the upscale Bellwether Hotel (Tom Glenn was a manager for the port). At the Harbor Center, be sure to check out the flounder, urchins, sea stars, crab, anemones, octopi and friends at the Marine Life Center—a big little local gem of a place. To extend the walk, wander up Roeder Ave. a few blocks to C. St. and cross to Maritime Heritage Park and lower Whatcom Falls nearby (*see also Hikes #19 and #21*). Long ago, a pedestrian overpass was proposed from the Harbor to Broadway up on the bluff— still a great idea that ought to be pursued.

THE COAST—
9. South Bay Trail

Distance: 1 - 6 miles round trip   Time: Allow 1 - 4 hours

Season: Year-round

Bellingham's longest waterfront trail and greenway system, the South Bay Trail is still being developed, with a major over-water link south of Boulevard Park planned for 2004 or 2005. The corridor connects Fairhaven and the Padden Creek Trail to the south with the downtown area and Whatcom Creek Trail to the north (*map, p. 88*). The route passes through scenic Boulevard Park where the new public pier would connect the south end of the existing walkway to the soon-to-be-refurbished Taylor Street Dock. This will rectify a major disruption in the South Bay Trail that occurred in early 2001 when the quasi-reptilian mucky-mucks—rather, our good friends—at Burlington Northern Santa Fe Railway abruptly barri-

South Bay Trail at Boulevard Park.

caded two existing railroad crossings at either end of the park. A thousand people complained and the northerly crossing has since been fixed, and nicely so, thanks to the demands of the citizens, the mayor and city staff. Unfortunately, the city blinked on the southern crossing. (The author believes that the public may have established a permanent right to cross at both locations a long, long time ago; thus we may have been too quick to allow a fat-cat corporation to bully us away from our own waterfront. The trail should have remained open at least until the new southern link was completed.)

From the south, the new Village Green park in Fairhaven makes a good start. At 10th and Mill Streets walk north on the obvious trail to another short section of 10th St. and, in two blocks, the entrance to South Boulevard Park. The old route dropped to the railroad here, but since that crossing is now officially closed, continue to the street end and turn left on Bayview Dr. Find the waterfront path at the bottom of the hill, across the tracks. A left here traverses the existing pier to steps climbing up a steep rocky point above the tiny beach at Easton Cove—a great view and resting perch. To continue north, follow the shore around the park to a large tower and bridge leading to the upper park area (1.0 mile from Fairhaven). Or stay left to cross the tracks again (when safe). This section follows an old railroad grade dubbed "Miracle Mile" that leads a mile, of course, to the impressive Wharf Street Trestle, passing several spurs and stairways leading up to the Boulevard, South Hill and the university area (via Pine St.). The main trail continues to Railroad Ave. (2.4 miles from Fairhaven) and a future link with the Salish Coast Trail (*Hike #6*). Head back, or walk another five blocks to York St. and the Whatcom Creek Trail just beyond (*see Hike #20*).

Tнε Coast—
10. Post Point

Distance: 1 mile round trip   Time: Allow 1 hour
Season: Year-round

From Marine Park at the west end of Harris Ave. in Fairhaven, this short popular walk follows the beach along the railroad tracks (may be impassable if the tide is up) south to Post Point (*map, p. 88*). At lower tides, it's a pleasant 0.5-mile stroll one way to the low-lying rocky point in the distance. Continuing farther on the tracks is not recommended since it could be difficult to get out of the way of a passing train. Again, our good railroad friends think they own everything and would prefer that you and I had no access at all to mile after mile of our public shores. They should not be allowed that convenience, especially when it's to the detriment of the public's inextinguishable right to reasonable access to public land or water. That said, no guidebook author can guarantee when or where such rights will be upheld. As a matter of common sense, avoid the tracks and walk the beach at a lower-low tide instead. In winter, hundreds, maybe thousands of ducks, scoters, and grebes, mergansers, and a few loons, eagles and kingfishers can be seen. Even a grey whale, though rarely seen in Bellingham Bay, is not unheard of. This walk can be combined with the Padden Creek Trail (*Hike #25*), or with a stroll to the Alaska Ferry terminal north of Harris Ave.

Post Point.

THE COAST—
11. Teddy Bear Cove

Distance: 0.8 - 2.2 miles round trip   Time: Allow 1 - 2 hours
Elevation gain: 200 - 300 feet   Season: Year-round

Teddy Bear Cove, below Chuckanut Dr. south of Bellingham, may sound like a singular place, but there are two small coves here lying north and south of a small rocky headland. The cove to the north was also known as Brickyard Beach since this was the location of an intermittent brick-making operation from 1915 to 1925, as the residue on the beach suggests. Among the public, the beach had been a popular place to frolic for generations, and was well known locally as a nude sunbathing beach—but not anymore. A proposed housing development in the late 1980s inspired citizens to take action to save the area. The land was acquired by the Whatcom Land Trust and happily turned over to Whatcom County Parks.

This hike is short, but steep. Parking is not permitted where the trail leaves Chuckanut Dr. (*map, p. 96*). "No Parking" signs seem to appear and disappear, making it difficult to tell where parking is allowed. To be safe, park 0.6 mile north at the North Chuckanut Mountain Trailhead, walk up the obvious trail to California St., cross and follow the Interurban Trail to the Teddy Bear Cove junction (**0.6 mi**). Cross Chuckanut Dr. (when safe) and hike steeply down a half-dozen switchbacks to the railroad tracks. Cross (when safe) to the two coves and headland. Across Chuckanut Bay, the Clark Point

peninsula is also largely protected from development, as is Dot Island to the south.

Teddy Bear Cove.

THE COAST—
12. Wildcat Cove

Distance: 0.5 - 1 mile round trip   Time: Allow 1 hour
Season: Year-round

The storm-swept rocky shore at Larrabee State Park is one of the more wild and scenic places in western Whatcom County. Eroded 50 million-year-old sandstone lines the water's edge, capped by evergreen forests of douglas fir and madrone. The beaches and tide pools below invite curious kids and adults to experience marine ecology up close among communities of sea stars, mussels, barnacles, crabs and anemones. The park is the state's oldest and offers great opportunities for hiking, rock climbing, camping (some walk-in sites), kayaking, wildlife viewing, picnicking and photography.

To sample this intriguing landscape, drive five miles south of Fairhaven or bike the Interurban Trail (*Hike #28*) to the park's main entrance (if the hefty $5.00 parking fee is still in effect, direct your

Chuckanut coastline near Wildcat Cove.

complaints to the governor and state legislature, not the park staff).
Walk down a path left of the bandstand and through a short tunnel
beneath the railroad tracks. Stairs lead down to an easy trail that
follows the shore a short distance north and south. Go left 0.1 mile
to a rocky point and one of the loveliest sunsets in the region, marred
only by the misplaced construction of a house at Whiskey Rock. At
the junction below the tunnel, go right 0.1 mile to a fine beach,
popular in summer. If the tide is way out, you can wander the beach
and sandstone outcrops a bit more to the giant rock wall and boat
launch on Wildcat Cove. This is a popular launch for kayaks, while
the rock wall attracts roped-up climbers. A spur trail heads up briefly
for a view. The boot track beyond is used by climbers and dead ends
at dangerous drop-offs (not recommended). From the parking area,
one can walk up the old south entrance road to find a foot trail next
to a gate that leads to Clayton Beach (*see Hike #13*).

THE COAST—
13. Clayton Beach
Distance: 1.2 - 2.2 miles (or more) round trip   Time: Allow 1 - 2 hours
Season: Year-round

Clayton Beach was an outstanding addition to Larrabee State Park
in the late 1980s as a direct result of grassroots citizen action to
save the area from development (much of the credit goes to Arnie
Klaus). The area had been used by the public for many years, and
was perhaps appreciated most for its wild and undeveloped character. A fancy parking lot was built along Chuckanut Drive some time
ago, but the trail has not been satisfactorily upgraded. Muddy or
steep sections and an informal railway crossing can be expected.
Nevertheless, most of the trail is easy to walk despite mud and standing water in the rainy season (cards and letters to our state representatives— ask them to secure long-overdue funding for needed
trail repairs, including a new pedestrian bridge over the tracks.) When
improvements do occur, care must be taken to ensure that the tran-
quillity and wild character of the beach—the same qualities that fu-
eled the citizen effort to save the area—are not compromised.

Sandstone shore at Clayon Beach.

To access the beach, park at the signed trailhead on Chuckanut Dr. near MP 14, just south of the park entrance (*map, p. 96*). Cross the highway (when safe) and descend stairs to the old Interurban Trolley grade. A link to and from the main park area intersects the grade a few yards to the right. For the beach, head left across the bridge through forest and possible mud holes (generally okay in summer) to a short, steep rock slab (may be slippery). Scramble down, angle left and cross the railroad tracks when safe (note that passenger trains are unusually quiet and fast, so look carefully), or use the pedestrian overpass if it ever gets built. Follow the path leftward to the big sandy beach and unique sandstone formations, 0.6 mile from the start. Low tides allow much exploring north and south. At lower-low tides, adventurous hikers may be able to walk/ scramble northward some distance along the shore, but try not to crush the cute critters clinging to the crud.

URBAN AREAS

Jim Kaemingk Sr. Trail at Fishtrap Creek in Lynden.

14. Jim Kaemingk Sr. Trail (Fishtrap Creek)

Distance: 1.0 - 3.2 miles round trip   Time: Allow 1 - 2 hours
Season: Year-round

Former Lynden Mayor, Jim Kaemingk Sr., a strong advocate for trails, helped lead the development of what was originally called the Fishtrap Creek Trail. To recognize the mayor for his commitment to a quality community in Lynden, the city recently renamed the trail in his honor. The trail is a work in progress, but at 1.5 miles and growing, it merits a visit almost anytime of the year. The wide, paved path crosses the city more or less on a diagonal, from northeast to southwest, is linked to neighborhoods, and has the potential to link with a future trail along the Nooksack River, assuming the usual concerns of adjacent landowners can be adequately addressed.

A good place to begin the walk is at Lynden City Park on the east side of 3rd St. (Depot Rd.), three blocks north of Main St. and 1.5 miles east of Guide Meridian. Plans call for extending the trail to the southwest, and area residents should voice their support to help make it happen. Until that portion is built, head east through the park. Go left at a junction in 0.4 mile to explore a short spur after crossing Fishtrap Creek—a once prolific salmon stream. Return to the main trail and reach Bender Rd. at 0.8 mile. The path continues up the creek and through Bender ballfields, ending near Aaron Dr. (**1.5 mi**). The trail is planned to connect soon with the new Heritage Park immediately to the north. Return via the same route.

15. RiverWalk

Distance: 0.5-mile loop   Time: Allow 1 hour
Season: Year-round

Ferndale's RiverWalk Trail, adjacent to the Nooksack River, is only a semi-interesting 0.5-mile loop at the moment, but there is good potential for this trail to be extended along dikes for some distance up and down the river, perhaps two miles or more, which would make the trail far more appealing. A 15-mile river trail to Lynden would be outstanding should it ever happen. Over the short term, a link west to Pioneer Park would create a much more meaningful urban trail system than what currently exists at Ferndale. There is a lot of interest in the community in providing more trails, and one can only hope that key landowners and elected officials will be supportive as well. From Main St. turn north on 2nd Ave., head up and over the tracks and turn right on Washington St. Find the trail next to a parking area in VanderYacht Park two blocks ahead. The loop has interpretive signs that offer interesting insights on the river environment and its history.

Urban Areas (Bellingham, Everson)—
16. Bay-to-Baker Trail

Distance: 3.0 miles (or more) round trip   Time: Allow 1 - 2 hours (or more)

Elevation gain: 100 feet (or more)   Season: Year-round

The dream of a west-to-east regional trail across Whatcom County has been a serious consideration for at least two decades, and very slowly, portions of the "Bay-to-Baker" Trail are beginning to materialize. The exact route for the trail has not been fully determined, but ideally it would follow an abandoned railroad grade, county road shoulders in some areas, and other alignments elsewhere (*see maps on p. 73 and 75, for the Bellingham portion*). The trail could link together eight communities: Bellingham, Everson, Nooksack, Lynden, Sumas, Kendall, Maple Falls and Glacier. Beyond Glacier, the route would follow old logging roads and a new trail through the National Forest to Shuksan Arm and and Heather Meadows. Part of the Salmon Ridge Nordic Ski Area trail system may be improved soon to provide a six-mile link to the meadows.

In the 1970s, Whatcom County Parks acquired a scenic 7.5-mile section of the old railroad grade from Maple Falls to Glacier for conversion to a multiuse trail. The project was sidetracked by private property claims, but was eventually settled in the county's favor. In the early 1990s, the author helped obtain a $120,000 grant for the county to develop the eastern 5-mile stretch from Boulder Creek to

Glacier. Public support in the community seemed strong, and more than 200 kids from the Nooksack Valley School District volunteered to clear brush and improve drainage along the route. Yet just before final construction was to go out to bid, several anti-trail residents circulated petitions, as if the sky was falling, and managed to stop the project. Today, there seems to be a renewed interest in the foothills for a low-impact trail and the benefits it could bring to the smaller communities, so the trail may happen yet.

In Everson and Bellingham, public right-of-way is in place and some design or construction has occurred. In Everson, watch for the trail (soon?) off the west end of Main St. In Bellingham, the west terminus of the route is at Little Squalicum Beach (*see Hike #7*). From the railroad trestle, the wide gravel path (left) can be followed 1.3 miles east to Northwest Ave. The next stretch to Cornwall Park, Bug Lake and Sunset Pond could materialize by 2004. In rural areas, residents along some portions of the route like the idea of a nice trail nearby and some have offered to donate land or trail easements across their portion of the old railroad grade. (People who live along the route can contact Whatcom County Parks for updates and information about selling or donating right-of-way for the trail.)

Sunset Pond, along the future route of the Bay-to-Baker Trail.

17. Cornwall Park

Distance: 1 - 3-mile loops   Time: Allow 1 - 2 hours
Elevation gain: Minimal   Season: Year-round

In north Bellingham, this 66-acre park hosts a compact 2.5-mile trail system, mostly barrier-free paved and unpaved, that offers an hour of easy sauntering among large trees, lawns and Squalicum Creek. Some paths form part of a fitness trail and others link facilities together within the park. Most trails are level, though there are a few small hills. Eventually, the park may host a portion of the Bay-to-Baker Trail (*see Hike #16*) which will help link Cornwall Park to the Birchwood and Columbia neighborhoods, and to Bug Lake and Sunset Pond. Find the park at the north end of Cornwall Ave., or off Meridian St. about one block south of Squalicum Pkwy., or on foot or by bike from the Puget neighborhood to the south. The paths can be wandered leisurely and aimlessly.

Forested path in Cornwall Park.

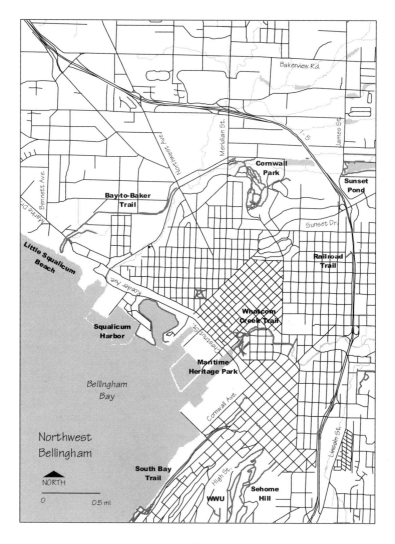

Northwest
Bellingham

NORTH

0   0.5 mi

URBAN AREAS (BELLINGHAM)—
18. Big Rock & Northridge Park

Distance: 0.5 - 3.0-mile loops   Time: Allow 1 - 2 hours
Elevation gain: Minimal - 400 feet   Season: Year-round

Northridge Park, north of Barkley Blvd., was undeveloped in 2003 but will likely see improvements soon, including a small trail network linked to neighborhoods. Some gravel paths exist already, which can be combined with the steep trail along Barkley Blvd. and paths near Big Rock Garden to create a loop. As new trails fall into place, the area's appeal for an urban walk will certainly increase. Head north from Alabama on Sylvan St. and park near the end of the street. Walk left briefly to a tunnel under Barkley Blvd. that leads to a fork; stay left for a wildlife pond and loop leftward back to Barkley, then left up the sidewalk to the tunnel (0.5-mile loop). From the tunnel, one could descend nearly 300 feet in 0.5 mile to the Railroad Trail (*Hike #19*), or head back to Sylvan and the trail leading east into the woods. Informal paths in the forest can be explored in various directions (may be upgraded). If you find your way through the maze (heading generally southeast) to a good gravel path, you should be able to turn right and follow this to the big water tank near Big Rock Garden not far up the hill; a left spur leads to a good view of Lake Whatcom below Academy St. After an amble through

Big Rock Garden, walk down the entrance road to Sylvan St. and continue right three blocks to the start.

Duck Pond at Northridge Park.

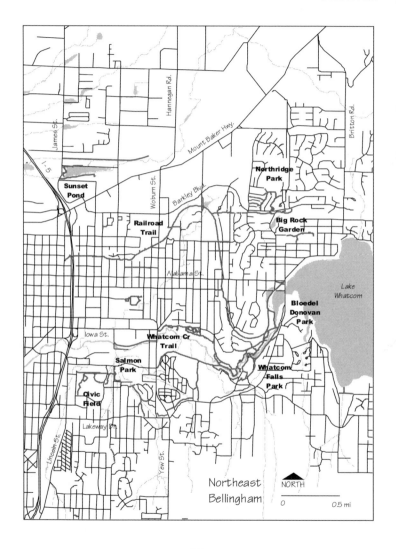

Northeast
Bellingham

NORTH

0   0.5 mi

URBAN AREAS (BELLINGHAM)—
19. Railroad Trail

Distance: 3.7 - 5.0 miles (or more) one way   Time: Allow 2 - 3 hours
Elevation gain (or loss): 250 feet   Season: Year-round

The trains that once made the run from Bellingham Bay to Lake Whatcom had nearly 300 feet of elevation gain to contend with, which explains why this route snugs up to Alabama Hill, traversing at just a two-percent grade to reach the lake with steam to spare. The route was abandoned long ago, and was improved for trail use by volunteers in the 1980s. It has since been upgraded to a high standard for hikers and cyclists. An expensive (and definitely warranted) new trail bridge over Alabama St. was completed in early 2003. A missing segment northeast of downtown requires some walking on sidewalks to complete the entire route. Return by bus or via the Whatcom Creek Trail (*Hike #20*).

Old railroad trestle over Whatcom Creek, near the Railroad Trail.

From Bloedel-Donovan Park, wander out to Electric Ave. and follow the sidewalk north (right) a short distance to find the Railroad Trail's east trailhead across the street (*map, p.75*). Formerly a railroad grade serving coal mines and sawmills on Lake Whatcom, the wide gravel path passes bird-rich Scudder Pond—kudos to the Audubon Society and Mrs. Armitage. Walk 0.3 mile past the pond to a junction of two wide paths; stay right. (A slightly longer, but nicer, option is to take the first left past the pond on a narrow, winding trail and follow this to a bridge over Whatcom Creek. But don't cross; instead, head right to the main junction noted above.) The Railroad Trail heads right again at the next major junction (**0.6 mi**). But first, go left briefly and left again to see the frail remains of a large railroad trestle still spanning Whatcom Creek (**0.7 mi**). Let's hope the city makes at least a minimal effort to preserve this unique bit of our town's heritage. Return to the Railroad Trail and continue past Rhododendron Way, then stay right at Texas St. to find a nice view from the new pedestrian overpass at Alabama St. (**1.6 mi**). Several spurs lead to adjoining neighborhoods. At the St. Clair stormwater basin (**2.2 mi**), a right leads east 0.5 mile and nearly 300 feet up the hill to Northridge Park (*Hike #18*). The Railroad Trail continues to the I-5 overpass and trail's end at Sunnyland Memorial Park (**3.7 mi**). The park's trees were planted by mothers who lost sons in WWI. For the final segment downtown, it's necessary to follow neighborhood streets south about five blocks to Kentucky St. and west five and a half blocks to a paved trail on the left next to the high school, just west of Franklin St. (*map, p. 73*). Head south, jog right to cross Ohio St., and find the trail again off Ellis St. sandwiched between two fences. This leads to York St. and Railroad Ave. (**5.0 mi**) which can be followed five more blocks to the South Bay Trail (*Hike #9*).

20. Whatcom Creek
Distance: 0.8-mile loop or up to 5 miles one way   Time: Allow 1 - 3 hours
Elevation gain (or loss): 100 - 400 feet Season: Year-round

Trails along Whatcom Creek—perhaps Bellingham's best-loved natural gem—offers several easy to moderate walks of a few miles or less, to a 5-mile trek from Lake Whatcom to Bellingham Bay. The latter will become increasingly attractive as the city completes some of the missing trail sections between Racine St. and I-5 (hopefully in 2003 or 2004), and from there to downtown (a bit later). For now, two longer options combine trails and street sections, passing through several parks, and touching the estuary at Bellingham Bay with a possible return route by bus or via the Railroad Trail up Alabama Hill (*Hike #19*). An extensive trail system between Bloedel Donovan Park and Whatcom Falls Park offers a variety of loops past wetlands, wildlife ponds, waterfalls, time-sculpted sandstone, tall trees, a fish hatchery, and picnic areas. "Whatcom," a native term suggesting "noisy waters," is a perfect moniker for this wild urban creek as it descends more than 300 feet in four miles, right through the heart of Bellingham.

Sadly, tragedy struck Whatcom Creek June 10, 1999 when Olympic Pipeline Company's underground fuel pipeline ruptured at Whatcom Falls Park, resulting in a catastrophic explosion that took the lives of three young people and destroyed over a mile of riparian and aquatic habitat, hundreds of trees, and thousands of fish, birds, mammals, amphibians and other wildlife. A major restoration effort is underway to assist in the recovery of the Whatcom Creek ecosystem (avoid all closed areas).

Despite the damage, the trails are open and well worth exploring. For the shortest walk to the exquisite stone bridge at Whatcom Falls, head out Lakeway Dr. and turn left (north) at the park sign at Kenoyer Dr. The falls is near the parking area with additional trails leading to more waterfalls up and down the creek. One idea for a short walk is to cross the bridge, turn left and follow paths closest to the creek to Whirlpool Falls, then up the stairs to a wide path; turn right to return to the stone bridge (0.8-mile loop).

Stone bridge at Whatcom Falls.

For the longer lake-to-bay trek, begin at Bloedel-Donovan Park at the north end of Lake Whatcom (*maps, p. 73 and 75*) and follow the path south along the landscaped berm to another path across Electric Ave. This leads quickly to a bridge over Whatcom Creek. Just ahead, make a sharp left (downhill) then left again to view a dilapidated railroad trestle hovering over the creek like an old dream. Retrace your steps and go left again on a path that leads back to the creek and a kids fishing pond and bridge. Cross and continue straight ahead (left leads around the pond and back to Bloedel-Donovan Park). Follow trail and road past the trout hatchery and on to the stone bridge below Whatcom Falls (**1.0 mi**). Cross, stay left along the creek, then at a wooden bridge there is a choice to be made. Once the Whatcom Creek Trail is completed to I-5, it will make more sense to *not* cross the bridge; instead, head downstream past another falls and up a few steps to a junction (**1.4 mi**). Left here and left again leads to two overlooks of the lower gorge with information about the 1999 fire. This is followed by a long flight of steps down a hillside to Woburn St. (**2.1 mi**). Cross at the light, head left then right and continue to Racine St. and the end of the trail in early 2003 (**2.6 mi**). One may have to follow sidewalks for 1.2 miles from here to reach the downtown section of the Whatcom Creek Trail.

Back at the wooden bridge, a second option is to cross and head right along a wide path to Bayview Cemetery. Either walk south and west through the cemetery to Old Woburn St., or hike around the cemetery on path and sidewalk to the same location. Turn right on Wildflower Way to find the Salmon Park Trail a block down the hill, 1.3 miles from the wooden bridge. See Hike #21 for the route to Geri Fields, then walk the obvious paved path west to Moore St. where a jog left then right brings you to Lincoln St.; turn right. This becomes Meador and leads to State St. Cross to Kansas and in two blocks go right on Ellis St. Walk a few yards and look left for the Railroad Trail contained within two fences. Follow this across Whatcom Creek to a junction; turn right (from the wooden bridge, it's 3.1 miles to this point). Cross Cornwall Ave. and continue on the trail the last mile through downtown. From Grand Ave., take the path on the north side of the creek to reach an overlook and superb salmon trail that is dedicated to the memory of Liam Wood, an inspired young fisherman who perished in the 1999 disaster. Cross Dupont St., descend stairs to another bridge below Lower Whatcom Falls, Maritime Heritage Park, and the last bit of path along lower Whatcom Creek. (*See also Hike #22.*)

UrBan AReas (BellinGHam)—
21. Salmon Park
Distance: 1.2 - 3.3-mile loop   Time: Allow 1 - 2 hours
Elevation gain: Minimal or 200 feet   Season: Year-round

Midway between Lake Whatcom and the Bay, the forks of Cemetery Creek converge in a large area of wetlands before emptying into Whatcom Creek northeast of Civic Field. A small network of trails provide limited access to undeveloped "Salmon Park." A planned link to the Whatcom Creek Trail will enhance the walking potential considerably. One could begin at several locations, but to make a bit more of a trip out of it, try starting near the Arne Hanna Aquatic Center just east of I-5 and north of Lakeway. Take Lincoln St. to Potter, turn right, then left on Moore St. for one block to find the wide trail leading into the woods (*map, p. 75*). The trail splits and rejoins on the way to a paved path at Geri Fields. Head right to Puget St. and cross to the next section. Stay left at a junction, cross a bridge, and go right at the next (left here should eventually connect with the Whatcom Creek Trail). At Toledo Ct. (**0.6 mi**), turn left a block to pick up the next section. Cross another bridge and turn right. At the next junction, a right leads up to Lakeway Dr.; left goes to Wildflower Way, two blocks from the cemetery (**0.9 mi**).

For a good loop, walk up Wildflower Way to Old Woburn St.; turn right, then cross to a paved path on the left. Follow this up Lakeway, cross at the light and go left briefly to find more paved trail leading past the cemetery and along Lakeway Dr. again. Just after a cemetery entrance, take the wide gravel path heading north to another wide path (**1.9 mi**). Right here leads to Whatcom Falls Park (*see Hike #20*), but go left for the loop. Walk this corridor to Woburn St.; cross and head down the hill and west on Fraser St. past a resi-

dential area to a path on the left in the woods. Walk this briefly to a junction (**2.8 mi**) and go right to return to Geri fields and the start of the hike (**3.3 mi total**).

Salmon Park.

URBAN AREAS (BELLiNGHAM)—
22. Historic Bellingham

Distance: 2.0-mile loop (or more)   Time: Allow 1 - 2 hours
Elevation gain: Minimal   Season: Year-round

For this walking tour of Bellingham, the emphasis is on historic buildings in the downtown area and in the Columbia neighborhood. Lower Whatcom Falls, a fish hatchery, a museum, two parks and a lot of beautiful century-old Victorian homes exist along the route. In the residential areas, keep an eye on all the chimneys: no two look quite the same.

The fountain on W. Holly St. in front of Maritime Heritage Park makes a good starting point (*map, p. 73*). Walk to the amphitheater and note the 1892 French Victorian building up on the bluff—now the Whatcom Museum of History and Art. This landmark once served as City Hall for the town of New Whatcom and later Bellingham. Head left toward the creek on a nicely landscaped path. Pass a totem pole, native plant interpretive signs, salmon art and a viewpoint before reaching the footbridge at the base of Lower Whatcom Falls. The falls represents the birth of Bellingham since it was the useful energy of the falls that attracted Captain Henry Roeder and his partner, Russell Peabody, to establish a lumber mill here in 1853. They called their new town "Whatcom," after the Indian name for the creek's noisy waters. To imagine the history, walk up the creek under the Prospect St. bridge to Grand Ave.; make a U-turn to the left and return to Prospect (*see also Hike #20*). Cross and drop down the steps to the hatchery, then angle right up a diagonal walkway to the Old Village Trail (**0.6 mi**).

Next, pass the ancient George Pickett house at 910 Bancroft, built in 1856 out of lumber from the Roeder mill. Pickett came to Whatcom in 1855 to establish Fort Bellingham and was also caught up in the "Pig War" of the San Juan Islands. He joined the Confederacy in Virginia in 1861, soon to become the famed Major General who would lead an Army division of thousands to their doom in "Picket's Charge" in the Battle of Gettysburg. At H. St., jog right, then left at the striking Theater Guild building to reach Broadway and Elizabeth Park (**1.0 mi**). Walk through the park (donated by

Former City Hall, now Whatcom Museum of History and Art.

Captain Roeder in 1883) to Walnut and Washington, heading west on the latter. In the Columbia Neighborhood, many historic homes have been beautifully renovated. Watch for identifying plaques, but respect the residents' privacy. Turn left on Utter St. to see the attractive Shields House (1895) and the Loggie House (1893), whose early owner operated the largest cedar mill in the world in the 1920s. His daughter, Helen, was a well known Pacific Northwest artist. Continue on Utter past the Countryman houses (1897, 1901) and turn left at Eldridge Ave.—or keep exploring the neighborhood.

The Jenkins House at 1807 Eldridge was owned by the postmaster and father of a mayor of New Whatcom. Pass St. Paul's Episcopal Church at 2116 Walnut St. (the older wood building was built in 1884 for $1,300). Check the good view of Squalicum Harbor off the end of Broadway at W. Holly St. (**1.5 mi**). On June 15, 1792, Lieutenant Joseph Whidbey entered the bay while on a reconnaissance for Captain George Vancouver. Vancouver named the bay for Sir William Bellingham, an English Navy officer. Continue down W. Holly past the Aftermath Club (1905), a meeting place for socially active, intellectual women. Pass the First Baptist Church building (left) at 1311 I St., the oldest church in Bellingham, and the Lottie Roth Block (1890), a great example of Chuckanut sandstone construction.

Turn left on E St. to see the oldest brick building north of San Francisco. Built in 1858, the Richards Building (1308 E. St.) has been a general store, bank, warehouse, courthouse, jail, post office, taxidermy, newspaper company, outdoor equipment store, wood shop, gallery and who knows what else over its long life. Go back across West Holly to the old Great Northern Freight Depot, a long white building at E St. and Roeder Ave. Walk south and notice the attractive brick depot nearby, formerly a station for passenger trains. Continue walking up W. Holly St. to Maritime Heritage Park to complete the loop (**2.0 mi**), perhaps exploring the shops of "Old Town" rife with history, local charm, antiques and oddities.

URBAN AREAS (BELLINGHAM)—
23. Sehome Hill Arboretum

Distance: 2.0-mile loop (or more)   Time: Allow 1 - 2 hours
Elevation gain: 300 feet (or more)   Season: Year-round

This hike near Western Washington University features a 165-acre natural arboretum, sandstone outcrops, a tunnel, and a view tower overlooking the city. Sehome Hill was logged off in the 1870s, later becoming a city park and finally a nature preserve in the 1970s. Douglas fir seems to be overpowering the opportunistic hardwoods, stealing their sunlight, and promising ongoing ecological change in

View from Sehome Hill Arboretum.

the forest community. There are several means of access and a number of side trails and short loops that can be explored, so the loop described below is just one idea of many. There are about five miles of trails on the hill (*map, next page*). One can also combine the walk with a tour of the outdoor sculpture museum at the university (call ahead for information or explore on your own). To avoid throngs of students on campus, try weekends or late afternoons.

From Samish Way, take Bill McDonald Pkwy. to 25th St., the first right after the high school. Most of the year, students may be hogging the public parking slots here, so head up the road 0.8 mile to the upper parking lot. A couple of short paths lead 0.2 mile northward to the view tower (well signed). For the real hike, maybe save the view for later and instead look for a sign pointing to WWU. Follow the gravel path left along the west side of the parking lot opposite the radio tower. The path, Douglas Fir Trail, winds gently down through an attractive mix of douglas fir, big leaf maple, sword ferns, red elderberry, snowberry and salal. Stay on the main trail, bypassing several forks that branch to the left. A four-way intersection ap-

85

pears about 10-15 minutes from the start (**0.6 mi**); go straight (a path to the right offers a shortcut to the return route). The main path curves sharply to the left, passing low sandstone cliffs popular with rock climbers, before reaching the road (**0.7 mi**). (A trail continues down to the Parkway where one could jog left to Ferry Ave., turn right and head down the hill two blocks to find the north end of the trail to Connelly Creek Nature Area; *Hike #24*.)

At the arboretum road, turn right, then right again in 200 yards, just outside the gate, and follow the path up a couple of steps and left on the better trail. Soon, pass the shortcut route coming down from the right (**1.0 mi**) and continue to an intersection with a campus road; take the path on the right and continue north. Beyond, several spur trails access the university and its historic buildings, sculptures and landscape. The mostly paved Huntoon Trail gradually rises through a mixed forest of red alder, big leaf maple, Oregon grape, salal, oceanspray and a variety of ferns and wildflowers (in spring and early summer). Just past a wide flat of pavement, take the second right, a paved fork rising the last 0.1 mile to the view tower (**1.8 mi**). The view of the city, bay and harbor is impressive: Vancouver Island, the Gulf Islands, Canadian peaks, Mount Baker and part of the North Cascades are all visible on a good day. From the tower head right on a paved path leading back through a tunnel to the parking lot (**2.0 mi**).

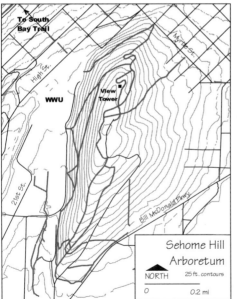

86

24. Connelly Creek Trail

Distance: 1 - 4 miles round trip   Time: Allow 1 - 3 hours

Elevation gain: Minimal   Season: Year-round

With only a couple of short missing links, this trail system through Bellingham's Happy Valley and the Connelly Creek Nature Reserve now links Sehome Hill to the north with the Interurban Trail to the south (*map, next page*). To walk only the nature reserve, take 32nd St. to Donovan Ave. and head two blocks west to 30th St. to the signed shoulder parking area. Follow the path north, and stay left at the first junction, right at the next. Cross the skinny creek undergoing recovery work for salmon, a small flood-control dam, and an unusual grove of Sitka spruce before reaching another small trailhead at Douglas Ave. (**0.6 mi**) Just before the latter, one can angle right, cross Taylor Ave., and walk the access driveway and path north through Joe's Garden and into forest for the last stretch to Ferry Ave. (**1.0 mi**). Walk up the street, cross Bill McDonald Pkwy. and head left briefly to find a good trail leading into the Sehome Hill Arboretum (*Hike #23*). For the Interurban link, return to the Donovan Ave. trailhead, walk west about three blocks to find the trail on the left. This 0.2-mile path leads past a play area and over a bridge across Padden Creek before reaching Old Fairhaven Pkwy. Cross, then walk 0.3 mile west to find an access to the Interurban Trail south of the Parkway (2.0 miles from Sehome Hill). Most of the missing links could be completed in fairly short order.

Connelly Creek Nature Area.

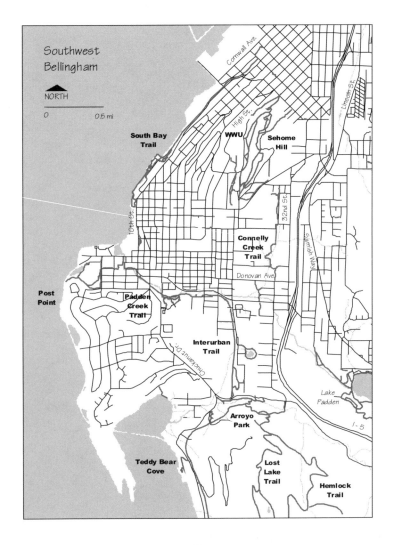

Southwest
Bellingham

NORTH

0   0.5 mi

South Bay
Trail

WWU

Sehome
Hill

High St.

Cornwall Ave.

Lincoln St.

10th St.

32nd St.

Samish Way

Connelly
Creek
Trail

Donovan Ave.

Post
Point

Padden
Creek
Trail

Interurban
Trail

Chuckanut Dr.

Lake
Padden

I - 5

Arroyo
Park

Teddy Bear
Cove

Lost
Lake
Trail

Hemlock
Trail

URban AReas (BeLLiNGHam)—
25. Padden Creek & Historic Fairhaven
Distance: 2.4 miles (or more) round trip Time: Allow 1 - 3 hours
Elevation gain (or loss): 100 feet   Season: Year-round

The hike along the lower reach of Padden Creek on Bellingham's southside is one of the nicer gems in the city trail system. In fall, it is a great place to watch chum salmon coming up the creek by the hundreds, if not thousands, to spawn. The route offers several destinations and connects with the Fairhaven Historic District, as well as other urban routes (*see Hikes #9, #10 and #27*). From the tennis courts at Fairhaven Park, walk down the steps and go left along Padden Creek, crossing it three times on foot bridges. At a four-way junction go left; straight ahead leads to 14th St. and right leads 0.2 mile to the Interurban Trailhead, an alternate starting point. Continue, walking under the 12th St. bridge, crossing Padden Creek

Padden Creek at Fairhaven Park.

over a pair of large culverts. Round the 10th and Donovan intersection (**0.4 mi**) and take the trail back down into the canyon (a right spur leads to Harris Ave. in Fairhaven). The next section contours along the creek through the multi-layered forest canopy, passing an interesting historic marker on the way. Cross the creek to a junction; right goes to Harris Ave., Fairhaven and Padden Lagoon. Pass a marsh with bird boxes, continue across 6th and 4th Streets, and head left at the wastewater treatment plant (right goes to Harris Ave. and the Alaska Ferry terminal). Take either fork ahead to explore the loop trail to a saltwater lagoon (**1.2 mi**). Right here leads, again, to Harris Ave.; left to Post Point (use caution, of course, if crossing the tracks).

Take any of the spurs to Harris Ave. to wander among the historic markers, buildings (some recent, but nice, imitations), and the new Village Green in the heart of it. The area suffers a bit from too many cars, and could use a bit more green space, but it's otherwise quaint and fun to explore. Highlights include the old double-decker bus shipped here from England in the 1970s; old red bricks down the center of the street, leftover from the trolleys; the Mason Block (a.k.a. Sycamore Square, 1890); Waldron Building (1891); Nelson Block bank building (1900); Pythias Building (1891); Morgan Block (1890), and the Terminal Building (1888)—Fairhaven's oldest commercial building. Fairhaven was originally envisioned as the western terminus of the Great Northern Railroad and owes its beginning to the land speculators and developers whose moneyed dreams never

quite materialized. The town was platted in 1883 by "Dirty Dan" Harris. By 1903 it had merged with the rest of Bellingham.

Terminal Building.

90

26. Lake Padden

Distance: 2.6-mile loop   Time: Allow 1 - 2 hours
Elevation gain: Minimal   Season: Year-round

The 2.6-mile loop around placid Lake Padden is one of the more popular year-round walks (and jogs) in Bellingham. The trail is wide, well maintained, and has quarter-mile markers for those who might want to train or monitor fitness. This is a good place to calculate your ideal walking pace. (A comfortable 2 MPH pace means 30 minutes per mile, or 7.5 minutes per quarter-mile. For 3 MPH, walk a mile in 20 minutes or a quarter-mile in 5 minutes, and so on.) The lake is also a favorite among paddlers, swimmers and quackers.

From Bellingham, drive or peddle south on Samish Way about 2.2 miles from its bridge over I-5. Take either of two entrances into the park and find the path near the lake (*map, next page*). Hike either direction and generally follow the main trail closest to the lake. The route otherwise needs little description. The south shore involves a few easy hills and is heavily wooded. The north shore is low-lying and level. Near the lake outlet on the west end, a wide gravel spur leads along the creek for 0.4 mile to a short 0.3-mile loop at the end. Someday (we can hope) this trail may be extended down-canyon to Happy Valley and the Connelly Creek and Interurban Trails. Lack of an obvious corridor has stymied the idea for now. For other trails in the area, including a more difficult 6-mile loop taking in Padden Ridge, see the next listing (*Hike #27*) or look for the large trail map near the mouth of Ruby Creek by the ballfields.

Lake Padden.

27. Padden Ridge

Distance: 5.8-mile loop

Time: Allow 3 - 4 hours

Elevation gain: 500 feet

Season: Year-round

In addition to the loop trail around Lake Padden, a number of other trails exist along the ridge between the lake and I-5. To get acquainted with some of these consider the loop described here. These trails are popular with mountain bikers and equestrians, and some trails have suffered as a result. Nevertheless, efforts have been made (and more are needed) to improve the trail system, reduce damage, and make the area much more suitable for shared use.

See the previous listing, Lake Padden (*Hike #26*), for directions to the park. For the longer loop, start at the tennis courts. Head right along the lakeshore, pass several spurs, cross Padden Creek, and walk uphill to a junction with a horse trail; stay right (left is the easy lake loop). Gain the ridge at a fence line and head left. Continue straight then right at a four-way junction (**0.7 mi**; left returns to the lower lake loop). Stay right again at the next fork to begin a section that may be very muddy in the wet season unless its been rebuilt. The trail climbs moderately through a pleasant forest of

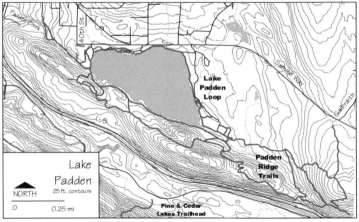

Padden Ridge Trail.

Douglas fir and cedar. Stay right again to pass beneath a giant rotten log—the "fallen tree arch". Look for a rare seven-foot diameter old-growth douglas fir tree and a Pacific yew nearby. Beyond, the trail descends to another junction (**1.8 mi**); stay right to continue the hike, or left to reach the lower lake trail. Go right at the next junction (**2.0 mi**); again, left leads to the lake loop nearby.

From this junction, begin a series of messy, short switchbacks up to the ridge crest where the trail improves considerably. At a powerline corridor (**2.9 mi**), check the uncommon view of I-5 and the Chuckanut Mountain area. Pass under the powerlines to another junction just in the woods. The longer loop heads right. (A shortcut follows the old road left, which leads back to the powerlines, passes a link on the right, and re-meets the longer loop at a tee 0.4 mile away.) For the longer loop, stay right on the narrow path and right again at the next junction (**3.1 mi**); a left here leads 0.5 mile back to the powerline. Continuing right, follow a winding mountain-bike path gradually up (ignoring minor spurs) and angling left at two large fir trees before another junction (**3.6 mi**); stay left (right leads 0.4 mile to the mountain bikers' preferred trailhead on Samish Way). Descend 0.3 mile to a junction, head right, and skip the next left to reach the powerline tee with the shortcut noted earlier (**4.1 mi**). This final leg of the hike descends gently through maturing forest, rotting stumps and verdant wetlands, crossing a small bridge before reaching the big trail map near the lake and ballfields (**4.6 mi**), an alternate starting point. Follow the obvious trail along the lakeshore to return to the tennis courts (**5.8 mi**).

Chuckanuts

Interurban Trail in winter.

CHUCKANUTS—
28. Interurban Trail

Distance: 2.8 - 12.7 miles round trip   Time: Allow 2 - 6 hours
Elevation gain: Minimal - 300 feet   Season: Year-round

The historic Interurban trolley was the first rapid-transit system between Bellingham, Mt. Vernon and points south. Now, the old rail corridor is used by hikers and bicyclists coming and going between Fairhaven, Arroyo Park, Larrabee State Park, and the Chuckanuts. One can begin near the tennis courts at Fairhaven Park, at the main Interurban Trailhead (described here), or 1.2 mile south at the Arroyo Park trailhead on Old Samish Hwy. just off Chuckanut Dr. (*maps, p. 88 and next page*). Except for a short section through Arroyo Park, the path is generally wide and well maintained.

From the signed trailhead on Old Fairhaven Pkwy. near 20th St., walk up the gravel path to a wide sidewalk; go left (right leads 0.2 mile to Fairhaven Park). Cross 22nd St. and pass a former trailhead sign (**0.3 mi**). Turn to the south through forest and wetlands, passing several spurs on the left. The first leads a few yards to 24th St.; jog right then left to reach Hoag Pond (**0.7 mi**), a 0.4-mile sidetrip. The next two spurs offer a 0.3-mile loop through an area dedicated to Clarita Moore, a passionate environmental educator who brought her students here many decades ago. Continue south to cross Old Samish Hwy. (switchbacks) to Arroyo Park (**1.2 mi**). The trail drops down to a bridge over Chuckanut Creek, a salmon stream and a good turn-around point for the shorter walk (**1.4 mi**). Or, cross the bridge and climb to the old original grade where a very large trestle once spanned the valley. Continue across California St. (**1.9 mi**) and pass a junction leading down to Teddy Bear Cove (**2.4 mi**; *see Hike #11*), then hike a long stretch to where the trail makes a big dip and crosses Fragrance Lake Creek (**4.4 mi**). Keep walking to intersect the Fragrance Lake Trail at Larrabee State Park (**5.6 mi**). Either head right into Larrabee State Park (*see Hike #12*), or go straight, then left on a narrow path to the Clayton Beach Trailhead (**6.1 mi**; *see Hike #13*).

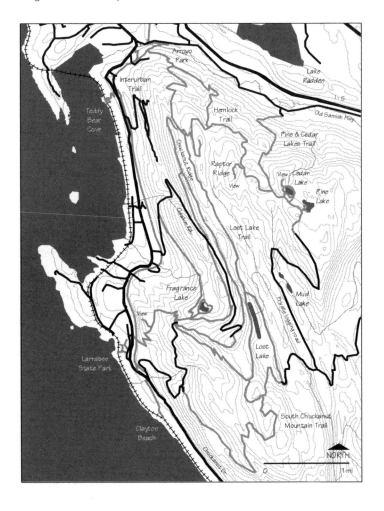

Chuckanuts—
29. Pine & Cedar Lakes

Distance: 4 - 6 miles round trip   Time: Allow 3 - 5 hours
Elevation gain: 1,300 - 1,600 feet   Season: Year-round

Two very pleasant lakes and views of the San Juan Islands and even Mount Rainier on a clear day make this a rewarding hike almost any time. Cedar Lake has a loop trail around it and Pine Lake has a small island-peninsula with campsites nearby. Eventually, an improved trail system may connect this area with Lost Lake, Larrabee State Park, and Lake Samish.

From Fairhaven (12th St. & Old Fairhaven Parkway), follow Chuckanut Drive (SR 11) south 1.3 miles, turning left on Old Samish Hwy. Continue another 1.9 miles to the signed trailhead and parking area on the right (*elevation: 300 feet*). The broad path, an old logging road, is quite steep for the first mile. At a flat, either go straight (steep), or left on a newer trail (more gradual). The trails rejoin and finally level out at the Cedar Lake/Hemlock Trail junction (**1.6 mi**).

Lily pads on Pine Lake.

A right here leads to Raptor Ridge and Arroyo Park (*see Hike #30*). Stay left to find the Cedar Lake Trail (**1.9 mi**), or keep walking to reach the spur to Pine Lake (**2.2 mi**); continuing right leads to private, logged-off timberland above Mud Lake, about two miles away.

The spur to Cedar Lake (*elevation: 1,520 feet*) descends moderately in 0.1 mile. Hike either way around the lake and watch for a spur on the west end leading up to views. The path may be hard to follow in the dense thicket of young trees, but you should be able to find a glimpse of Bellingham, Pine Lake, the Cascades and the San Juan Islands from various vantage points. The spur to less visited Pine Lake is also very short. Approach quietly to avoid scaring off the ducks or other wildlife. No trail circles this lake, but the island-peninsula near the west edge is a fine spot to spread out the picnic. Several campsites exist near the shore and fishing is permitted in season at both lakes. Allow four hours to hike the entire route.

Chuckanuts—
30. Hemlock Trail & Raptor Ridge

Distance: 5.2 - 9.6 miles round trip   Time: Allow 3 - 6 hours
Elevation gain: 1,300 - 1,600 feet   Season: Year-round

Hemlock Trail is the name given to the old logging road that ex tends four miles from the end of California St. (no parking) to the Pine and Cedar Lakes Trail, including a 0.7-mile section of new trail that was built in the late 1990s to complete the link. The 0.4-mile Raptor Ridge Trail leads from the Hemlock Trail up to an excellent viewpoint (*map, p. 96*). In 1999, the author along with 40 volunteers from the Bellingham Mountaineers, Sierra Club and others constructed the 0.4-mile footpath to Raptor Ridge—a name given to the wooded ridge and high cliff band at the end of this scenic, moderately steep, wildlife-sensitive trail. Hawks, eagles, owls, ravens and turkey vultures are often seen or heard in summer.

If Raptor Ridge is the destination, the shorter, but steeper, approach is from the Pine and Cedar Lakes Trailhead (2.6 miles total). The easier, but longer, route via Arroyo Park is 4.8 miles. If starting at Pine and Cedar Lakes Trail (*see Hike #29*), go right at the Hem-

Trail volunteers at the Raptor Ridge overlook.

lock Trail junction (**1.6 mi**), on a level grade—a remnant of railroad logging in the 1920s. The Hemlock follows it for 0.3 mile before dipping down past old bridge stringers (logs), rounding a bend, and climbing slightly to a junction with the Raptor Ridge Trail (**2.2 mi**). Turn left, ambling through the woods, crossing a bridge, climbing stone steps (watch your head), passing grottos, and otherwise communing with sandstone on the way to a panoramic view of the Oyster Creek watershed—the wild heart of the Chuckanuts (**2.6 mi**).

If starting at Arroyo Park, cross Chuckanut Creek and go left at a junction (sign post). The road above is Hemlock Trail; head left and pass the turnoff to Lost Lake (**1.4 mi**). Continue along the road which soon steepens. At a major tee junction with a signpost (**3.2 mi**), turn left on a level grade; right leads a mile to a view atop Madrone Crest, or 1.2 miles to North Lost Lake Trail (*Hike #33*), via the Salal Trail. Continuing left from the tee, find the Raptor Ridge Trail shortly after leaving the old road grade (**4.4 mi**), and turn right for the final ascent to the view (**4.8 mi**; *elevation: 1,600 feet*). Use caution at the overlook—there's a very long drop (maybe constrain the kids and pets). Be extra cautious in strong wind, snow or ice.

CHUCKANUTS—
31. Fragrance Lake

Distance: 2 - 5 miles round trip   Time: Allow 2 - 4 hours
Elevation gain: 1,000 - 1,800 feet   Season: Year-round

A favorite year-round hike for many locals, the Fragrance Lake Trail passes through deep forest on the way to a pleasant loop around the lake. Years ago, an earthen dam was built to raise the lake level, but it weakened in a storm, gave way and sent a wall of water raging down the mountain. Several homes were destroyed in the vicinity of today's Chuckanut Fire Station. The Interurban Trolley, which just happened to be passing by, was badly damaged.

There are three approaches to the lake (*map, p. 96*). The most popular begins at the west trailhead on Chuckanut Dr. near the main entrance to Larrabee State Park, 5 miles south of Fairhaven (well signed). Another, the north access, begins 0.7 mile up the Cleator

Fragrance Lake.

Rd., on the right just before a gate. The third begins about 2.5 miles up the same road. One can also combine the Fragrance Lake hike with a visit to Chuckanut Ridge (*Hike #32*) or Lost Lake (*Hike #33*).

Beginning at Chuckanut Dr. (*elevation: 100 feet*) across from the main entrance to the State Park (possible parking fee). Hike up a few dozen paces to the Interurban Trail, cross and follow the gently ascending route to a junction (**0.9 mi**). A left takes you 0.2 mile to a good viewpoint of the islands. Return to the junction and continue a mile on a gradually steepening path. Cross a small stream and reach another junction near the old Fragrance Lake Road, now closed (**1.9 mi**). The lake trail drops down slightly to another junction near the lake (**2.1 mi**). Go left on boardwalk or straight to complete the easy 0.5-mile loop around the lake (*elevation: 1,020 feet*). The north approach climbs steadily on an old fire road, passes a small waterfall and reaches two junctions with narrow paths leading down to the left. Both meet the lake loop near its outlet. Or stay on the ridge crest for a good view of the lake (high cliffs: use caution). This path descends to the 1.9-mile junction near the old Fragrance Lake Road (**2.0 mi**). The east approach is the shortest but less interesting. The path off Cleator Rd. is well marked and descends gently along the old road to the same junction above the lake.

Chuckanuts—
32. Chuckanut Ridge

Distance: 2.2 - 9.8 miles round trip   Time: Allow 1 - 6 hours
Elevation gain: 200 - 600 feet (or more)   Season: Year-round

Thanks to the acquisition of land along Chuckanut Ridge by county and state park agencies in the 1980s, this scenic trail has become one of the more popular routes in the Chuckanuts. Much of the trail is rough and passes very close to cliffs, so due caution is in order. Approach from the west or south off Cleator Rd., or from the north by way of Lost Lake Trail (*Hike #33*). The ridge trail's north end link to the Lost Lake Trail was recently reconstructed, improving the potential for longer treks (*maps, p. 96*).

To reach the west or south trailhead, take Chuckanut Dr. four

Chuckanut Ridge Trail (and Bean).

miles south of Fairhaven to High Line Rd. (a.k.a. Cleator Rd.). Drive 2.0 miles up to Middle Ridge Trail, the easier approach, partly hidden on the left (*elevation: 1,060 feet*). Expect a good view of the bay and islands in 0.5 mile and the ridge at 0.9 mile. Or, drive to the road end at Cyrus Gates Overlook (3.5 miles) and walk back down the road (possible new trail here) to the last road switchback and the ridge trail. In less than 100 yards is a partial view of Mount Baker and Lost Lake—a stones throw away but 600 feet below. The 300-foot cliffs of Oyster Dome (*Hike #35*) are visible to the southeast three miles away. Continue north generally near the ridgetop, eventually passing a junction with Middle Ridge Trail (**2.8 mi**; or 0.9 miles via Middle Ridge; *elevation: 1,460 feet*). The ridge becomes skinnier and more dramatic, with pleasant spots to sit and soak up the scenery—but watch the edge! Up and down rocky trail offers great views north and east: Bellingham, Lake Padden, Mount Baker and Lookout Mountain.

The trail descends to a relatively flat area and bends to the right to drop off the ridge on a new trail, passing large blocks of sandstone before connecting with the Lost Lake Trail a few yards north of Salal Trail (**3.9 mi**; or 2.0 miles via Middle Ridge; *elevation: 1,200 feet*). The Salal Trail provides a good link to the Hemlock Trail and Madrone Crest viewpoint (*see Hike #30*). Go left on the Lost Lake Trail to reach California St. in a mile and Arroyo Park beyond. A right takes you to the lake in 2.4 miles, with a long loop option back to the south end of Chuckanut Ridge. That southwesterly end of the ridge trail is just above the gate next to the west end of the Lost Lake Trail (2.5 miles from Lost Lake). From there, climb the lower ridge a short mile to the upper Cleator Rd. parking lot.

Chuckanuts—
33. Lost Lake

Distance: 5.5 - 11 miles round trip   Time: Allow 4 - 8 hours
Elevation gain: 1,100 - 1,500 feet   Season: Year-round

The lands surrounding Lost Lake were studied in the mid-1990s for possible new trail links in order to provide a well linked trail system in the Chuckanuts, including Mount Blanchard to the south. Eventually, new sections of trail may connect the Lost Lake area with Chuckanut Ridge, Pine and Cedar Lakes, and perhaps Samish Park to the east. While most hikers follow old logging roads to and from Lost Lake, loops and side trips are described for enjoying a little more of the Chuckanut wilderness. The usual approach is from the southwest via Fragrance Lake Trail (*Hike #31*). However, the northern approach from Arroyo Park and the Hemlock Trail is also described (*map, p. 96*).

Southwest approach: Hike the Fragrance Lake Trail to the junction at 1.9 miles, then walk down the old Fragrance Lake Rd. 200 yards to an old log-

Wet-weather cascade near Lost Lake.

ging road on the left with a white gate—the official Lost Lake trailhead (**2.0 mi**). Walk this old road with partial winter views of Samish Bay and the San Juan Islands to a saddle, gaining 450 feet (**3.4 mi**); stay left. Note the path to the right is the optional return route. From the saddle, it's a 400-foot descent to the lake and a junction at its north end (**4.5 mi**). Make a sharp right to reach the lake (continuing straight takes you to California St. in 3.4 miles). A 0.2-mile walk through dense damp vegetation brings you to the soggy lake shore (*elevation: 1,182 feet*). Follow the trail left up a short bank and south along the narrow rocky ridge rimming the lake's east shore to good views and rest stops (**4.8 mi**). The rock can be slick where it hugs the edge of small cliffs. The outlet stream flows across rocky slabs disappearing over a mostly invisible waterfall into the forest below. Either return the way you came or take the North Lost Lake Trail back to Arroyo Park.

To continue the lake loop, follow the low ridge past logged areas and 0.3 mile past the south end of the lake to an old road bed (**5.4 mi**). In another 0.3 mile, turn right on a path just before the old road bed starts to curve to the left (goes to Bloedel timber lands and logging roads to Lake Samish). Follow the path a winding mile through quiet forest, regaining 400 feet of elevation; stay right at trail junctions; or go left to explore older forest and more views from logged-off lands. The way curves north to the saddle where you rejoin the main trail (**6.7 mi**); this should be the old road grade you walked on the way to the lake; turn left. Take care not to lose your bearing; the forest can be disorienting.

North approach: To reach Lost Lake from the north, begin at Arroyo Park (*elevation: 100 feet*), crossing Chuckanut Creek on a bridge. After a short climb beyond the bridge, grab an obvious trail on the left contouring up through forest and a few mud holes to California St., an unpaved former logging road. Turn left on this road and right at a road junction nearby—this is the north end of the Lost Lake Trail (**1.4 mi**). After several switchbacks when the grade settles, look for the Chuckanut Ridge Trail on the right (**2.4 mi**). The 0.5-mile hike to the top and a short jaunt south for a view make this a worthy side trip. Or just continue south to the junction near Lost Lake (**4.6 mi**) and the lake beyond (**4.8 mi**).

Lake Samish from the lakeshore trail.

Chuckanuts—
34. Lake Samish

Distance: 0.6 - 1.5 mile loop   Time: Allow 1 - 2 hours
Elevation gain: 100 - 300 feet   Season: Year-round

A couple of short paths at Lake Samish Park can be combined into a single one-hour stroll. So while the hiking is limited, the forest, lakeshore, stream, waterfalls and other features make it easily worth the trouble. From the North Lake Samish I-5 exit, head left and down through curves to a fork; stay right on North Lake Samish Rd. to find the park on the right just before the bridge that crosses the northwest end of the lake. From the upper parking area, cross the gravel road and look for the path above, then angle left to a waterfall viewing platform. It's just a trickle in summer, but more impressive in the rainy season. Continue up several switchbacks (0.2 mile) to a rocky perch in a pipeline corridor for a nice view and a rest. Then head toward for the woods and a fork; right goes up 0.2 mile to the "Eagle's Overlook" and a partial view through the trees; left is more scenic, gradual and crosses the creek on a bridge. At a junction with an old grade, right leads up toward "Eagle," and left works back down to the road. Head right on the road to the path on the left just before the park boundary. Follow this down to the lakeshore and walk this scenic stretch 0.2 mile back to the start.

CHUCKANUTS—
35. Oyster Dome

Distance: 3.6 - 7.2 miles round trip   Time: Allow 3 - 5 hours
Elevation gain: 400 - 1,900 feet   Season: Almost year-round

There are several approaches to the Blanchard Mountain area of the southern Chuckanuts, including Oyster Dome, the giant ta-lus field, Lily and Lizard Lakes and more *(for the east approach see Hike #36.)* Among the rewards are a whole lot of rock and out-standing views of Bellingham and Samish Bays, Georgia Strait, the San Juan and Gulf Islands, Skagit Valley, and the North Cascades and Olympic Mountains. The so-called bat caves, which are really just large crevices in the giant boulder field, require spelunking skills to be explored. Avoid them from fall through spring so you don't inad-vertently disturb a highly sensitive bat species known to use the area. For this hike, the giant talus and a spectacular viewpoint high above are the recommended destinations.

The easiest approach is from the Samish Overlook, although most hikers prefer to start well below at the Pacific Northwest Trailhead

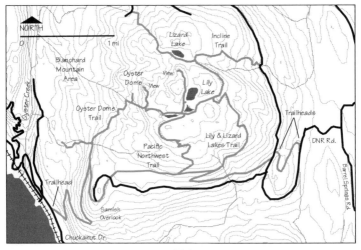

(PNT) on Chuckanut Drive. From Fairhaven, follow Chuckanut Dr. (SR 11) several miles south of Larrabee State Park and beyond the hairpin bridge at Oyster Creek. Park at a turn-out across from the trail at MP 10.1 (*elevation: 150 feet*) The signed trail climbs steeply through maturing second-growth forest. The path soon enters a large clearcut (at least the views are good) and keeps climbing below a hang-glider launch at the ridgetop called Samish Overlook. The trail works left not so steeply and re-enters the forest. At a junction (**1.8 mi**), a sharp right goes 0.5 mile to the overlook and the shorter approach (*see Hike #36 for directions and a possible loop*). But keep going straight at this junction. Cross a couple of small streams and pass a less conspicuous junction (the old trail on the left leads down about 1.5 miles to an unpaved, possibly restricted, private road and Chuckanut Dr. just north of the PNT trailhead). Keep heading up past a small cascade and two large rock outcrops on the left.

Shortly after the second, watch for a signed spur trail to the left

Samish Bay from Oyster Dome.

(**3.0 mi**). This leads 0.1 mile to the giant talus field where the high cliffs of Oyster Dome lean out precariously over a stark landscape of house-sized boulders. Explore this broad heaping pile of rubble with care. Wet or moss-covered rocks offer poor footing; and deep holes and crevices, some hidden beneath thick vegetation, threaten to swallow those of us with shorter attention spans. The geology here is much different that the rest of the Chuckanuts. Instead of 50-million year old sandstone, the Blanchard Mountain area is comprised of metamorphic rock. Return to the Talus Trail junction to make the final steep push to a tee at the top (**3.2 mi**; *elevation: 2,060 feet*). Lily Lake is an easy mile to the right. Go left and up another 200 feet to find the top of Oyster Dome and the best view in the Chuckanuts (**3.5 mi**). Mt. Rainier is visible on the clearest days. The area may be dangerous to rambunctious kids or pets, or to the rest of us if windy or snowy (if icy, the rock slabs should be avoided altogether).

CHUCKANUTS—
36. Lily & Lizard Lakes

Distance: 8 - 11 miles round trip   Time: Allow 4 - 8 hours
Elevation gain: 700 - 1,300 feet   Season: Almost year-round

Two quiet lakes in a heavily forested setting are the reward for this moderate hike up the east flank of Blanchard Mountain. The trail is also the eastern approach for Oyster Dome (*see Hike #35*). From I-5, take the Alger exit (#240), go west 0.4 mile and turn left on Barrel Springs Rd. In another 0.7 mile, turn right on a good gravel logging road (trail sign). Pass the lower horse trailer parking area, and continue to the upper Lily and Lizard Lakes Trailhead in less than two miles, just after a spur road on the left which goes to Samish Overlook (about two miles away). There is a good view of Mount Baker near the trailhead. Walk back down the road a few yards to the trail sign (*elevation: 950 feet*).

The route is in good condition, well marked and easy to follow on mostly gentle grades. Pass a junction (**1.5 mi**) where a connector heads left to the PNT (also called Max's Shortcut) in 0.6 mile and Samish Overlook in 1.6 mile. Continue right to the lakes junction

(**3.3 mi**); Lily is left, Lizard's right. Many of the trails in this area follow old logging railroad grades, as evidenced by a few ties and an occasional steel rail. It is about 0.5 mile to Lily Lake at 2,020 feet, and 1.0 mile to Lizard Lake at 1,862 feet. There are campsites at both lakes. From Lizard Lake, the PNT continues past the outlet and descends to logging roads. A major new 7-mile trail from Lizard Lake to Lost Lake ("Lost–Lizard Trail") is also in the planning stages.

On the way to Lily Lake, pass another spur on the left in about 0.4 mile known as Max's Shortcut that goes to Samish Overlook and passes the connector mentioned above (for a possible loop). The Lily Lake spur is just beyond this point on the right. The spur leads along the north side of Lily Lake to a less obvious path that keeps going up for a good view. Stay left at a somewhat inconspicuous fork (right goes 0.3 mile to Lizard Lake, another loop idea) and climb to a scenic rock outcrop 0.4 mile from the lake (*elevation: 2,220 feet*). Back at the main trail, one can head west a mile to access Oyster Dome. One could also begin a nice loop at the Samish Overlook (*elevation: 1,360 feet*) to find a signed trailhead on a landing just below the first hang-glider launch (a good place to watch these brightly-colored modern teradactyls ride the wind. Hike from the landing to the tee junction near the top of Oyster Dome; turn right to Lily Lake, then right again just after the turn-off to the lake on the PNT, or Max's Shortcut. This leads back to the Samish Overlook road. Cross and walk this short trail to the landing.

Lily Lake.

Lowlands & Foothills

Old-growth forest at Berthusen Park.

37. Berthusen Park

Distance: 1 - 4 miles round trip   Time: Allow 1 - 2 hours
Elevation gain: None   Season: Year-round

Lynden's largest park, Berthhusen, is actually outside of town, about a mile west of Guide Meridian, off Badger Rd. The 236-acre park was donated to the city in 1944 upon the death of Hans Berthusen with the stipulation that this original homestead be preserved intact as an example of both the human and natural history of the region the Berthusens loved. Bertrand Creek, a salmon stream undergoing restoration, snakes through the forest, where large red cedar and douglas fir trees provide a welcome refuge. There are about five miles of trails to explore and plenty of loops and links to confuse the newcomers. Some are open to horses. Eagle Loop (0.8 mile), and the Owl Trail (3 miles) are partly signed.

Enter the park off Berthusen Rd., 0.2 mile south of Badger Rd. Watch for a box of trail maps, then continue across the bridge and park. One idea is to park near the end of the access road and look for the Berthusen Grove Nature Trail, a hiker path, on the right. This route winds among the larger trees, and spurs invite further rambling. Longer, meandering loops extend south of the same road, mostly in second-growth forest. The map (and signs) may be a little confusing here, so a sense of direction (or even a compass) can come in handy. Near the road bridge over the creek, watch for the magical, carved black bear crawling out of a stump.

38. Terrell Creek Marsh

Distance: 1.0 mile round trip (or more)   Time: Allow 1 hour (or more)
Elevation gain: None   Season: Year-round

A visit to Birch Bay State Park usually means a walk on the beach (*see Hike #4*), but this 0.5-mile loop in the woods to the edge of the Terrell Creek Marsh makes a worthy diversion. The beach, the woods, the marsh and the creek done together encompass a diver-

Terrell Creek Marsh.

sity of habitats—a birder's mini-paradise. In spring, the marsh and creek serve as a critical flyway for hundreds of great blue herons that occupy one of the largest nesting colonies in the Northwest, not far inland from the mudflats of Birch Bay. (The nesting area is off-limits and has no trail, but is regularly monitored by wildlife biologists.) Bring the bird book and binoculars, and in an hour or two you might see 30 or more species of birds almost anytime of the year, though the species will vary considerably from season to season.

From I-5, take Grandview Rd. 6.9 miles to Jackson Rd.; turn right, then left in 0.7 mile on Helweg Rd. The small, signed trailhead is on the left near the east entrance to Birch Bay State Park. One can also walk east on the park road from the beach area or campground. The loop is straight-forward, beginning in a hardwood forest of alder, birch, big-leaf and vine maple, then our most common conifers, Douglas fir, western red cedar and western hemlock. Keep an eye out later for a pocket of Sitka spruce trees, and some non-native English holly. The trail quickly reaches the broad marsh. The area is low-lying, and though this point is more than two miles upstream from the mouth of Terrell Creek, it is still subject to tidal influence. On the return, look for an unmarked path across the road that can be followed past a gnarly cedar tree back to the campground; from there go left to the road. Turn right for the beach and creek (named for an area homesteader). The creek may actually run backwards during higher tides. Along with many birds, muskrat are commonly seen as well. Except for the walk described, the park is unusually devoid of trails.

Lowlands & Foothills—
39. Tennant Lake

Distance: 1.0 mile loop   Time: Allow 1 hour
Elevation gain: 50 feet (tower)   Season: Year-round

This walk includes a viewing tower, a unique boardwalk through the marsh, a fragrance garden, interpretive center (the former Nielsen homestead) and game reserve, adjacent to the nationally listed Hovander Homestead (*see Hike #40*). These areas together occupy 720 acres. Enjoy a mile of pleasant ambling and excellent birding in winter through early summer. Hunting season keeps the boardwalk closed part of the fall and winter, but the trail is generally open from mid-January to early October. From I-5 exit #262, head west 0.5 mile, turning left on Hovander Rd. immediately past a railroad overpass. Angle right on Nielsen Rd. (signs) to reach Tennant Lake Interpretive Center and the parking area.

Begin the walk in the fragrance garden then head up the 50-foot view tower (maybe bring binoculars). Those not inclined or able to climb the steps can see the view by way of a remote and fully maneuverable video camera. When open, take the path over a bridge to the boardwalk; a viewpoint is 50 yards to the left at a fork. Stay right to begin a long loop that weaves an interesting course through the shadowy swamp (watch your step). Move quietly to see perching and aquatic birds and maybe a muskrat. Listen for the metallic songs of red-winged blackbirds, the rattling warble of marsh wrens, high-pitched trills of winter wrens, and maybe the eerie shudder of a bald eagle. Back at the parking lot, a signed path goes 0.5 mile west to Hovander Homestead.

Tennant Lake tower.

Lowlands & Foothills—
40. Hovander Homestead

Distance: 1.4-mile loop (or more)   Time: Allow 1 - 2 hours
Elevation gain: None   Season: Year-round

A visit to Hovander Homestead Park, listed on the national register of historic places, is easy to combine with Tennant Lake (*see
Hike # 39*). There are turn-of-the-century farm buildings, a view
tower, the old Hovander farmhouse full of antiques, plus gardens,
lawns, animals, shelters and picnic areas. The river is close by and
offers a bit of exploring as well. See Hike #39 for directions to the
park and turn right just before the Tennant Lake Interpretive Center. From the big barn, check out the view tower then head south
across lawns toward the trees lining the river. Stroll leftward in the
grass to find a good trail on the dike. Follow this, a portion of the
Salish Coast Trail (*see Hike #6*), to a junction with an old road (**0.6
mi**) and turn left (straight continues to Slater Rd.); beware of hunters in season. At the Tennant Lake area (**0.9 mi**), the loop turns left
along a nice trail leading back to the barn (**1.4 mi**). Watch for beaver, muskrat, eagles, acrobatic swallows, lone woodpeckers, and
happy warblers flitting in the brush. For a more extended walk, head
toward the river but walk upstream this time, generally along a dirt
road next to the fields, with occasional spurs to the river bank. This
path continues one mile to the public boat launch off Hovander Rd.
(a vehicle use permit is required to park here).

*Nooksack
River at
Hovander.*

Lowlands & Foothills—
41. Nooksack River

Distance: 1 mile round trip (or more)   Time: Allow 1 hour (or more)

Elevation gain: None   Season: Year-round

There are only a few places to wander along our own Nooksack River, including its three forks. The North Fork carries meltwater from Mount Shuksan's Nooksack Cirque, and from six glaciers on the north and west flanks of Mount Baker. The arms of the South and Middle Forks are essentially wrapped all the way around the Twin Sisters Range. Most of western Whatcom County is drained by the river, which means a lot of what we do on the land impacts the river and the salmon and other wildlife that depend on it. In the lower sections, many miles of dikes and levees, designed to tame the bigger flows in flood season, also provide excellent opportunities for riverfront trails—an idea that has been floating around for years and which some communities are now beginning to talk up more seriously. The "Chain of Trails" concept being studied by the Foothills community and the Whatcom Council of Governments includes this idea of a long-distance river trail linking all the river's cities and towns (for details, see www.wcog.org/projects/). Hopefully this enthusiasm will solidify into real improvements on the ground over the next several years. Much depends on the concerns and cooperation of farmers and other landowners along the river, but if their concerns can be responsibly addressed, we may be able to provide at least some areas where people can really enjoy the river up close.

Until then, some of the parks and hikes listed in this guide will give you at least a glimpse of the mighty Nooksack. Best options currently are at Ferndale's RiverWalk (*Hike #15*), Hovander Park (*Hike #40*), Horseshoe Bend (*Hike #55*), and Nooksack Cirque (*Hike #84; see also Hikes #7, #15, #48, #50, #74, #75 and #76*).

Lowlands & Foothills—
42. Galbraith Mountain

Distance: 2 - 10 miles (or more) round trip   Time: Allow 1 - 6 hours
Elevation gain: 200 - 2,000 feet   Season: Year-round

The north end of Lookout Mountain east of Bellingham is also called Galbraith Mountain—mostly private lands managed for timber. Mountain bikers began to make use of the area some years ago. Many trails have been constructed to link with the road system and the mountain is etched with a veritable maze of mountain bike routes, some of which may be of interest to hikers. Check local bike shops for a map of the area (*see also* www.galbraithmt.com). Keep in mind that the bikers' enthusiasm and hard work are what created the trail system. And while trails have been informally open to public use, this *is* private land and there is no guarantee that your presence will be welcome indefinitely. The hiking potential is good in the sense that there are many miles to explore, but maybe not so good considering that there is hardly any real forest. There are some views, but not much else of interest.

If that's enough to entice you to go, there are at least two places to check out. On the south end near Lake Padden, one can walk up a gated road that leads to a couple of communication towers with pretty good views. From Samish Way, a mile east of Lake Padden, take Galbraith Lane a short distance to a junction with shoulder parking on the left (*elevation: 740 feet*). Walk the road to the right, then go left at a gate and follow this several miles to the top, gaining 1,000 feet on the way. There are numerous road grades and trails branching off the main route, some vaguely interesting, some not, and it may take a certain amount of trial and error to get acquainted with the area. It can be a long walk home if you get disoriented, so a map is definitely helpful. After passing the first tower, reach a junction where a left heads up to a second tower, and right contours around a slope to a sea of clearcuts with a view of Mount Baker.

On the north end, it may be best to park at Whatcom Falls Park, then cross Electric Ave. to Birch St. and walk this south across Lakeway Dr. to its end, a few blocks from the park. Look for a trail leading south along the base of a slope (recent construction may have altered the location). At a nearby junction go left on the "Miranda Trail" which leads up to a ridge. Turn right, and continue south to powerlines and good city views. Again, there is an extensive web of roads and trails to choose from, so note every junction to be sure you can find your way back down. On weekends, you will likely encounter others who can help with directions. Working up and to the east you may stumble on a nice view of Lake Whatcom from an old landing, two to three miles from the park.

Lowlands & Foothills—
43. Stimpson Nature Reserve

Distance: 2.5-mile loop   Time: Allow 1 - 2 hours
Elevation gain: 300 feet   Season: Year-round

This path to a large beaver pond and mature forest in a 138-acre DNR Natural Resources Conservation Area in the Lake Whatcom watershed, has been enjoyed by area residents for decades. The Whatcom Land Trust recently received a 116-acre donation of adjacent land from the Stimpson family, purchased another 80 acres next to it, while also receiving 16 acres from the university, to create a reserve complex of 350 acres. The trail was scheduled for reconstruction in 2003, along with some new sections to produce an attractive 2.5-mile loop. The first 0.2 mile to the pond should be wheelchair accessible. Look for a small parking lot on Lake Louise Rd., 1.6 miles south of Lakeway Dr. (*map, next page*). The reserve will protect the ecology of the area while accommodating environmental education and recreational access. This is a sensitive area for wildlife so please don't disturb anything. Larger groups of ten or more should first contact Whatcom County Parks.

Beaver pond.

Lowlands & Foothills—
44. Lookout Mountain

Distance: 9.2 miles round trip   Time: Allow 6 - 9 hours
Elevation gain: 2,300 feet   Season: Almost year-round

The long wooded ridge between Lake Whatcom and I-5 southeast of Bellingham is Lookout Mountain, and at one time there actually was a fire lookout on the south summit. Today the site is adorned with an unsightly communication tower, the disappointing fate of so many local high points. The young forest also has recovered to the point that there is no real view to be had. However, the north summit, one foot taller and also crowned with towering space junk, still offers a fine vista—if you don't mind all the infrastructure peering over your shoulder. The trek is a longish road walk on state land, perhaps more enjoyable fall through spring when trails in the North Cascades are still buried in snow.

From Bellingham, take Lakeway Drive to Austin St.; turn right. This soon becomes Lake Louise Rd. Watch for a gated unpaved road

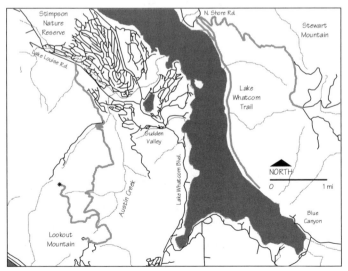

Mount Baker and Twin Sisters Range from Lookout Mountain.

and dilapidated house on the right 2.5 miles south of Lakeway (*elevation: 460 feet*). This is the edge of the former Olson property that the city of Bellingham was able to acquire as part of its watershed acquisition program designed to help protect the lake and our drinking water supply from the impacts of development. Park in a safe place (don't block the gate) and walk up this road. Curve left and passing a beaten path on a road grade to the left (**0.6 mi**), an alternative Sudden Valley approach. Continue straight up the main road and stay left on the more level grade at a fork (**1.1 mi**). The route steepens, passing a pretty waterfall in the canyon below. After a long, moderately steep slog up the road, the grade finally eases off before reaching a fork with a green box (**3.1 mi**); left goes to the south summit. Head right instead and follow this up to a saddle (**3.6 mi**) where it's possible to wander left a few yards on lumpy ground to a great view of Lake Samish, the Chuckanuts, the San Juan Islands and Olympic Mountains. Just ahead, there are good views to the east of Mount Baker and the Twin Sisters Range. Just below the top, the road forks again (**4.3 mi**); stay right (left is restricted). The grade circles around to a rocky summit perch at the foot of a tower (**4.6 mi**; *elevation: 2,677 feet*).

Lowlands & Foothills—
45. Squires Lake & Alger Alp

Distance: 1 - 6 miles round trip   Time: Allow 1 - 3 hours
Elevation gain: 100 - 1,000 feet   Season: Year-round

In 1995, with the assistance of the Whatcom Land Trust, the Whatcom and Skagit County park departments, various volunteers, an anonymous cash donor and others, an 80-acre parcel surrounding Squires Lake near Alger became our newest public park. Loop trails and spurs lead around the lake (*elevation: 400 feet*), to a beaver pond, and along a sandstone ridge in second-growth forest. The stroll to the lake is short, but moderately steep, while most of the balance of the trail system involves only minor ups and downs. The walk has become popular on weekends, but is good any time of the year. Visit mid-week for a chance at a little more solitude.

From I-5, take south Lake Samish exit #242 and go east 0.7 mile on Old Hwy 99; the trailhead on the left. The trail splits twice, but soon reconnects, leading to the bridge at the lake outlet (**0.3 mi**). The lake loop and other trails have benches and are well signed. Other loops and spurs lead to the beaver pond and up a wooded ridge past the park boundary (**0.5 mi**, *from trailhead*). One can continue on the latter to an old logging road that doubles as a segment of the Pacific Northwest Trail. The PNT also passes through the Chuckanuts and the Mount Baker area and is an attempt to link trails all the way from the Pacific coast to the Continental Divide (see www.pnt.org for details). To continue to the 1,315-foot summit locally known as Alger Alp, stay on the main logging road (go straight

where a road drops right (**1.3 mi**), then right at the next, left at the next. Great views of many lakes, and from the summit (**2.3 mi**), Alger and the Skagit valley.

Squires Lake.

Lowlands & Foothills—
46. Lake Whatcom

Distance: 2 - 6 miles round trip   Time: Allow 1 - 3 hours
Elevation gain: 100 feet   Season: Year-round

This three-mile walk along Lake Whatcom is a local favorite, with the trail rarely more than a few feet from the lake. There are several small pretty waterfalls, some big cliffs above the trail, and a few large trees to gander at. The route generally follows an old railroad grade that once carried coal from Blue Canyon, while connecting Bellingham sawmills with the timber brought down from the Lake Whatcom and South Fork Nooksack watersheds. The trailhead, on 271 acres of county park property adjacent to Smith Creek, could potentially serve a future trail network connecting the lakeshore with high rocky bluffs, small stands of older forest, wild gorges, and pretty waterfalls (*see also Hike #47*).

From the intersection of Alabama St. and Electric Ave. in Bellingham, follow North Shore Dr. around the lake to Agate Bay; stay right, then left in 2.5 miles (trail sign) to find the trailhead just past the bridge at Smith Creek (8 miles from Alabama St.; *map, p. 118*). Two paths lead the same distance down to the lake: the one on the left near the gate is narrower and steeper; the one

Lake Whatcom.

to the right is wide and gentle (barrier-free). Walk either route in pleasant forest of cedar and maple to reach the old Blue Canyon railroad grade (**0.3 mi**). Pass a waterfall framed in mossy rock walls (**1.0 mi**) and cross a bridge, soon passing below high cliffs. Ahead are a few large Douglas fir trees, some more than six feet in diameter, mixed with cedar, maple and interestingly, madrone trees which are more common on west-facing saltwater shores. Cross another creek with a partly hidden double waterfall (**1.4 mi**). Reveille Island is across this narrow neck of the lake. The deepest part of the lake, at 328 feet, is a mile south of here—the bottom is slightly below sea level. Cross a third creek, a good turn-around for a shorter walk (**1.8 mi**), or go another 1.2 miles to an abrupt end of the trail at private property. Blue Canyon Rd. is not far beyond, but the county has been unsuccessful in securing an easement to complete the trail—even though a well designed path would likely enhance property values. (Anyone who can persuade the owners to sell a narrow easement for the trail will be an instant hero.) On the return, there are several good spots along the lakeshore for a lunch break.

Lowlands & Foothills—
47. Stewart Mountain

Distance: 7.0 - 9.6 miles round trip   Time: Allow 4 - 7 hours
Elevation gain: 2,100 - 2,600 feet   Season: Almost year-round

While not exactly a fairyland for hikers, the trudge up Stewart Mountain, east of Lake Whatcom, nevertheless offers a good workout almost anytime of the year, and excellent views of the lake. It is a big place with much state land, many miles of logging roads, and a BPA transmission line corridor—not exactly paradise, but interesting enough. There are several good places to access the area, including the Lake Whatcom Trailhead (described here), and an equestrian trailhead off Y Rd., a mile north of North Shore Rd. (*map, p. 118*). The latter is open to hikers, but is of primary interest to horseback riders. For directions to the preferred Lake Whatcom Trailhead, see Hike #46 (*elevation: 360 feet*).

From the parking lot, head up the obvious road grade left of a

Low clouds over Lake Whatcom.

trail, passing through two gates and reaching the first good view at a switchback (**0.2 mi**). The road soon meets the BPA corridor (**0.4 mi**) and a view down into Smith Creek. Continue up the main road past several towers, then into in the woods and back out to the towers with a good view of the north half of the lake and much of western Whatcom County (**1.5 mi**). Pass under the crackle-buzz-pop of the lines to another good view in the next mile. The road soon levels off and reaches the best view of the trip, this time more comfortably away from the transmission lines (**3.5 mi**; *elevation: 2,500 feet*). This is a good resting point and turn-around. The mountainside drops steeply to the sprawling lake, Reveille Island and part of Bellingham. Lookout Mountain guards the opposite shore (*Hike #44*), while the Olympics and B.C. Coast Range are prominent in the distance.

If it's still too soon to stop, one may be able to continue along the road 0.5 mile to a junction with two roads on the left; the second leads across Jones Creek to a gate and private timberland beyond (Crown Pacific). Please note that a written permit is required to continue past the gate (normally available at CP's guard station on Y Rd., a mile south of Mt. Baker Hwy.). Once you're legal, stay left at the next fork where the Twin Sisters Range comes into view. This spur rises to the 3,000-foot crest of Stewart Mountain. Take a left fork for a great view of the Sisters, Mount Baker and the South Fork Nooksack valley (**4.8 mi**).

Lowlands & Foothills—
48. South Fork Nooksack River

Distance: 1 - 6 miles round trip   Time: Allow 1 - 4 hours
Elevation gain: 200 feet   Season: Year-round

Except for the mud holes near the start, the South Fork trail offers an enjoyable, albeit primitive, walk near the river. A friend reported that during a high-water period he once encountered salmon slithering across the trail. Late summer or early fall is the best time to visit, although cold clear winter days when the ground is frozen are also nice. When there's snow, the route makes a possible cross-country ski tour. The people of Whatcom County recently had the good fortune of securing several hundred acres along the South Fork Nooksack, largely through the work of park staff and the Whatcom Land Trust, and donations from the Syre and Nesset families, which will add tremendously to the public's ability to enjoy and preserve the natural values and rural historic character of the area for generations to come. New trails along the South Fork should materialize in the not-to-distant future.

From Highway 9, two miles south of Acme, drive east on the Saxon Road 3.5 miles to its end near the Skookum Creek Fish Hatchery. Park across the bridge and begin walking southward along the old road closest to the river. In 0.5 mile, a long stretch of large mud holes may require minor detours through woods to avoid wet feet. Overgrown side roads and paths provide access to beaver ponds and gravel bars. Edfro Creek is crossed in a mile and Cavanaugh Creek at 2.3 miles, just before the old site of Dyes Ranch. The area is rich in marsh habitat and wildlife. Between the two creeks, the river flows through a narrow, but hard-to-access rocky gorge once mis-considered as a possible dam site. The old road can be followed into Skagit County where it emerges into an area of huge clearcuts.

Lowlands & Foothills—
49. Canyon Lake Cr. Community Forest

Distance: 2 - 9 miles round trip   Time: Allow 2 - 6 hours
Elevation gain: 200 - 2,200 feet   Season: April - November

One of the more ambitious land conservation efforts undertaken by the Whatcom Land Trust (WLT), Whatcom County Parks and Recreation, and Western Washington University is the 2,300-acre community forest reserve at Canyon Lake. The reserve contains one of the oldest stands of Alaska yellow cedar in the Northwest, with trees nearly 1,000 years old. Most of the watershed above the lake has been logged and roaded, but the 600 acres of old growth that remained are now protected. Public and private funds were raised to meet the $3.6 million purchase price. WLT holds a conservation easement on the property, and the county and university jointly own and manage it for recreation, research and environmental education. Four miles of old logging roads were converted to trails; a new 1.2-mile path was constructed through a portion of the old growth; and a 2-mile loop trail was built around the lake (construction was

Twin Sisters from the ridge above Canyon Lake.

still underway in early 2003). The trees, the lake, good views, some waterfalls, and an abundance of plant fossils are key attractions (no camping). The road to the lake is generally passable to most vehicles, but it can be rough, steep and narrow in places.

From Mt. Baker Hwy. at MP 16.9 turn right on Mosquito Lake Rd. and follow this 1.8 miles to Canyon Creek Rd.; turn left. The 6.5-mile route to the Canyon Lake Trailhead is well signed. In case any signs grow legs, stay left at 0.5 mile, drive slowly past several homes, and stay left at a fork in 1.0 mile (the gate here is open 6 am to 9 pm). Go left again at 2.2 miles, right at 3.3 miles, and right at 3.7 miles. The main road seems to curve left at the last main junction, but continue straight on well traveled road 2.8 miles more to the trailhead (*elevation: 2,300 feet*). Trails are limited to hikers only.

For the 2.0-mile lake loop, head for the outlet stream at the edge of the parking lot. Once the trail is open, cross the bridge and follow the lakeshore, passing small waterfalls, climbing slightly, and entering a nice patch of old-growth forest in the first 0.5 mile. Cross Canyon Lake Creek, assuming the bridge is in place (**1.0 mi**) and continue up an easy grade to the upper trail (**1.5 mi**). Left here leads 0.5 mile back to the parking area.

For the upper trail, pass by the gate near the parking area to reach the lake loop junction (**0.5 mi**). Continue up the old road on a moderate grade past rocks, fossils (help preserve them for others),

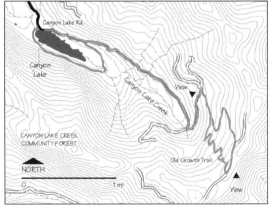

a nice view of the lake, and several creeks with pretty cascades. The second bridge crosses Toboggan Creek, sliding down its bedrock course (**1.3 mi**). Round a switchback and reach another bridge just past an impressive view of the lake and valley (**2.5 mi**). Turn right at a junction and find the trail to the old growth not far beyond (**2.9 mi**). Head right here (*elevation: 3,800 feet*); the return route comes down the old road. The path winds upslope past many large western hemlock and Alaskan cedar trees—considered very old for this kind of forest community. The path breaks out of the trees and into a clearcut at the ridgecrest (**4.1 mi**). On a good day, the view of Mount Baker, the Black Buttes and the Twin Sisters Range is fabulous. After a break, head left (northeast) about 0.3 mile to a fork; stay left to descend 0.8 mile to the lower end of the old-growth trail, 2.9 miles from the trailhead. On the drive down the mountain, watch for a good view of all three forks of the Nooksack River far below.

50. Racehorse Falls

Distance: 0.8 mile round trip   Time: Allow 1 hour
Elevation gain: 100 feet   Season: Almost year-round

This is a short, rough walk along the creek through an attractive vine maple and cedar forest. From Mt. Baker Hwy., turn right on the Mosquito Lake Rd. (MP 16.8), then left in 1.1 mile on North Fork Rd. In winter, a wide shoulder at the one-mile point makes a good place to stop and look for bald eagles feeding on spawned out salmon. Turn right in 4.2 miles, just before the creek, and park at a road bend in 0.1 mile.

The slightly hidden trail is on the left. Really, there are two—take the second. Stay right in 50 yards (try the left on the return), and in 50 yards more go right again on a narrow path right before a dip (straight leads to the creek nearby). Minor clambering over rocks and logs and past mud holes lead upstream partly in a flood channel. Ten yards before the creek, a rough path goes right and hugs the steep hillside. A few logs are crossed before the falls come into view. Scoot over rocks to a tiny beach just below the falls (**0.4 mi**). A

Raceborse Falls.

slightly better view is had from the top of an obvious rock ramp, although it may be slippery and hazardous when wet or icy, so stay to the right. Watch out for devils club, and avoid the ramp altogether if you're unsure. The noisy waterfall is not huge but the setting is unique and well worth the effort. Below the falls, Racehorse Creek is an important salmon stream.

Lowlands & Foothills—
51. Ostrom Conservation Site

Hiking distance: 1.0 mile round trip   Time: Allow 1 hour
Elevation gain: None   Season: Year-round

Students from the Nooksack Valley School District recently developed this 0.5-mile interpretive nature trail on a 39-acre site east of Everson donated by the Ostrom family to Whatcom County Parks in 1983. It straddles both South Pass Rd. and Breckenridge Creek and has been used for environmental education programs for years. The site has also been identified as a potential trailhead for Sumas Mountain. The nature trail winds through a second-growth forest of cedar, fir and hemlock, with many other species of trees, shrubs, ferns and flowering plants represented. Students also produced a very nice trail guide (may or may not be available at the trailhead). To find the Ostrom Conservation Site, follow South Pass Rd. 3.8 miles east from its junction with SR 9 in Everson, and watch for the sign and small parking area on the left. The trail is easy to follow and could be conveniently combined with a visit to Sumas Mountain, Lost Lake or Silver Lake (*Hikes #52, #53 and #54*).

52. Sumas Mountain

Distance: 3.4 - 9.8 miles round trip   Time: Allow 3 - 7 hours
Elevation gain: 1,000 - 3,000 feet   Season: April - November

The arduous hike up Sumas Mountain is a local classic and a great spring conditioner for those aiming for more serious summer ascents in the North Cascades. The woods are gorgeous most of the way up, with small meadows, rocky outcrops and splendiferous views of western Whatcom County, the Fraser River valley, and B.C. Coast Range. This place really deserves to be set aside as a reserve or perhaps even a state park. Botanists take note: native plant diversity is extraordinary. The land is managed by DNR—a scary notion considering all the recent logging activity on the mountain's north end—where the best hiking is. There are potentially 1,000 to 2,000 acres that ought to be protected, although some of those living at the foot of the mountain might argue for more (Sumas Mountain sprawls across more than 25,000 acres). Like Blanchard Mountain in the

View from Sumas Mountain.

Chuckanuts, the north end of Sumas Mountain is among the best of the best. The agency, however, is much better designed for removing trees. Let's hope we can save it for ours and future generations. (Cards and letters should go to our state senators and representatives.) Ironically, the name Sumas is said to mean "land without trees"—yikes. Presumably, the name originally described the floodplain below, not the mountain.

A new hiker trailhead has been proposed at the Ostrom Conservation Site which may not yet exist in 2003 (*see Hike #51 for directions*). The Ostrom trailhead will include an obvious sign showing the route up Sumas Mountain. If no such sign exists, then head back down South Pass Rd. for the unofficial trailhead off Sealund Rd., 1.3 miles to the west (2.5 miles east of SR 9). Turn south on Sealund Rd. and in about 0.2 mile park on the skimpy shoulder near the last obvious house (*elevation: 350 feet*). Please respect the owner's kindness and don't block that driveway or the driveway that continues ahead. If there's not room, find another place back toward South Pass Rd. The path leads east just outside a fence line. This stretch can be very muddy from fall through spring (rubber boots advised; stash them at the other end).

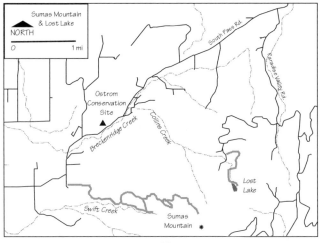

The trail soon improves and bends to the south to merge with an old road grade with occasional muddy sections. Skip a spur on the left, cross Hardin Creek, then head left at a junction near the next creek (**1.1 mi**; the right fork leads to the "gold mines" loop described below). The path steepens but the tread is good to a big flat in the forest surrounding the old Friendly Cabin—John Friendly helped build it (**1.4 mi**; *elevation: 1,250 feet*). Continue eastward briefly to a fork on the hillside (**1.6 mi**): go left for the summit or right for the loop to the mines. For the latter, the trail traverses southward, sidles past two small drainages, and drops slightly to a junction in 0.2 mile. Experienced hikers can climb left on skinny trail to a marginally interesting old mine shaft which may or may not be safe to enter (expect standing water, a low ceiling and essential darkness if you go). The mines were apparently "salted" with gold in a bogus money-grubbing scheme. Back at the junction, continue down along Swift Creek for 0.2 mile to a spur on the left that descends to an old vault and former building site. This path quickly rejoins the mine loop and reaches the junction with the main trail just ahead (below Friendly Cabin).

For the recommended summit option, the upper mine loop junction beyond the cabin is where the climbing gets serious. The path is steep, gaining a 1,000 feet in less than a mile. The trail splits in 0.3 mile; *left* is short and steep and passes through a small meadow with a faint trail (head straight up the slope); *right* makes a longish traverse on good trail and is more gradual; they rejoin near a mossy outcrop above (**2.4 mi.**, *from trailhead*). It helps to take a look back at each fork to remember which way you came. After a brief respite, the trail steepens again, eases off in a slightly brushy area then runs up close to the steep north face of the mountain, then meadows just above (**4.4 mi**; *elevation: 3,000 feet*). The views to the north, then west and east are outstanding, from the San Juan Islands to Vancouver and Mount Baker. Wildflowers are a-blazing in spring and early summer. An intermittent boot track continues south about 0.4 mile along the ridge crest with pocket views (including Mount Baker) above a near-vertical drop to the east. This path quickly fades at a recent clearcut—the end of the line.

Lowlands & Foothills—
53. Lost Lake (Sumas Mountain)

Distance: 1.8 miles round trip   Time: Allow 1 - 2 hours

Elevation gain: 400 feet   Season: April - November

One of two good hikes on Sumas Mountain, Lost Lake (not to be confused with Lost Lake in the Chuckanuts) is a short jaunt on poor trail. This assumes, of course, that the DNR road leading up to the area is not gated, as the agency is often prone to do. A portion of the lake and lovely forest around it (207 acres) were donated to Whatcom County school kids in 1918 by Aron Molinder for the study of "birds, plants, trees and all forms of natural life." The Bellingham Herald recently noted the words on his tombstone in the Nooksack cemetery: "Know more believe less." The site is adminsitered by Nooksack Valley School District. An uncommon old-growth forest here plus maturing forest on Sumas Mountain creates a rare opportunity for a landscape-scale reserve with exceptional ecological, scenic and recreational value (*see also Hike #52*).

From South Pass Rd., about seven miles east of SR 9 (near Everson), turn south on Paradise Valley Rd. which quickly becomes

a steep, unpaved logging road. Swing right up the hill at 1.7 miles, climbing into recent clearcuts with wide views of the Fraser River valley, Abbottsford and the B.C. Coast Range. Stay right at 3.5 miles on a coarse gravel road (park if not driveable). Continue another 0.2 mile (keep left at a fork) to the unmarked trail on the left (*elevation: 2,300 feet*). Unfortunately, portions of the route have been impacted by ATVs. Cross

Lost Lake in the fall.

two creeks in the first 0.5 mile to easier ground, then up again to a third crossing just below the lake (**0.8 mi**). Go left across the creek and amble leftward briefly to a perfect rock perch above the shore (**0.9 mi**; *elevation: 2,700 feet*). The quiet forested lake offers a fine refuge from the devastated hills below. The shussshhh of the creek may be the only sound. Some older maps show a trail coming up from the east, but it's not easy to spot. The trail to the lake is somewhat braided so glance again at each junction on the way in and out.

Lowlands & Foothills—
54. Silver Lake

Distance: 1-mile loop (or more)   Time: Allow 1 hour (or more)
Elevation gain: 200 feet (or more)   Season: Year-round

For a routine, if not refreshing, walk in the park away from town next to a sizeable lake, add Silver Lake Park to your to-do list. The park entrance is about 3.5 miles north of Maple Falls. Leave Mt. Baker Hwy. at MP 25.8 and follow Silver Lake Rd. to the park; turn right and head for the lodge 0.5 mile ahead. There is a map of the park on a board near the lodge, or maybe try the following loop. Head north through lawns and cross a tiny cove on an interesting bridge, then pass above some cabins, partly on a paved road and go left on another. Pass through a dip then at the top of a hill (**0.2 mi**), turn right on a trail leading through alder forest. At a junction near campsites, turn left (straight goes to the horse camp). The path climbs about 200 feet to what used to be a good view, but which the trees have since retaken. Head left at the next junction (**0.5 mi**), cross the entrance road, and go left through woods to a grassy area with a picnic shelter next to the lake. Turn northward (left) through the grass for more path leading back to the start (**1.0 mi**). Earlier, upon reaching the entrance road, a longer alternative would be to walk right to the park entrance at Silver Lake Rd., turn left and follow the road 0.2 mile to another trail on the left. This leads around the south end of the lake and connects to logging roads and horse trails on Black Mountain where much more rambling is feasible.

MOUNT BAKER AREA

Vine maple, Horseshoe Bend Trail.

55. Horseshoe Bend
Distance: 0.5 - 5.4 miles round trip   Time: Allow 1 - 4 hours
Elevation gain: 100 - 200 feet   Season: Almost year-round

A nice hike even on a crummy day, this easy trip is suitable for families almost any time of year. The trail winds along the North Fork Nooksack River at the edge of a deep forest. A rushing tumult of melting snow and glaciers, the river seems to be building momentum here for the hard push across the lowlands to Bellingham Bay. The reach is popular with kayakers who slalom through rapids near the SR 542 bridge.

Park at the trailhead on Mt. Baker Hwy. (MP 35.4) across from the Douglas Fir Campground (*elevation: 1,000 feet*), 1.8 miles east of the Glacier Public Service Center (*map, next page*). The trail begins at the bridge and meanders upriver along noisy whitewater crashing over boulders and bedrock. Sword ferns and moss form a thick carpet beneath a dense second-growth forest of red cedar, douglas fir, hemlock, vine maple and red alder. In early summer trillium, wild ginger, bunchberry, twin flower and Indian pipe share the damp forest floor with devils club, salmonberry and other shades of green.

Cross Coal Creek (**0.2 mi**) and continue as far as conditions allow, since the old trail deteriorates somewhat in the first mile. Or, push on to the namesake bend in the river beyond (**1.2 mi**). Just around the bend turn right on an old road (or simply head back). In 100 yards the trail goes right (may be brushy) another 1.5 miles and ends at a point where the tread disappears over the edge of a large washout next to the river. This section is not maintained, was in rough condition in late 2002, and can be difficult to locate in summer (due to vegetation). Thus the lower section of trail is the better walk. There are no great views of surrounding peaks, but the rushing water, especially in spring, makes it one of the best river walks in the county.

MOUNT BAKER AREA—
56. Church Mountain

Distance: 8.4 miles round trip   Time: Allow 5 - 6 hours
Elevation gain: 4,100 feet   Season: July - October

*C*hurch Mountain, named for the rock steeple at its summit, is very prominent from Mt. Baker Hwy. about a mile east of the Glacier Public Service Center. It is a fairly strenuous climb—the trail gains 1,000 feet per mile on the way up to the old lookout site. Although the building was removed in 1967, its location on Church Mountain (built in 1928) was strategic to fire control in the Nooksack watershed. This lovely rocky ridge is the western extremity of the High Divide, a 10-mile ridge system of uninterrupted meadows reaching all the way to Yellow Aster Meadows above Swamp Creek (*see Hikes #58 and #64*). The upper end of the trail was recently upgraded. Camping possibilities are sparse. Carry extra water after midsummer.

Turn left off Mt. Baker Hwy. at MP 38.8, just beyond Fossil Creek

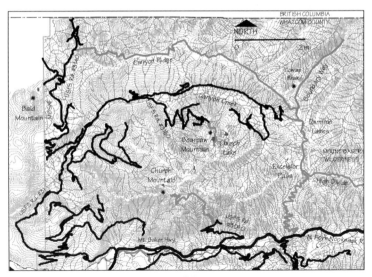

Wildflowers in the mist.

onto USFS Rd. #3040. The road may be rough and steep but is usually passable to most cars. In 1.8 miles, cross the creek bed (park here if not driveable). The trailhead is 0.9 mile farther, at the road end (*elevation: 2,000 feet*). The trail follows the old logging road initially, then enters a shadowy wilderness for the long ascent to the meadows and first good views (**3.0 mi**). After contouring westward another 0.5 mile, the trail switchbacks up the final wildflower slopes toward the rocky point above. The final few steps are literally carved out of the rock face. The top, a flat rocky veranda at 6,100 feet, makes a fine munching place (**4.2 mi**). Soaking up the views... Mount Baker, the Nooksack Valley, Mount Shuksan and countless distant peaks on both sides of the international border. Close by to the west is the summit of Church Mountain with its near vertical walls. Experienced cross-country hikers may find a way to descend 500 feet to the north to reach Kidney Lakes and Whistler Lakes (*see Hike #57*). By midsummer, carry extra water, since the high ridge becomes very dry, especially on the south side.

MOUNT BAKER AREA—
57. Church Lake & Bearpaw Mountain

Distance: 1.4 - 3.4 miles round trip Time: Allow 3 - 7 hours
Elevation gain: 300 - 1,300 feet Season: Mid-July - October

At the west end of the High Divide, the alpine lakes and meadows between Church Mountain and Bearpaw Mountain comprise a seldom visited wilderness, contrasting sharply with massive logging scars that characterize much of the Canyon Creek valley. Clearcutting occurred at very high elevations here (near 5,000 feet). An uneasy benefit, however, is better access to Church Lake and the meadows surrounding Bearpaw Mountain. Strangely, this portion of the Divide was not included in the 1984 Washington Wilderness Act which designated lands to the east as part of the Mount Baker Wilderness.

To access the area, drive two miles east of Glacier on Mt. Baker Hwy., turning left at MP 35.6 onto Canyon Creek Rd. #31 (*map, p.136*). Follow this narrow paved road about 10 miles, then take the right fork onto USFS Rd. #3160. Near a bridge in 0.4 mile, the road is slide prone and may be very rough beyond here, if passable at all.

Bearpaw Mountain from USFS Rd. #3160.

Stay right at 2.2 miles and left at 3.9 miles. The road ends at a saddle at the upper edge of the clearcut, about 4.4 miles from Canyon Creek Rd. (*elevation: 4,800 feet*).

The bumpy approach may be difficult, but the hike certainly isn't. The unmarked trail continues to the right (south) through open forest, ascending into subalpine country. The high cliffs of Bearpaw's north peak loom above azure Church Lake (**0.7 mi**; *elevation: 5,100 feet*). The path is less obvious as it climbs the long curving ridge that begins southeast of the lake (feasible camping). Experienced hikers can wander meadows and rock to the southwest to a 6,062-foot summit and views of High Divide, Mount Baker and Mount Shuksan (**1.7 mi**). The more adventurous hikers with good map and compass skills could continue on a descent to discover a number of small lakes and wild meadows leading to potential campsites at Whistler and Kidney Lakes. Church Mountain rises sharply beyond.

Mount Baker Area—
58. Excelsior Pass & High Divide

Distance: 5.0 - 8.2 miles (or more) round trip   Time: Allow 3 - 6 hours
Elevation gain: 1,200 - 3,500 feet   Season: July - October

There are two approaches to this extensive alpine ridge, the northerly one via Damfino Lakes being a tad easier to hike (2,500 feet less elevation gain; *map, p. 136*). Both lead to exceptional meadows and good views of Mount Baker, the North Cascades, and peaks of the B.C. Coast Range. From Excelsior Pass, one can wander this heather and wildflower ridge for miles either way. Since there are at least five trails which access the High Divide area, numerous day hikes and overnight trips are possible. Note that the snow on north-facing slopes takes longer to melt, which means the longer south route may be mostly snow free several weeks earlier than the north.

The south trailhead is on the Mount Baker Hwy. at MP 41.1, 7.5 miles east of the Glacier Public Service Center (*elevation: 1,800 feet*). This steep wooded trail climbs 3,500 feet in 4.1 miles to the pass. Most of the route is in heavy forest, breaking out into meadows the last mile. But to reach the shorter northern start, turn left on Canyon Creek Rd. #31 at MP 35.6 and drive this 7.6 miles and go right, then left at a fork in 10 miles; trailhead is to the right 5 miles farther (*elevation: 4,300 feet*). The trail meets the Boundary Way/Canyon Ridge Trail just before Damfino Lakes; stay right (*see Hikes #59 and #60*). From the tiny lakes (ponds), the muddy trail is easy to follow and gently climbs to drier meadows for two miles, before reaching the 5,300-foot pass (**2.5 mi**). From here, one can hike up several hundred feet to higher viewpoints in either direction. The old Excelsior Lookout site is 0.2 mile to the east and 400 feet above. The fire lookout was built in the mid-1930s and removed in 1968. Mount Baker, Chowder Ridge and the heavily crevassed Roosevelt Glacier are prominent to the south, as is Mount Shuksan to the southeast.

If you're good with a map, it's feasible to ramble westward near the ridge top for several miles toward Church Mountain (more difficult), or eastward on the High Divide Trail to Welcome Pass, five miles from Excelsior Pass (*see Hike #64*). There's good camping along the ridge and at Damfino Lakes. Up high, carry extra water. Snow is usually gone and wildflowers are at their peak by late July.

Mount Baker Area—
59. Boundary Way

Distance: 4.6 - 12.6 miles (or more) round trip   Time: Allow 3 - 8 hours
Elevation gain: 1,000 - 2,800 feet   Season: July - October

The hike up the Boundary Way Trail offers a quiet alternative to the more popular Excelsior Ridge Trail, reached from the same trailhead. South-facing slopes also mean a somewhat earlier snow-melt, compared to the north-facing slopes of Excelsior. The slightly adventurous jaunt to the summit of Cowap Peak makes a fine outing in its own right where the jagged North Cascades appear bunched up like waves on a stormy coast. Glacier lilies are profuse as soon as the white stuff melts, followed by a host of other alpine wildflowers.

Follow Mount Baker Hwy. (SR 542) to MP 35.6, about two miles past the Glacier Public Service Center, and turn left (north) on Canyon Creek Rd. (USFS Rd. #31; *map, p. 136*). In about 7.6 miles, cross the creek on a bridge and head right. Continuing up Canyon

Tomyhoi Peak from Cowap Peak.

Creek Rd., stay left at a fork in 10 miles, and reach the signed east trailhead on the right at about 15 miles (*elevation: 4,300 feet*).

Walk briefly in second-growth forest, then old growth to a junction (**0.5 mi**); stay left (right goes 150 yards to Damfino Lakes and Excelsior Ridge; *see Hike #58*). At the next junction (**0.9 mi**) head right; left is Canyon Ridge (*Hike # 60*). The Boundary Way Trail leads through a linear opening in the forest, dropping slightly to reenter the woods on the left, then quickly emerges into open meadows beneath the long rocky ridge of Cowap Peak. Tomyhoi and the Border Peaks loom to the east. The trail angles up and right to reach a junction at the ridge crest at 5,300 feet (**2.0 mi**). A short, steep narrow section should be passable. At the ridge top, the old trail begins a long gradual descent to nowhere and disappears after a mile or so. The better bet is to head left up the ridge to the summit crest (**2.3 mi**). Steep snow may require an ice axe in early summer. The first summit point offers a scenic lunch counter. The true summit (*elevation: 5,658 feet*) nearby requires a careful step across an exposed spot. The panorama is sumptuous: Mount Baker, Mount Shuksan, Excelsior Ridge, Bearpaw Mountain, Canyon Ridge, Bald Mountain and more. The area seems to be missing good campsites.

MOUNT BAKER AREA—
60. Canyon Ridge

Distance: 5.2 - 7.5 miles (or more) round trip Time: Allow 3 - 6 hours
Elevation gain: 1,000 - 2,200 feet Season: Mid-July - October

The 7.5-mile-long Canyon Ridge Trail is probably best hiked from east to west but can be done as a through hike with a possible key swap in the middle for two parties starting at opposite ends. The east portion tends to be in better condition with better views, so the most practical option may be to walk from the east end to a high point, then retrace your steps to the start—a good add-on to the walk up Boundary Way Trail. See that listing (*Hike #59*) for directions to the east trailhead (*map, p. 136*). The route is well signed. Go left at the first junction (**0.5 mi**) and left at the next (**0.9 mi**). The trail rounds the ridge and breaks into meadow (**1.5 mi**) then attains the ridge, rising in and out of trees to the first good high point at 5,300 feet (**2.6 mi**), followed by ups and downs in trees or not to other vistas and a crest at 5,200 feet (**4.0 mi**) with excellent views—barely a mile south of Canada. Heavy logging activity is evident in the lower watersheds both north and south of the border. Beyond, the trail is largely in forest and smaller openings, losing about 1,200 feet in 3.5 miles.

For the west trailhead, follow Mount Baker Hwy. (SR 542) to MP 35.6, about two miles past the Glacier Public Service Center, and turn left (north) onto the Canyon Creek Rd. (USFS Rd. #31). In about 7.6 miles, cross the creek on a bridge and turn left. The road is rough and may not be passable for some standard cars; stay right at 6.1 miles and continue two miles to find the west trailhead over a

saddle at the end of the road (*elevation: 4,100 feet*). Trail improvements on the ridge are ongoing year to year. Carry extra water if running the complete ridge. There are reasonable campsites at several locations.

Canyon Ridge from Cowap Peak.

MOUNT BAKER AREA—
61. Heliotrope Ridge (Mount Baker)

Distance: 6 - 8 miles round trip   Time: Allow 4 - 6 hours
Elevation gain: 1,400 - 2,300 feet   Season: Mid-July - October

Also called Mount Baker Trail, this popular route for hikers and climbers alike offers one of the best places to get up close and personal with a river of ice, namely, the Coleman Glacier. For just a moderate effort, the scenic rewards are plenty: ancient forest, wildflowers, mountain streams and waterfalls, the Coleman and Roosevelt Glaciers, Mount Baker, and the Black Buttes. From Mt. Baker Hwy., a mile past the town of Glacier, turn right (south) at MP 34.3 on Glacier Creek Rd. #39. Follow this narrow winding road eight miles to the obvious trailhead on the left (*elevation: 3,700 feet*).

The trail gradually climbs through open forest to a series of switchbacks and waterfall views before passing the site of the old Kulshan Cabin (**2.0 mi**). The former log cabin was built by the Mount Baker Club in 1925 when getting there required a ten-mile hike from

Coleman Glacier and Mount Baker.

Glacier. The cabin was rebuilt in 1949, then, sadly, was dismantled in the late 1980s. Just beyond, the path leaves the forest where views quickly improve. Stay left at a junction (**2.2 mi**) for the easy stroll across what are avalanche slopes in winter and spring, and stream-hopping terrain in summer, to the brink of a lateral moraine overlooking the Coleman Glacier (**2.5 mi**). The edge is loose and sloughing away so be cautious, and by all means stay off the glacier (unless you're an experienced climber with a rope team, ice axes, crampons and the like).

This is one of the iciest scenes you'll find in the North Cascades. Beaten paths up and down the moraine and through rocky meadows offer more exploring. Or, return to the earlier junction and hike up the hogsback—the climbers route up the mountain. Snow and ice blocks the way for hikers at about 6,000 feet. The Heliotrope Ridge crest is a half-mile to the west. Beware of high water, steep snow (with drop-offs below), thin snow bridges and avalanches in late spring and early summer.

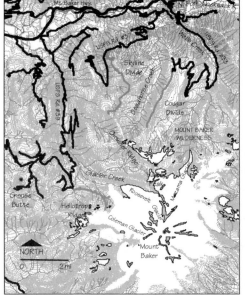

62. Skyline Divide

Distance: 5 - 14 miles round trip   Time: Allow 3 - 10 hours
Elevation gain: 1,400 - 3,200 feet   Season: Mid-July - October

Skyline Divide has long been a favorite for veteran North Cascade hikers, thanks to broad green meadows, alive with wildflowers much of the summer, and panoramic high points with vistas from Mount Baker to Canada. As moderate hikes go, this one is as popular as any in the region. For more wildness and less people, try a weekday or head up early on the weekend, ahead of rush hour. Cooler days in fall, before the snow hits, is also good. To access the trailhead, follow Mt. Baker Hwy. a mile past Glacier and turn right on Glacier Creek Rd. at MP 34.3. Then make an immediate left on the Deadhorse Creek Rd. (USFS Rd. #37). The road parallels the North Fork Nooksack River for several miles then rounds a number of switchbacks before reaching the trailhead in just under 13 miles (*elevation: 4,400 feet; map, p. 144*). The trail is on the left a few yards up the road. Carry extra water after mid-summer.

Mount Baker and the Black Buttes from Skyline Divide.

The hike is steep at first, then eases off in old-growth forest for 1.5 miles before reaching a small opening around 5,200 feet. The path soon crosses the wilderness boundary and meets the meadowy crest of the ridge, at one of those places where your whole body involuntarily just says "wow" (**2.1 mi**; *elevation 5,800 feet*). From here on, the views never let up: Mount Baker, Mount Shuksan, the conspicuous "table" of Table Mountain, and Church Mountain and the High Divide to the north. At a junction, a path tracks left in meadowland, an easy stroll for 0.3 mile (campsites and a possible turn-around point for the easier trek). The main trail to the right steepens toward two high points, both are nice vantage points. The main path skirts the higher one on the west (or go up steeply for 200 feet and over the top), then descends slightly to a saddle (**3.5 mi**). Cougar Divide's green meadows are visible to the southeast, the next ridge over. A fork goes left to gentle ground, water, wildflowers, marmots and campsites in the upper Deadhorse Creek basin.

For the equally scenic upper ridge, continue on the right fork up a steep section (not too difficult) to more meadows and easy trail. Several humps on the ridge offer places to lunch and lounge. Chowder Ridge is the rugged stuff and icy crags to the south leading toward the volcano. Unless snow-covered, a reasonable path continues around a ridge to the right, regaining the view, with more tread to go (**6.0 mi**). The deteriorating path trods along the southwest slope (and crest) of Chowder Ridge for another two miles or more to Hadley Peak, encountering some loose rock and steep gullies. This section is not recommended for casual or inexperienced hikers.

MOUNT BAKER AREA—

63. Cougar Divide

Distance: 7.0 miles round trip   Time: Allow 4 - 6 hours
Elevation gain: 1,200 feet   Season: Mid-July - October

This pleasant trail is not easy to get to, but it does provide a comparable, less populated alternative to the heavily used Skyline Divide Trail to the west. The trailhead is high (*elevation: 4,800 feet*) and the views are good much of the way. It's a very long bumpy drive to the trailhead, though most small cars should do okay if the road has been recently graded. From Mt. Baker Hwy. (MP 40.7), turn right on the Wells Creek Rd. #33 and continue across the bridge beyond Nooksack Falls. At a road junction, make a hard right and follow this up the Wells Creek valley to a bridge at six miles and a view of Mount Baker and the Hadley Glacier. From here its another six miles and 2,000 feet up a winding rough road to another junction; stay left. Just beyond, follow a right fork a short distance to the trailhead on the left (*elevation: 4,800 feet; map, p. 144*).

The trail is not regularly maintained but is in fair condition as it gently climbs southward through old snags in a miniature subalpine forest. A high knoll (5,382 feet) offers a great view and suitable turn-around point for a short walk (**0.7 mi**). The path meanders through unusual volcanic terrain to a point where the ridge drops slightly to a wooded area. Watch for the trail below to the left. For the next mile the path is generally good and stays close to the ridge crest in thick forest. At several points a short steep slippery section or fallen log may be discouraging but passable.

After a small pond, a meadow is crossed on a side slope before gaining the crest again. From here the views of Mount Shuksan, Mount Baker, Hadley Peak and Chowder Ridge are scenic and impressive. The trail ends where Cougar Divide intersects rugged Chowder Ridge in colorful, fragile and often soggy meadows (**3.5 mi**; *elevation: 6,000 feet*). Camping is not recommended. Stay on the trail and don't build any fires. More experienced hikers can wander up to the southwest through rock and snow to more views at the ridge crest near Chowder Ridge (*see Hike #62*).

Mount Baker and Chowder Ridge.

MOUNT BAKER AREA—
64. Welcome Pass

Distance: 5 - 8 miles (or more) round trip   Time: Allow 4 - 6 hours
Elevation gain: 3,000 - 3,600 feet   Season: Mid-July - October

*O*ne of several access routes to the meadowlands of the High
Divide, the Welcome Pass Trail is the most grueling. Endless
short switchbacks—67 of them—go almost from trailhead to summit. After an easy half-mile along an old road bed, expect to gain
2,400 feet in the next two miles to the pass, making Welcome Pass
one of the steepest trails in the North Cascades. As always, the views
on top help ease the pain of getting there. Welcome also offers an
eastern approach for an extended 11 to 13-mile hike along the Divide, beginning or ending with the northern or southern leg of the
Excelsior Pass Trail (*see Hike #58*). Starting such a trek at Welcome
helps avoid an otherwise knee-pounding descent. Note that water
can be scarce late season.

The trailhead is near the end of USFS Rd. #3060 just west of
Silver Fir Campground. Turn left off the Mt. Baker Hwy. at MP 45.8
and drive 0.7 mile to the trailhead and parking area just beyond
(*elevation: 2,200 feet*). If undriveable, park in the highway turn-out

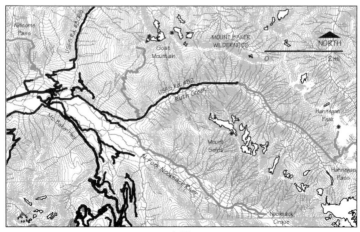

On the trail above Welcome Passs.

nearby and walk up the road. Follow the old logging road that nature is slowly reclaiming up to the former trailhead where the path abruptly heads right and steepens. Cross the wilderness boundary at the end of the logged-off area, and continue in old-growth forest, up and up and up. The trail runs along a ridge crest near the half-way point, then around switchback #60, there are finally some enticing views to enjoy: Mount Shuksan across the North Fork Nooksack River, and Mount Baker through small breaks in the trees. If you've been counting switchbacks, the crest will be very close by the time you round #67. The trail empties into open meadows at a pass—a welcome sight indeed (**2.5 mi**; *elevation: 5,200 feet*). Views include most major peaks in the region. Tomyhoi Peak is to the north. If that isn't enough, head steeply up the boot track to the right (east) to an even better view into the North Cascades. Or, wander more easily to the west as far as time and gumption allow, through a delectable landscape of meadows, ponds, and subalpine timber. Note that it's about six miles from Welcome Pass to Excelsior Pass (a ridge crest view in 1.5 miles makes a good turn-around).

MOUNT BAKER AREA—
65. Gold Run Pass & Tomyhoi Lake

Distance: 4.4 - 8.8 miles round trip   Time: Allow 4 - 7 hours
Elevation gain: 1,800 - 3,500 feet   Season: July - October

The old mining trail across Gold Run Pass is part of a century-old network used by prospectors in an area that once seemed to promise rich diggings. Scattered relics and adits (mine entrances, often never finished) speckle the hillsides and basins, evidence of a dedicated search for the mother lode. Today, the hike from the road to the pass is a moderately easy day trip. Beyond, the big drop to Tomyhoi Lake adds 1,700 feet of elevation to gain on the hike back out, which means few dayhikers actually make it to the lake.

From Mt. Baker Hwy. at MP 46.4, turn left on the Twin Lakes Rd. and drive 4.5 miles to the signed trailhead at a switchback (*elevation: 3,600 feet*). The

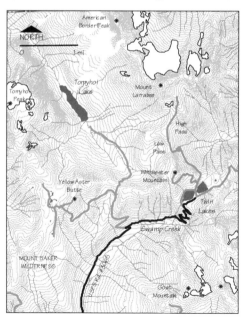

path begins climbing immediately, wandering in and out of a large avalanche slope, with a view of Goat Mountain to the southeast, then Mount Baker to the southwest. Back in the forest, the trail enters the Mount Baker Wilderness and soon reaches a large basin with some open areas. In the fall of 2002, we flushed a tiny saw-whet owl feeding on a mouse next to the trail. Ignore a faint path on the left just

Mount Baker from the pass in October.

before a campsite. The trail steepens then meets the signed junction
with the Yellow Aster Butte Trail (*Hike #66*) on a meadowed slope
(**1.9 mi**). Continue up through trees briefly to the pass (**2.1 mi**;
elevation: 5,360 feet). Wander left a few yards to a better vantage
point of the Border Peaks and Mount Larrabee to the north. A boot
track leads another 0.1 mile up and to the left to a wider view of
surrounding peaks, including Mount Baker, Mount Shuksan,
Tomyhoi Peak and the mile-long lake below. The trail to Tomyhoi
Lake heads downslope from the pass, steeply at first then easier
through meadows and forest to the south end of the lake and campsites near the shore (**4.3 mi**). The impressive east wall of Tomyhoi
Peak rises almost vertically 3,200 feet above the lake. On the way
back up, there is also a possible connecting route to Low Pass (*see
Hike #68*).

MOUNT BAKER AREA—
66. Yellow Aster Butte

Distance: 6.6 - 8.0 miles (or more) round trip   Time: Allow 4 - 7 hours
Elevation gain: 2,000 - 2,600 feet (or more)   Season: July - October

The old Keep Kool Trail to Yellow Aster Meadows, popular as it was, is no more. Veteran hikers may recall the swampy lower meadows that made trail maintenance a particular challenge, and the clearcut that destroyed the lower section of trail. The good news, though, is that the "new" trail to the meadows and the namesake butte above is relatively dry, even more scenic, and entails 600 feet less elevation gain. Not surprisingly, the hike is a bigger draw than before. Don't go on a pleasant summer weekend looking for solitude. For that, try mid-week or in the fall when the mountain ash and blueberry bushes are radiant against stark green mountain hemlock trees and golden grasses retreating into winter. The hike can be easily combined with a visit to Gold Run Pass (*see Hike #65*).

See Hike #65 for directions to the Yellow Aster/Tomyhoi Lake Trailhead (*elevation: 3,600 feet; map, p. 150*). On the drive in, the Butte is visible to the north at about 2.5 miles. The trail to Yellow

Yellow Aster summit and Mount Larrabee.

Aster shares its approach with the Tomyhoi Lake/Gold Run Pass Trail to a signed junction (**1.9 mi**). From there, head left on an easy grade for the traverse westward and gradually upward through magical parklands and rock gardens with views of Mount Shuksan and Goat Mountain's two sharp summits. Soon enter a small, flat basin with a snowfield (possible avalanche debris) and interesting rock outcrops that seem folded and mashed. The trail drops slightly to cross a small stream then climbs out of the bowl to higher meadowland, wild-flowers, and views of Mount Baker. The path turns north, passes a tarn on the way to a junction with the summit trail (**3.3 mi**). Head right up a moderately steep, then very steep path to the rounded south summit of the 6,100-foot Butte and the full panorama (**3.5 mi**). Experienced scramblers can descend slightly to the north and follow the boot track along the ridge to the slightly higher north summit (**3.8 mi**). From the junction below the Butte, one can de-scend several short, steep switchbacks to a broad basin of many tarns, campsites (no fires), minor diggings, and a web of trails to explore. Don't forget the way back up. Something to ponder: rocks in the meadows belong to the Yellow Aster Complex—the oldest known rocks in North Cascades, at more 400 million to one billion years old. A climbers path heads north up the long ridge leading to Tomyhoi Peak (the summit is a serious climb, not a hike).

MOUNT BAKER AREA—
67. Winchester Mountain & Twin Lakes

Distance: 3.6 - 8.4 miles round trip   Time: Allow 3 - 6 hours
Elevation gain: 1,300 - 2,900 feet   Season: Mid-July - October

The lookout atop Winchester Mountain is an impressive vantage point that offers sprawling views of major peaks, lakes and the high country north of Mount Baker. By the time the snow has melted away (maybe by mid-July), it is a popular place, especially on fair summer weekends. To avoid crowds, plan your visit on a weekday or wait until fall. To reach the trailhead, turn left on the Twin Lakes Rd. #3065 off Mt. Baker Hwy. at MP 46.2, 12.7 miles east of the Gla-cier Public Service Center. At a junction, stay left; it's 4.4 miles to a

Twin Lakes and Mount Larrabee.

parking area at the Gold Run Pass/Tomyhoi Lake trailhead. The road is often washed out beyond, so walk (or drive?) the remaining 2.4 miles to Twin Lakes (*elevation: 5,200 feet; map, p. 150*). The lakes can be snow-covered into July. Distances shown above depend on whether the road is driveable or not. This historic "mine-to-market" road served the Lone Jack Mine southeast of the lakes—the most successful (so to speak) of the mines in the region. Prior to completion of the road in 1950, access to the area required a long slog up Swamp Creek from the North Fork Nooksack River, or perhaps a scenic trek from the west along the High Divide. Today, however, the road is a bit of an eyesore and should probably be removed.

A good trail passes between the lakes, contouring the southeast slope of Winchester to meet the Low Pass/High Pass Trail (**0.2 mi**; *see Hike #68*); continue straight (left) for the lookout. The trail climbs moderately through scenic sloping meadows with occasional steep rocky sections. Near the ridge crest, lingering snow in early summer requires an ice axe (and the ability to use it) due to steep snow and dangerous cliffs below; if unsure, turn back. The ridge crest is just above (**1.5 mi**). Here, at 6,000 feet, the views improve greatly. The final short switchbacks lead up the southwest side of the mountain to the restored lookout cabin at the summit (**1.8 mi**; *elevation: 6,521 feet*). The views are tremendous: (clockwise from north) Canadian and American Border Peaks, Mount Larrabee, Goat Mountain, Mount Shuksan, Mount Baker, the Nooksack River valley, Tomyhoi Peak and Tomyhoi Lake. The lookout, built in 1935 was saved from ruin by, and is maintained by, volunteers of the Mount Baker Hiking Club. Without their efforts, the building may have disappeared by now, as is the case with most of the old fire lookouts of the North Cascades. Expect much company, especially on nice weekends.

MOUNT BAKER AREA—
68. Low Pass & High Pass

Distance: 3 - 8 miles round trip   Time: Allow 2 - 6 hours
Elevation gain: 700 - 1,800 feet   Season: Mid-July - October

The abandoned Gargett Mine on the southern flank of Mount Larrabee has collapsed, but a few old relics litter the diggings. Almost continuous views on the way to Low Pass and High Pass make this one a charm.(*See Hike #67 for directions to Twin Lakes; map, p.150*). At the junction 0.2 mile above Twin Lakes, stay right (left goes up Winchester Mountain). Follow the path over a shoulder, descending briefly while traversing a steep northeast slope (turn back if icy). The red pyramid of Mount Larrabee above High Pass dominates the view. In another mile, a series of switchbacks through wildflowers gain about 400 feet to Low Pass (**1.5 mi**). (For a possible loop trip around Winchester Mountain, experienced cross-country hikers can descend to the southwest to meadows and traverse to the Gold Run Pass-Tomyhoi Lake Trail 1.3 miles away. Head left and over the pass back to the Twin Lakes Rd. - about 7.5 miles total.)

From Low Pass, the trail climbs the subalpine ridge crest and skirts a knoll, reaching High Pass (**2.5 mi**; *elevation: 6,000 feet*). The Gargett brothers mine and remnants are visible to the north about 250 feet below, reached by a steep trail. Tomyhoi Lake shines against the 2,500 foot high cliffs of Tomyhoi Peak. Continue on a less used path up and east about 0.8 mile to a remote perch and a closer view of the precipitous Pleiades ridge east of Mount Larrabee. The lookout can also be seen atop Winchester Mountain. A combined trip to High Pass and Winchester Lookout requires a full day, but its not an unreasonable outing for ambitious types.

Mount Larrabee and High Pass.

MOUNT BAKER AREA—
69. Goat Mountain

Distance: 5 - 8 miles round trip   Time: Allow 4 - 7 hours
Elevation gain: 3,000 - 4,100 feet   Season: July - October

One of many good hikes in the upper watershed of the North
Fork Nooksack River, Goat Mountain is as enjoyable and challenging as its neighbors. The trail leads to big meadows with good
views of Mount Shuksan and surrounding peaks. The lower meadows can melt out in late May or June, while the upper slopes often
remain snow-covered into July. Prospectors scratched out a few no-
glory holes more than a century ago, and a fire lookout once stood
at the 4,100-foot level (removed in 1963). The trailhead, at 2,500
feet, is slightly lower than most, but moderate grades make the going reasonable. From Mt. Baker Hwy (SR 542), turn left at MP 46.5
onto the Hannegan Pass Rd. Stay left at a fork to find the small
trailhead at 2.5 miles (*elevation: 2,500 feet; map, p. 148*).

The trail switchbacks up the south slopes of the mountain on a
steady rise for a mile, eases off briefly, then steepens again as it
traverses northward. More switchbacks lead past openings and
patches of slide alder before entering the lower meadows (**2.0 mi**).
The trail may be rough and wet in places (some reconstruction is
scheduled for 2005) as it winds among huckleberries and scattered
trees, and steepens to pass a good campsite (on the right next to a
clump of trees). A rocky outcrop nearby (head right; **2.5 mi**) makes

a good turn-around or
resting perch with
great views south and
west, from Mount
Shuksan to Mount
Baker and beyond. Or,
continue up the main
path along a meadowy
ridge to the base of the

*White-tailed ptarmigan
at Goat Mountain.*

156

upper mountain (**3.0 mi**). From here, the trail deteriorates to a narrow boot track as it traverses left across a very steep meadow, not recommended for casual or less experienced hikers (carry water). The path leads up steeply to a ridge crest and a false summit above (**4.0 mi**). Steep rock, snow or ice blocks further progress.

MOUNT BAKER AREA—
70. Bagley & Chain Lakes

Distance: 1.5 - 9 miles round trip   Time: Allow 2 - 6 hours
Elevation gain: 200 - 2,000 feet   Season: July - October

Between Mount Baker and Mount Shuksan a major trail system offers easy to moderate walks and hikes and many loop possibilities from less than a mile to 20 miles or more. Easier walks include a 1.5-mile loop around lower Bagley Lake with a stop at the new Heather Meadows Visitor Center inside an historic building perched on a rocky overlook. The longer hike to Chain Lakes is extraordinary (and popular) summer and fall.

    Drive Mt. Baker Hwy. to the Mount Baker Ski Area and turn right

Lower Bagley Lake and Table Mountain.

at the big map sign (MP 54.6) and right again in 0.1 mile to the parking lot (*elevation: 4,200 feet*). Follow signs to Bagley Lakes (right). The trail drops to the lower lake and heads for the dam at its outlet. Turn left before crossing and wander a half-mile to the double-arch stone bridge. For an easy loop either go left uphill to the obvious visitor center and return via the Wild Goose Trail (*see Hike #71*), or cross the bridge and head back along the west side of the lower lake to the dam. To reach Chain Lakes, cross the bridge and head southwest around the upper lake, climbing 1,100 feet to a slope above the rocks of Herman Saddle (**3.0 mi**). Chain Lakes are 500 feet down the other side (**4.0 mi**; good camping; no fires). Mazama, Iceberg (the largest), Galena, and Hayes Lakes lie quiet in a magical setting. Turn back at the pass or the lakes, or for a more ambitious loop, continue on to Ptarmigan Ridge Trail (*Hike #73*), a mile beyond Mazama Lake. About 0.3 mile south of Mazama Lake, a left fork at some downed trees (not maintained) switchbacks up to a good viewpoint on the northwest shoulder of Table Mountain, 800 feet above the lakes. At the Ptarmigan Ridge junction, walk left 1.2 mile to reach Artist Point, and left again at the restrooms to follow the Wild Goose Trail (*Hike #71*) back to the start.

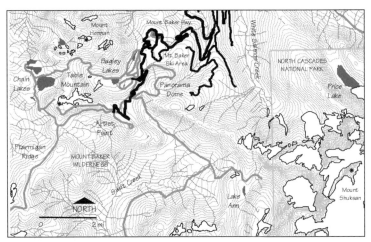

MOUNT BAKER AREA—
71. Wild Goose Trail & Table Mountain

Distance: 1.5 - 6 miles round trip   Time: Allow 2 - 5 hours
Elevation gain: 300 - 1,700 feet   Season: July - October

The trail to Wild Goose Pass (a.k.a. Austin Pass) and Artist Point at the end of the Mt. Baker Hwy. offers an aerobic and beauteous alternative to driving all the way up there (*see Hike #73 for directions to Artist Point; map, p.158*). The hike up Table Mountain is much easier from there but you will miss some great hiking below. You could also begin at the Heather Meadows Visitor Center below Table Mountain where a 1.5-mile loop and a 0.7-mile interpretive loop, the Fire and Ice Trail offer continuous views throughout. But if a bigger workout beckons, park at the lower Bagley Lakes trailhead immediately past the ski area (*see Hike #70*).

The Wild Goose Trail heads leftward and upward, passing a faint spur on the left to Panorama Dome (*Hike #72*). Follow the Wild Goose markers through a picnic area near the visitor center, angling

Mount Shuksan from Table Mountain.

left toward the highway at the road junction (**0.7 mi**). The trail climbs below and parallel to the highway to Austin Pass (**1.0 mi**), then bends right to climb stone steps to easier going beyond. Tall cairns mark the way. Cross the road then reach Artist Point near the restrooms (**1.5 mi**). Cross the lot to the northwest (toward Table) to find the trail leading to the summit of Table Mountain (another path left goes to Ptarmigan Ridge and Chain Lakes). The trail climbs 500 feet in less than 0.5 mile up the east end of the mountain. Zigzag up through short, exposed lava cliffs. The mountain itself is a remnant of an ancient lava flow that was actually deposited in a valley whose walls have long since eroded away. The path reaches a crest at meadows and panoramic views (**2.0 mi**); angle left to continue along the flat-tened summit for another 0.6 mile before fading into rock or snow. There are numerous rocks and slabs for lunch breaks. Some maps show a trail going down the west end, but it has largely vanished in a rock slide and dangerous snow slope. There is no easy descent to Chain Lakes from here, although experienced scramblers with an ice axe might manage it (if unsure, don't chance it). The Forest Ser-vice has no plans to reconstruct the old trail.

MOUNT BAKER AREA—
72. Panorama Dome

Distance: 3 - 4 miles round trip   Time: Allow 2 - 3 hours
Elevation gain: 800 feet   Season: July - October

This short hike through the Mount Baker Ski Area offers worth while views and good berry pickin' in late summer. From the parking area noted in Hike #70, follow the Wild Goose Trail to where it nears the road (**0.4 mi**). Turn left on a faint boot track and cross the road to the well marked trailhead next to a ski chair. The trail drops slightly into Galena Canyon then traverses and climbs Pan Dome to its top (**2.0 mi**; *elevation: 5,000 feet*). Either turn around here or pass the ski patrol hut to another path leading southeast to a small saddle below Shuksan Arm. Curve right (west) and descend to the Lake Ann trailhead at Austin Pass (**3.0 mi**). The Wild Goose Trail is across the road for the return to the trailhead (**4.0 mi**).

73. Ptarmigan Ridge

Distance: 6.2 - 9 miles round trip   Time: Allow 4 - 7 hours
Elevation gain: 400 - 1,000 feet   Season: Mid-July- October

The trailhead for Ptarmigan Ridge is located at Artist Point, one of the most scenic paved places anywhere in the Cascades Range. Drive 57.2 miles east from Bellingham to the very end of Mt. Baker Hwy. (usually snow-covered until mid-July). From the southwest corner of this alpine parking lot, follow the Chain Lakes Trail across the south face of Table Mountain toward Mount Baker (*map, p. 158*). In 1.2 miles, a junction is reached; stay left for Ptarmigan Ridge; the right goes the short way to the lakes (*see Hike #70*). The trail drops slightly and contours the broad ridge on its northwest side before crossing to the southeast (**2.2 mi**). A small spur ridge is reached: a good viewpoint and turn-around (**3.1 mi**). It's a 400 foot gain to here. Even in August, hikers may encounter marginal weather with poor visibility and patches of snow over the trail, possibly requiring an ice axe (and the ability to use it). Snow, rain and wind can be serious hazards any time of year; turn back if conditions should deteriorate. There is no protection in case of bad weather (several trail travelers have met their maker here).

When free of snow (usually August-September), the upper portion of the ridge can be easily followed all the way to Coleman Pinnacle and the rocky meadows of Camp Kiser just beyond (**4.5 mi**; good campsites). The entire trail is high and wild with great views of the Rainbow and Park Glaciers. Take care to keep your bearings.

*Coleman Pinnacle
in winter.*

MOUNT BAKER AREA—
74. Elbow Lake & Bell Pass

Distance: 3 - 9 miles round trip   Time: Allow 2 - 6 hours
Elevation gain: 300 - 1,300 feet   Season: May - October

Located in old-growth forests on the Sisters Divide between Mount
Baker and the Twin Sisters Range, Elbow Lake can be reached by
either of two approaches: on the south from a road near the South
Fork Nooksack River, or from the north at a bridge over the Middle
Fork of the Nooksack. Water flowing north and south from this moderate divide allows a major river system to nearly surround the Twin
Sisters Range as if it was an island. Elbow and tiny Hildebrand and
Doreen Lakes nearby are situated at the headwaters. The southern
route can be an easy one mile stroll from the road end, or a more
extended four-mile hike from Pioneer Horse Camp, somewhat comparable to the north side trail. Both roads are gated over the winter
and spring to protect elk herds. Trail improvements are ongoing.

North approach: From Mt. Baker Hwy. at MP 16.8, turn south on
Mosquito Lake Rd. and continue 4.6 miles to Porter Creek Rd. (#38);

Always friendly gray jays, also known as "camp robbers".

angle left. In two miles, the North Twin Sister comes into view. Stay right at 4.2 miles and left at 4.7 miles (slide area here, road may be rough but better beyond). At 9 miles is the best view from a road of the mile-wide Sisters Glacier and the South Twin Sister. The seasonal road closure (from December 1st through June 15th) begins near MP 10; the signed trailhead is on the right at 11.4 miles (*elevation: 2,100 feet; map, next page*).

Hike to a footbridge across the river, then head up into old-growth cedar and hemlock forest above Green Creek. Soon the grade eases and crosses two small streams, then passes a great view of the Green Creek Glacier and the middle peaks of the Sisters Range (**2.0 mi**). The peaks, left to right, are Cinderella, Little Sister, Skookum and the South Twin Sister (partially hidden). The way heads up Hildebrand Creek, reaching Hildebrand Lake (or bog) and the larger Elbow Lake just over the divide (**3.4 mi**; *elevation: 3,400 feet*). There are campsites around the southeast side of the lake.

South approach: From SR 20 near Concrete (MP 82.4), follow the Baker Lake Rd. north just over 12 miles and turn left on USFS Rd. #12. Reach Wanlick Pass at MP 8 where a seasonal gate is closed from November 1st to July 1st. At MP 13.5 pass the Pioneer Horse Camp on the left. Go left to find the lower south trailhead at the end of a spur (*elevation: 2,200 feet*). The trail fords Bell Creek in 0.2 mile which can be difficult in early summer when the creeks are high. This 3.5-mile trail meets the upper Elbow Lake Trail about 0.7 mile south of the lake (the junction may be more vague from above). For the upper trailhead, including Bell Pass, continue up USFS Rd. #12 to its end, where it's an easy 1.3-mile stroll through deep forest along a quiet creek to the lake.

Bell Pass: (Note this route is popular with equestrians in late summer and fall.) From the upper south trailhead, walk 0.2 mile to a junction; turn right and continue through a forest of large conifers to Bell Pass (**2.0 mi**). Here the trail enters subalpine meadows and climbs to a junction with Ridley Creek Trail (*Hike #75*) and the Mazama Park Horse Camp (**3.6 mi**). The main trail turns south on switchbacks to the 4,800-foot pass below Park Butte (**4.4 mi**). From Mazama Park, an old trail also continues toward Mount Baker, Baker Pass and the Railroad Grade (*see Hike #80*).

MOUNT BAKER AREA—
75. Ridley Creek & Mazama Park

Distance: 10 - 16 miles round trip   Time: Allow 8 - 12 hours
Elevation gain: 2,200 - 3,200 feet   Season: Mid-July - October

Perhaps better appreciated by thicker-skinned veteran hikers, the Ridley Creek Trail leads up the southwest slope of Mount Baker from the Middle Fork Nooksack River to Mazama Park and Baker Pass—a kind of backdoor approach to the meadowlands that separate the forests from the glaciers. These meadows can also be reached more easily from Morovits Meadows (*see Hike #80*). The route involves a potentially difficult river crossing, not recommended for less experienced hikers. The trail is rough and brushy in places, and was to be reconstructed in the mid-1990s, but was delayed over concern that the new trail might adversely impact potential habitat for grizzly bears, a protected species under the Endangered Species Act. Given how rarely these majestic creatures are encountered in the Cascades, it makes sense to give them every chance to recover their population to a sustainable level. At the same time, the trail does

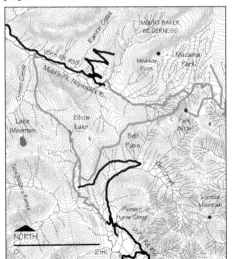

need work, including minor relocations, to reduce erosion. The bears and biologists should eventually come to agreement on how best to do that. Some wandering in high meadows, partly on old trails, is also feasible.

The trailhead is at the end of the Middle Fork Nooksack River Rd. (USFS Rd. #38). For directions, see the Middle Fork approach for Elbow Lake (*Hike*

#74), but continue to the end of the road (note the seasonal road closure from December 1 to June 15). The trail quickly drops to a footlog crossing of the Middle Fork Nooksack River—not for the faint of heart, and not recommended if slippery or when the river is running high. Remember that, in summer, streams often rise in the afternoon and fall overnight. Assuming the log hasn't been knocked out in a flood, it should not present much of a challenge to most experienced hikers. If unsure, maybe try another hike—say, Bell Pass via Elbow Lake Trail.

The trail leads up through forest with occasional openings, eventually breaking out in the lower meadows of Mazama Park and a junction with the Bell Pass Trail, near a horse camp (**4.0 mi**). The main trail climbs to the pass below Cathedral Crag and Park Butte. With good route-finding skills, one could also wander 1.5 miles northward in meadows to Meadow Point , Mazama Lake, or the ridge above overlooking the Black Buttes and the spectacular gorge of the Deming Glacier (caution near the edge, it might not be solid). The towering Black Buttes, remains of an older volcanic cone, rise in near vertical walls 4,000 feet above a tumbling mass of ice. Across the gorge, look for moving white specks: mountain goats grazing on impossible ledges. It's also possible to wander partly on old trail up to Baker Pass east of Cathedral Crag, and to the Railroad Grade beyond.

MOUNT BAKER AREA—
76. Three Lakes & Bear Lake

Distance: 3.6 - 7 miles round trip   Time: Allow 3 - 6 hours
Elevation gain: 1,200 - 2,100 feet   Season: July - October

It was once possible to drive to the shore of these tiny subalpine lakes by way of mining and logging roads on the southwestern flanks of the Twin Sisters Range. But nature is fast reclaiming the road and returning it to wilderness. The trail is remote and not maintained. Yet this seldom-visited corner of the range may offer the best access for exploring its stark beauty and unusual geology. The entire range is composed of olivine-rich dunite, the largest such exposure of mantle rock in the Western Hemisphere.

The best approach is by a somewhat obscure trail on the east by way of Baker Lake (*see Hike #74 for directions*). Note this road is closed at Wanlick Pass near MP 8 from November 1 to July 1. Just past MP 12 on USFS Rd. #12, turn left on Rd. #1260. Cross the South Fork of the Nooksack River and drive or walk to the road end in a clearcut two miles beyond (*elevation: 2,800 feet*). There is a good view of Mount Baker here. The unmarked trail leaves from a

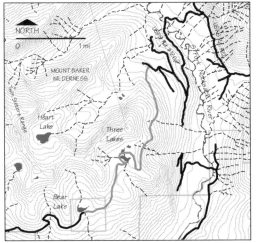

high point 150 yards before the road ends. It can be hard to follow in places and a few logs and boulders require some clambering. In a grassy area, the fading trail heads upslope to a more obvious trail above. After more contouring left-ward, the trail reaches an opening just over a

Three Lakes in the fall.

ridge crest with a good view. It dips slightly to forest then subalpine meadows surrounding the lovely lakes (**1.8 mi**; *elevation: 4,000 feet*). Be sure to memorize the route to the first lake so you can retrace your steps later. An old jeep track is encountered and faint paths wander the meadows. From a collapsed building on the south shore of the larger lake, walk an old road another mile southwest to reach placid Bear Lake.

Some cross-country wandering is possible for experienced navigators. From the first lake, climb 500 feet up boulder and talus slopes (Class 2 rock scrambling), toward a low point in the ridge northwest of the lakes, an excellent overlook of these lakes and Heart Lake in a glacial cirque to the west. This is the southwestern edge of the Mount Baker Wilderness and the views are exceptional. The area supports a significant elk herd; watch for their large deer-like tracks.

MOUNT BAKER AREA—
77. Shadow of the Sentinels

Distance: 0.5-mile loop   Time: 1 hour
Elevation gain: None   Season: Year-round

Shadow of the Sentinels is a short and enjoyable 0.5-mile loop on an accessible, year-round trail—well worth a visit anytime you're in the Baker Lake area. It is an interpretive nature walk with living exhibits ranging from giant Douglas-fir trees hundreds of years old to delicate maidenhair ferns sparsely scattered on the forest floor. The self-guided tour includes information plaques summarizing some of the important ecological relationships that are present in the forest. Children and adults should enjoy the walk, even on a rainy day.

To reach the trailhead, turn left (north) off the North Cascades Hwy. (SR 20) at MP 82.4 onto the Baker Lake Rd. The signed parking area is on the right in about 14.6 miles. The large trail sign includes several historical essays on early inhabitants of the Baker River area,

including the legendary prospector-guide, Mr. Joe Morovits. For giant cedar trees, try the Baker River Trail (*see Hike #88*).

You might notice patches of rusty-brown trees in the Baker Lake area. In recent years, surrounding hemlock forests here have been increasingly infested with something known to foresters as *hemlock looper*, and a serious outbreak was conspicuous here in 2002. Caused by moth larvae gorging on foliage, looper kills needles in vast numbers, giving the forest a gloomy, reddish-brown look and killing many of the trees that are invaded. Looper can increase with drought when the trees are stressed, but usually passes after about three years. A severe winter drought of 2000-01 may be a big contributor. Depending on the severity of the outbreak, hemlock stands as a whole can often survive the impact, but the jury is still out as to the lasting impacts of the current infestation.

MOUNT BAKER AREA—
78. Baker Hot Springs

Distance: 0.5-mile round trip   Time: 1 hour
Elevation gain: None   Season: Year-round

Baker Hot Springs once fed a small cedar-lined pool which had to be destroyed some years ago because of heavy use, abuse and high bacteria counts. However, the springs are unique in the Mount Baker area and worth a visit. A sizeable pool remains to enjoy the soothing relief of soaking ones hike-weary pedestals.

Turn left off Baker Lake Rd. (near MP 18) onto USFS Rd. #1130, just beyond the bridge over Boulder Creek. Follow this 1.6 miles to a junction; stay right, then right again at 3.9 miles on Rd. #1144. This road is proposed for closure to vehicles—a good idea that, due to the extra walking required, could help reduce the impacts to the hot springs from overuse. Drive (or walk) 0.5 mile to an informal parking area at the edge of a clear-cut, just past a sharp right bend. Look for the unmarked path leading up the bank and into the woods. The rough trail quickly improves in a deep forest of large cedars, vine maple and devils club on the way to the sulfurous steaming hot spring (0.2 mi). A bit of trivia: it is about seven miles from here to the steaming Sherman Crater atop Mount Baker. A rotted nurse log nearby supports a precarious row of western hemlock trees. Back at the last road junction, it is another 0.5 mile up Rd. #1130 to the Rainbow Falls viewpoint, a worthy side-trip. The old Swift Creek Trail is also nearby, 0.2 mile south of the hot springs parking area. The walking is limited, though. The bridge is missing at Rainbow Creek, less than 0.5 mile up.

MOUNT BAKER AREA—
79. Scott Paul Trail

Distance: 8.0-mile loop · Time: Allow 5 - 7 hours
Elevation gain: 1,700 feet · Season: mid-July - October

For a hike that combines great alpine country with a volcano and a pleasant saunter through old-growth forest try the Scott Paul Trail south of Mount Baker. The trail is a replacement and extension of the old Sulphur Moraine Trail. The present trail was designed by and named in the memory of a dear friend to many. Scott, a creative and respected trail planner-designer-builder, left our world prematurely in a trail construction accident in Oregon in 1993, at the same time this trail was being built. It's a gift to those who love wilderness that will be with us for generations. The hike is generally done as a loop using the lower two miles of the Morovits Meadows/Park Butte Trail (*see Hike #80*). Note that there are two seasonal bridges that are removed in the fall and replaced as the trails melt out in sum-

mer. If missing, the crossings can be more tedious, but generally doable for experienced hikers—assuming the water isn't too high.

From North Cascades Hwy. (SR 20) turn left at MP 82.4 onto Baker Lake Rd. In just over 12 miles go left again on USFS Rd. #12 (signed: Mount Baker National Recreation Area). In 3.6 miles turn right and reach the trailhead in 5.2 miles (*elevation: 3,350 feet*). From the signed trailhead at the

Climbers approaching Mount Baker's summit crater from the Easton Glacier.

restroom, hike 50 yards on the trail to Morovits Meadows and Park Butte, then turn right *before* crossing the permanent bridge over Sulphur Creek. The trail gently climbs through an ancient forest of silver fir and occasional hemlock giants to a subalpine ridge with a good view into the Cascades (**2.0 mi**). The trail rises above timberline and traverses west on gentle grades through meadow, rock and glacial moraines below a promontory called "Crag View," and the Squak and Easton Glaciers. Late summer, more experienced hikers may be able to explore another 1,000 feet or more of higher ground above the trail, depending on conditions. After topping out near 5,000 feet (**3.7 mi**), the path begins a 600-foot descent into the valley of Sulphur Creek, outlet of the massive Easton Glacier. Cross a small, seasonal suspension bridge on the way (**5.1 mi**). Rejoin the

Morovits Meadows Trail at a switchback (**6.0 mi**); stay left (right goes to Morovits Meadows, a huge moraine called the Railroad Grade, and Park Butte). Switchbacks lead one mile down to another seasonal bridge, and in a mile more, return to the trailhead (**8.0 mi**). Campsites are sparse in the higher meadows.

Paintbrush, a Cascades favorite.

Mount Baker Area—
80. Morovits Meadows & Park Butte

Distance: 5 - 12 miles round trip   Time: Allow 4 - 7 hours
Elevation gain: 1,400 - 2,500 feet   Season: mid-July - October

The trail through Schriebers Meadow, then up to the upper and lower Morovits Meadows, Park Butte and the Railroad Grade offers one of the best hikes in the Mount Baker area. Expect a lot of company on fair summer weekends (and horses late summer). There are many good destinations for a day hike and any number of variations are possible. The views are as dramatic as you'll find anywhere in the Cascades. The lower portion of this trail forms part of an attractive 7.5-mile loop with the Scott Paul Trail (*see Hike #79*). Campsites are available near tree clusters scattered about the meadows.

See Hike #79 for directions to the trailhead at Schriebers Meadow (*elevation: 3,300 feet; map, p.170*). An imposing view of the Railroad Grade (a glacial moraine), and the Black Buttes (remnant of a pre-Mount Baker volcanic cone) materializes near the trailhead. Head

Mount Baker and the Black Buttes.

Laast leg to Park Butte.

left at the restroom, pass the Scott Paul Trail, and cross Sulphur Creek on a bridge. Hike an easy mile of open forest and meadows to several small creek crossings in a broad basin. A removable bridge (only in place in summer) spans the worst of it (**1.0 mi**). The crossing can be treacherous during high runoff without the bridge, so turn back if necessary. The way switchbacks through forest to a junction with the Scott Paul Trail (**2.0 mi**) and edge of lower Morovits Meadow just beyond (**2.1 mi**).

At a junction in the broad meadow (**2.2 mi**), continue straight for Baker Pass and Park Butte, or head up the stone staircase to the right to view the snout of the Easton Glacier by way of the Railroad Grade—a lateral moraine leading smoothly up to the glacier. This is the climbers' route, and the home of hordes of hoary marmots. The Railroad Grade often melts out well before the meadows. It gains 1,000 feet or more in a long mile to a popular climbers' camp in a small basin just yards from the ice (stay off the glacier, of course; climbing the mountain requires ropes, specialized climbing gear, and a competent leader). Back at the first meadow junction, follow the main trail (left) to the upper meadows, a pass, and Park Butte Trail on the left (**2.7 mi**). The lookout, visible atop the 5,400-foot butte, offers an outstanding view of Mount Baker and the Twin Sisters Range. From this junction, it is another mile and a 500-foot climb to the historic lookout (**3.7 mi**); *elevation: 5,400 feet*). Built in 1932, it is nicely maintained by volunteers with the Skagit Alpine Club. Dos and don'ts are posted inside where a visitor register awaits your more profound ruminations. At the Park Butte junction, one can descend to Mazama Park which can also be reached from the Bell Pass and Ridley Creek Trails (*Hikes #74 and #75*).

MOUNT BAKER AREA—
81. Boulder Ridge

Distance: 6.4 - 8.4 miles round trip   Time: Allow 4 - 8 hours
Elevation gain: 1,900 - 2,900 feet   Season: mid-July - October

The trail up Mount Baker's Boulder Ridge was originally built by the Mountaineers in 1908, in advance of a summit expedition involving about 50 climbers from the Seattle area and beyond. In order to feed everyone, a cow was brought along for slaughter at the timberline camp. Thirty-nine alpinists, not including the cow, made the summit. They would probably find it just as amusing today that, because there are so many of us humans plunging into the wilderness, we must limit our groups to a dozen or less. And cows are now clearly discouraged. The Boulder Ridge Trail, nearly a century old, is in rough shape. Fortunately, it is scheduled for reconstruction sometime in the near future (perhaps in 2004). Until that happens, expect a muddy, well-used route with some very steep sections. The new trail alignment will bypass the worst—and most environmentally sensitive—places and eliminate a few ups and down, though the description here shouldn't change dramatically.

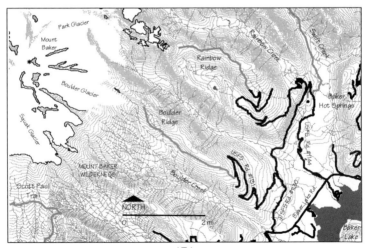

Mount Baker from below the cliffs.

From the North Cascades Hwy. (SR 20) at MP 82.4, head north on Baker Lake Rd. about 18 miles to USFS Rd. #1130, just beyond the Boulder Creek bridge; turn left. Stay left at a fork in 1.5 miles (signed) and follow USFS Rd. 1131 another four miles to its end (*elevation: 2,700 feet*). The trail briefly descends on an old grade, then climbs gently and enters old-growth forest (**0.3 mi**). After many ups and downs, a small stream is crossed (trail jogs left), before reaching a mile marker on a tree (**2.0 mi**) and the wilderness boundary just beyond. Cross a very wet meadow leftward (possible standing water) to pick up the trail again on the other side where it takes a sharp right then left (downed trees in late 2002 made it difficult to see, but it's obvious once you find it). The trail climbs and crosses a smooth rock slab near a waterfall (not difficult, but use caution—there's an exposed cliff below). Here, a very steep, gnarly section leads to easier ground above and finally a meadow opening (**2.7 mi**). The path improves and gently climbs to the crest of a moraine that offers a dramatic overlook of Mount Baker's eastern flank (**3.2 mi**; *elevation: 4,400 feet*). This makes a good turn-around point for a reasonable dayhike. Some ambling in the rocky meadows is feasible but remember where the trail is. Camping is a bit rugged.

The climbers' route continues northward on a boot track up the moraine to a low cliff band which presents a serious obstacle to hikers and is not recommended, especially when wet. Properly equipped, experienced climbers should be able to manage it (exposed Class 3 to 4 rock). There was an old rope hanging over the cliff in late 2002, but of course there is no guarantee it is safe to use. Turn back if you're not sure—it's always much harder coming down than going up. For those who push through this barrier, the skinny ridge above offers a number of good spots to munch and turn around—potentially a mile more hiking and 1,000 feet of gain, depending on conditions. Lingering snow in summer may require use of an ice axe and possibly crampons—and the skills to use them.

MOUNT BAKER AREA—
82. Rainbow Ridge

Distance: 5 - 7 miles round trip   Time: Allow 4 - 7 hours
Elevation gain: 1,200 - 2,700 feet   Season: July - October

While not quite as up close and personal to Mount Baker as some of the other hikes that lead up various flanks of the volcano, the trail along Rainbow Ridge offers a heap of high-end scenery. The ridge is named for the creek to the north and a namesake waterfall in the lower valley. The creek drains a steep canyon called Avalanche Gorge that is fed, of course, by the meltwater of the Rainbow Glacier. The downside of the hike: the lower portion of the trail is in very poor condition, muddy and slick and not maintained. Some minimal improvements to address erosion would seem desirable. Once on the ridge, the tread improves considerably.

To reach the trailhead, turn north off the North Cascades Hwy. (SR 20) at MP 82.4 and follow Baker Lake Rd. about 18 miles to USFS Rd. #1130 on the left, just beyond the Boulder Creek bridge. Turn here and stay right at a fork in 1.5 miles, and left at 3.9 miles. From a wide shoulder on the right at 4.4 miles one can view Rainbow Falls in the canyon below. At 6.0 miles pass a good view of Baker Lake, Bacon Peak and Mt. Hagan, and continue up the road,

Mount Shuksan from Rainbor Ridge.

staying left near its end at 9.3 miles to find the obvious trail off the end of a short spur (*elevation: 3,600 feet; map, p. 174*). Mount Baker rises high to the southwest. The first 0.5 mile is the worst, with steep, muddy sections to contend with even in dry weather. Meadow openings lead to the ridge crest and a much better trail, with excellent views to Mount Shuksan and the North Cascades (**0.7 mi**).

As the trail meanders over and around a few knolls and rocky outcrops on the way up the ridge, the views broaden to include Avalanche Gorge, the Rainbow Glacier and the dominating mass of Mount Baker. Several good tent sites are available along the ridge, including one with a perfect panorama from Mount Baker to Mount Shuksan (**1.7 mi**). After a house-sized rocky perch—a good lunch spot—the path descends briefly to a broad saddle at 4,600 feet (**2.5 mi**). Beyond, the trail fades, although experienced routefinders may be able to discern a faint boot track that leads steeply west then southwest to a craggy high point, almost 1,000 feet above, and a closer look at the Park Glacier ice cliffs (somewhat brushy). Water can be scarce in late summer. Use caution on the slippery descent.

NORTH CASCADES

Ruth Mountain from Hannegan Peak.

NORTH CASCADES—
83. Hannegan Pass & Peak

Distance: 8 - 10 miles round trip   Time: Allow 5 - 7 hours
Elevation gain: 2,000 - 3,100 feet   Season: Mid-July - October

Hannegan Pass, a popular trek, is one of three routes that access North Cascades National Park from the Bellingham area (*see also Hikes #84 and #85*). The Park boundary is five miles from the trailhead, just beyond the Pass. For overnight trips, Whatcom Pass and Copper Ridge are major contenders; permits are required. Hannegan Pass is a good destination for a day hike, but an extra effort takes you up Hannegan Peak for another amazing panorama.

The trailhead is at the end of the Hannegan Pass Rd. (#32), 5.5 miles from Mt. Baker Hwy. Turn left off the highway just before the Nooksack River bridge (MP 46.6); stay left at a fork in 1.5 mile (*elevation: 3,100 feet; map, p. 148*). The trail is nearly flat the first mile, then slowly climbs through fragrant avalanche slopes and forest, crossing several small streams along the way (can be tricky in early summer). Views keep improving: south across Ruth Creek are the sheer rock walls of Nooksack Ridge and Mount Sefrit; to the southeast, the solid white dome of Ruth Mountain at 7,106 feet. Bears are sometimes seen in the valley below. The trail passes a spur on the right to Hannegan Camp (**3.5 mi**), then steepens for the final climb to Hannegan Pass (**4.0 mi**; *elevation: 5,100 feet*). Portions of the trail are planned for reconstruction in 2005.

A steep trail to the north (left) leads up through woods and meadows to Hannegan Peak at 6,186 feet (**5.0 mi**). As you clear timberline the big panorama emerges: Mount Larrabee to the northwest, Mount Sefrit to the west, Mount Baker and Mount Shuksan to the southwest, Ruth Mountain to the south, Mineral Mountain, Mount Challenger, the Picket Range and Glacier Peak (on the horizon) to the southeast, Copper Ridge to the east, Mount Redoubt to the northeast and towering Slesse Mountain to the north, two miles inside Canada. From the Pass, overnight backpackers can descend one mile eastward to Boundary Camp and a junction with the Copper Ridge Trail (**6.0 mi**; *elevation: 4,400 feet*), or another 5.5 miles to the Chilliwack River (*see Other Hikes*).

NORTH CASCADES—
84. Nooksack Cirque

Distance: 7 - 13 miles round trip   Time: Allow 5 - 12 hours
Elevation gain: 500 - 1,000 feet   Season: July - October

This adventurous route requires a ford at the beginning across Ruth Creek which should not be attempted at high water. The Forest Service has no immediate plans to install a bridge over the creek. The hike is unique and best done late in the summer or fall when runoff is low and you can walk river bars much of the way. Despite inconvenient access and irregular maintenance, the route is still worth exploring. The North Fork of the Nooksack River finds its roots in the meltwater of Mount Shuksan's glaciers. Towering walls of rock and ice form a mile-wide glacial cirque at the head of the river where ambitious hikers are rewarded with outstanding views. The elevation gain is not great, but the approach can be tedious.

From Mt. Baker Hwy. (MP 46.5) turn left on Hannegan Pass Rd. (#32) just before a bridge. Stay right at a fork in 1.3 mile and continue about one semi-brushy mile to the trailhead where the bridge used to be (*elevation: 2,300 feet; map, p. 148*). If it's safe, cross (remembering that streams fed by snow and icemelt usually rise during the day and fall overnight). Enjoy the view of Shuksan, and walk the smooth gravel road to the old trailhead (**1.6 mi**) which leads down an overgrown logging road. The path soon enters a forest of large old trees (**2.4 mi**), some of which may be strewn across the trail sprouting mushrooms and impeding your progress. At the river and gravel bars (**3.5 mi**), a worse trail continues, intermittently, close to the bank through brush and over logs and side channels. However, the recommended route is up the river bed itself. This can only be done, of course, during low run-off when the river is down, though some knee-deep wading may still be necessary (maybe bring some beefy sandals). September and October are the best months for low water and fall colors.

When the gravel bars are negotiable, simply wander as far up the valley as you like, carefully marking and remembering the place you entered the river bed so you don't miss it on the return hike. It is another 2.5 to 3 miles to the best views deep in the cirque, although

Descending the river bed below Nooksack Cirque.

the scene is scenic all along the way. Icy Peak, Jagged Ridge and the East Nooksack Glacier dominate the skyline. Just beyond the point where a forested area ends on the left, it may be easiest to follow a series of dry side channels and bars that parallel the river on the left side. The final mile is more difficult due to the narrowing stream bed and some stubborn brush. When open gentle slopes scattered with boulders become visible (also on the left), head toward a house-sized overhanging boulder. The view is excellent. Seahpo Peak and the sheer Nooksack Tower pierce the sky. On the river, a certain amount of boulder-hopping can be expected. A walking stick offers some defense against wet rocks and slippery logs. An extra pair of wool socks aren't a bad idea either.

NORTH CASCADES—
85. Lake Ann

Distance: 8.6 miles round trip   Time: Allow 4 - 6 hours
Elevation gain: 1,900 feet   Season: July - October

In good summer weather, weekend hikers to Lake Ann at the foot of Mount Shuksan are likely to encounter climbers heading up or down this amazingly beautiful chunk of landscape. For the front-and-center view of Shuksan, it doesn't get much better than Lake Ann. On warmer afternoons, one can often hear and sometimes see large blocks of ice calving off the glaciers. The climb, of course, requires serious mountaineering skills and equipment in order to safely navigate the cliffs and glaciers. But you don't have to be a mountaineer to enjoy the spectacle.

From Bellingham, follow the Mt. Baker Hwy. about 55 miles to the trailhead on the left at Austin Pass (*elevation: 4,700 feet*), about one mile beyond the Austin Pass Picnic Area (*map, p. 158*). The trail is well marked and winds past a wooded knob then quickly descends

Swift Creek Valley near the Lake Ann Trailhead.

through forest for 500 feet to the wilderness boundary and gentle grades of upper Swift Creek. The trail levels out to a junction with the Swift Creek Trail on the right (**2.4 mi**; *elevation: 3,900 feet*). It's possible to wander this old trail for several miles, but it deteriorates rapidly as it descends into the steep lower canyon on the way toward Baker Lake. Bridges are missing on two major creek crossings (Swift and Rainbow) and the trail is no longer maintained (*see Other Hikes*). Stay left for Lake Ann. The trail immediately begins to rise in meadow and talus on moderate grades to the saddle above and a welcome view of the lake (*elevation: 4,800 feet*). The trail makes a brief descent to the icy lake—it can be clogged with ice well into summer. The view of Shuksan from the lake or from somewhat higher ground to the west is about as good as it gets. Just above the lake, the climbers trail contours toward the big cliffs and can be explored for 0.5 mile or so before running into more difficult climbing terrain. A number of campsites have been scratched out near the lake.

Noʀᴛʜ Cᴀsᴄᴀᴅᴇs—
86. Shannon Ridge

Distance: 7.2 - 7.8 miles round trip   Time: Allow 5 - 8 hours
Elevation gain: 2,500 - 3,300 feet   Season: mid-July - October

This arduous but scenic trail to the southern flank of Mount Shuksan is really a climbers route that is in dire need of reconstruction, which the Forest Service has tentatively scheduled for 2005 or 2006. Much of the trail has been beaten into the ground by heavy boots. In the forest, expect mud, rocks, logs and brush on the way to better trail in the meadows above. One would think that a trail this close to Mount Shuksan would offer a fantastic view of the mountain, but that's not the case. The mountain is in the way of itself, so to speak, so the better views are actually of Mount Baker and the sea of peaks that form the North Cascades. There is no clear destination here, and a rocky hump on the ridge may have to suffice. Do not, of course, proceed onto steep snow or ice or the glacier beyond unless you are an experienced and properly equipped climber.

From the North Cascades Hwy. at MP 82.4, turn north onto Baker

Shannon Ridge meadows.

Lake Rd. and follow this 23.5 miles to Shannon Point Campground; turn left here on USFS Rd. #1152. At 4.4 miles, stay right on Rd. #014 to find the signed trailhead 1.5 miles ahead (*elevation: 2,500 feet; map, p. 186*). The trail follows the old road grade for 1.6 miles where the path swings left up the hill briefly before entering old-growth forest (**1.8 mi**). The path may be confusing in a couple of places so look back occasionally to be sure which way to turn coming down. The path finally attains a level ridge crest and a huge view of Mount Baker (**2.8 mi**). The trail bends right, descends a little, then climbs to more open meadows. Watch for mountain goats on the rocky slopes of the ridge to the right. To the southeast are, left to right, Mount Blum, Mount Hagan's seven summits, and Bacon and Watson Peaks. Pass a boundary marker for North Cascades National Park (**3.6 mi**), and scamper up to a rocky bump in another 0.1 mile for a rest (*elevation 5,000 feet*). Campsites are marginal; permit required inside the park. Turn back here or continue up steeper trail, if passable, another 400 feet to a notch in the ridge, and head left to more sitting rocks (**3.9 mi**). The going is more difficult beyond and may be blocked, even in mid-summer, by lingering steep snow.

NORTH CASCADES—
87. Shuksan Lake

Distance: 4 - 6 miles round trip   Time: Allow 3 - 7 hours
Elevation gain: 1,900 - 2,500 feet   Season: Mid-July - October

A short, scenic, strenuous hike, the trail to Shuksan and Little Shuksan Lakes is as steep as any other listed in this guide. Nevertheless, three lovely lakes and unique views into some of the wilder parts of the North Cascades are worth the beating getting there. Overnight prospects are also good at both lakes. To find the trail, drive Baker Lake Rd. north from SR 20 about 24 miles to USFS Rd. #1160; turn left. Follow this winding gravel road to its end four miles up (*elevation: 2,900 feet*) where views of Mount Baker and Baker Lake offer encouragement for the work yet to be done.

The trail briefly negotiates an old clearcut, then with little rest, stays steep to the top of the ridge, passing a nice view of Mount Hagan and Mount Blum. The way leads around the west side of Little Shuksan Lake at 4,200 feet (**1.5 mi**), the meets another tiny lake. At a junction in meadows just beyond (**1.9 mi**), angle right for the grand view: Mount Shuksan's seldom seen Sulphide and Crystal Glaciers, Jagged Ridge, and Cloudcap (or Seahpo) Peak all to the north, the Baker River valley 3,500 feet below, plus Mounts Blum and Hagan, and Bacon Peak to the east and southeast.

From the junction go left on a fainter path to explore meadows, or head straight over the brink (so to speak) for the 600-foot descent through very steep terrain to the larger

Early summer near Little Shuksan Lake.

185

Shuksan Lake nestled in a remote canyon (**2.5 mi**). The trail may be rough and hard to follow, to the delight of every devout fisher-person. Bears are common in the area, as are several varieties of huckle-berries later in summer.

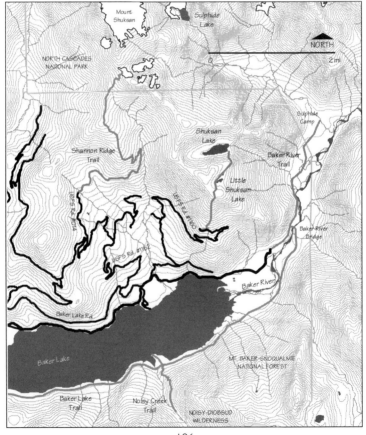

NORTH CASCADES—
88. Baker River

Distance: 5.2 miles round trip Time: Allow 3 - 5 hours
Elevation gain: 200 feet Season: Almost year-round

When the winters are mild, this easy trail may be open year-round, since it never exceeds 1,000 feet in elevation. Early mornings are the best time visit the large beaver ponds and a veritable rainforest of giant western red cedar and big leaf maple. A low angle sun on a clear morning reflects brilliantly through the rich green moss and shaded ferns on the forest floor. The walk is relaxed and suitable for most anyone. It enters North Cascades National Park so pets are not allowed. Turn left off the North Cascades Hwy. (SR #20, MP 82.4) onto the Baker Lake Rd. Drive 26 miles (mostly paved), making a left near the road end *(elevation: 700 feet).* The trailhead is well marked.

Walk the old road bed then enter old-growth forest on a mostly level grade before reaching the big cable-stay bridge spanning the Baker River (**0.6 mi**). The bridge is the start of the 14-mile Baker Lake Trail *(see Hike #89)*. Check it out but don't cross, and continue up-river. From the river bank, Mount Hagan is vis-

Western red cedar at Baker River.

ible high above. Several footlogs are crossed as you enter a seemingly enchanted forest of giant cedars (up to 12 feet in diameter). Sword, deer and lady ferns dominate the ground cover, but other ferns and numerous shade-tolerant flowering plants, such as trillium, wild ginger and bleeding heart, thrive on the damp forest floor.

Extensive beaver ponds are passed (**1.6 mi**), offering a good opportunity to observe wildlife (it helps to be quiet, patient and inconspicuous). Finally reach a camp with good sites at Sulphide Creek—the end of the trail (**2.6 mi**; *elevation: 900 feet*). In early summer, the creek is torrential from snowmelt originating in the cirque of Mount Shuksan's Sulphide and Crystal Glaciers to the northwest. Cloudcap (or Seahpo) Peak and Jagged Ridge are visible to the north. Later in summer or autumn, when the level of the creek has fallen, it may be possible to walk out onto gravel bars for much better views and a sunny lunch spot. A faint path leading upstream along the edge of the woods may offer access to the broad creek bed.

North Cascades—
89. Baker Lake

Distance: 4 to 14.3 miles

Elevation gain: 100 - 300 feet

Time: Allow 2 - 8 hours

Season: Almost year-round

An easy hike along the wild east shore of Baker Lake, this trail winds through a low-elevation old-growth forest with good views of Mount Baker and Mount Shuksan across a ten-mile-long reservoir. The 14-mile trail is accessible from either end of the lake, following the 1998 construction of an impressive 240-foot cable-stay bridge over the Baker River (some fascinating images of the construction of this bridge may be available on the Web at www.sahale.com). From the north, walk the first two miles to Hidden Creek bridge for an easy, pleasant outing, or hike 4.5 miles to Noisy Creek (*see Hike #90*) for an extra workout. Or, do it all from either end. Strong hikers could spot a bike at the south end for a 15-mile return via USFS Rds. #1107, #1106 and Baker Lake Rd. The trail itself is closed to bikes. For the north end access, see Hike #88.

From the south, cross Baker Dam (*see Hike #91 for directions;*

Cable-stay bridge over the Baker River (Baker Lake Trail).

map, p. 186), and follow USFS Rd. #1107 0.7 mile to the trailhead (*elevation: 1,000 feet*). The trail stays high to Anderson Creek (**1.6 mi**); 0.2 mile beyond, a short spur drops down to campsites and a good view from a lakeshore peninsula. In summer, it's not unusual to see dark streaks of mud and rock, or *lahar*, on Mount Baker's Boulder Glacier, emanating from the rim of Sherman Crater. The trail passes old fire scars that may have been caused by an 1843 eruption of the now sleeping volcano. Another 0.3-mile spur descends left to campsites at Maple Grove (**3.8 mi**). There is also camping north of Noisy Creek near the lakeshore (**9.8 mi**). Pass a nice waterfall at Hidden Creek (**12.3 mi**), then the big bridge (**13.7 mi**) on the way to the northerly trailhead at the end of Baker Lake Rd. (**14.3 mi**). If starting at the north end, walk the Baker River Trail (wide and flat) 0.6 mile to the really big bridge.

NORTH CASCADES—
90. Noisy Creek

Distance: 2.5 to 11 miles round trip   Time: Allow 2 - 6 hours
Elevation gain: 100 - 900 feet   Season: April - November

Noisy Creek was the focus of years of controversy over the poten
tial logging of an exceptional ancient forest along the creek's
lower reach which was recognized as an important ecosystem by the
public, and a valuable timber resource by the landowners. In 1990,
the Nature Conservancy, Congress and the U.S. Forest Service came
to the rescue. Surrounded by National Forest and Wilderness, the
big trees are now secure. A previous proposal to build a second trail
up the west side of the creek to create a loop has been dropped, at
least for now. There are no campsites along this trail.

The trailhead can be reached by small boat, or by walking the
Baker Lake Trail from either end (*see Hikes #88 and 89 for directions*). It's about 4.5 miles to Noisy Creek from the north, or about
9.8 miles from the southerly trailhead. For the easiest access, you
can cross the lake by boat from Shannon Creek Campground (possible windy conditions). Noisy Creek flows down the largest valley
directly across the lake, about 0.8 mile away and marked by an allu-
vial fan of gravel, cobbles and boulders (*elevation: 700 feet*). Disem-
bark and head left on the Baker Lake Trail nearby to find the
inconspicuous Noisy Creek Trail on the right at the crest of a ridge
shoulder just east of the creek (left leads to campsites near the lake).
The route leads away from the stream and is moderately steep, gaining 700 feet in the first mile. Along the lower stretch you will find a
huge western hemlock, red cedar and a Douglas fir tree over ten feet
in diameter that has stood here since before Columbus visited the
Carribean. The noisy cascading stream is reached again in about 1.5
mile (*elevation: 1,600 feet*). The last bit of trail descending to the
creek may be steep and rough. Enjoy the view—and the "noise."
This is the turn-around. Osprey, eagles and spotted owls are known
to inhabit the area.

NORTH CASCADES—
91. Watson Lakes & Anderson Butte

Distance: 3 - 8 miles round trip   Time: Allow 2 - 6 hours
Elevation gain: 1,200 - 1,800 feet   Season: July - October

*O*nce you arrive at peaceful Watson Lakes, you may have a hard time leaving. They are sizeable gems surrounded by fairy tale parklands where each bend in the trail reveals another placid scene. Autumn is very nice: brilliant red huckleberry leaves against still water reflecting tall trees and sky. Or head up the old lookout site instead, or do them both. From SR 20 (MP 82.4), head north on the Baker Lake Rd. about 13.8 miles, then turn right, crossing Baker Dam in another 1.5 mile. Turn left on USFS Rd. #1107 (sign), and continue 9.1 miles to a junction; stay left to reach the trailhead on the left at 10 miles (*elevation: 4,350 feet*).

The trail moderately gains 400 feet through hemlock-silver fir forest and a small meadow before meeting the Anderson Butte Trail on the left (**0.7 mi**). If going for the Butte, stay right at another apparent fork nearby. The trail to the old lookout site climbs steeply

Watson Lakes.

but is in good shape, reaching the scenic summit 500 feet and 0.5 mile above the junction (lookout was removed in 1964). The view includes Mounts Baker and Shuksan, and the Sisters Range to the west, Mounts Blum and Hagan to the northeast, and a shard of Baker Lake below. The original trail to the lookout started at Baker River.

From the Anderson Butte junction, the trail to the lakes drops slightly then gently climbs through a long narrow meadow with views of Mount Baker. Another descent through trees leads to a junction with the Anderson Lakes trail (**1.1 mi**). This optional side trip traverses through a green boulder field, reaching the lake in 0.5 mile. Another great view of Mount Baker is from the meadows across the outlet stream of Anderson Lake. Camping is feasible.

From the junction, the trail to Watson Lakes gains another 150 feet to a saddle at the edge of the Noisy-Diobsud Wilderness Area. The path then descends nearly 500 feet to a campsite at the edge of the smaller lake. Work left around the lake, clambering over a few logs, heading toward a beautiful isthmus of subalpine knolls between the two lakes (a privy nearby). The second lake is much larger and has a dramatic shoreline, including enchanted meadows and the high cliffs of Mount Watson (**2.5 mi**; *elevation: 4,400 feet*). Snow-covered Bacon Peak rises to the east and Anderson Butte is to the north. The elevation gain is only 600 feet each way, which makes this a suitable hike for families. Not surprisingly, the trail is kinda popular on summer weekends. There are a number of good campsites near the lakes. Portions of the trail system were recently upgraded.

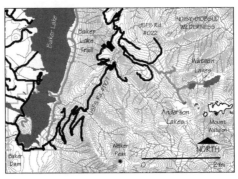

NORTH CASCADES—
92. Thornton Lakes & Trapper Peak

Distance: 10 - 12 miles round trip   Time: Allow 6 - 9 hours
Elevation gain: 2,200 - 3,700 feet   Season: Mid-July - September

Despite a moderately steep approach to the lakes, the views from the top of Trapper Ridge are worth the effort. The lakes require a steep 450-foot descent after a long hike up the mountain, although the cool water is a treat on a hot day. Good campsites are generally lacking. About 12 miles northeast of Marblemount, turn left (north) off the North Cascades Hwy. (SR #20) at MP 117.3 onto the signed gravel road paralleling the highway. In five miles, the road is blocked where the hike begins (*elevation: 2,700 feet*). The road may be rough in places.

Follow the old road bed through a large clearcut and across Thornton Creek (**1.0 mi**). Watch carefully for the marked trail on the left side of the old road (**2.3 mi**). Follow this through dense forest gaining 2,000 feet in the next 2.3 miles. Views improve con-

Close-up wildlife encounter—always memorable in the North Cascades.

siderably near the crest (**4.6 mi**; *elevation: 4,900 feet*). Just before topping out on the ridge (and a view of the first lake), a faint path to the right invites more experienced hikers to explore this scenic ridge northward perhaps 0.7 mile to the summit of Trappers Peak, 1,000 feet higher (don't go if still under snow; may be too dangerous). From Trapper, the view of Mount Triumph and the Picket Range are superb. One September afternoon the author, a friend, and four bears surprised each other at close range along this ridge while the six of us were feeding on huckleberries. Views of the Skagit River, Mount Triumph and the jagged Picket Range are humbling. From the trailhead to summit, it's about 5.3 miles with a gain of 3,200 feet. Back where the main trail overlooks the lake, scramble down a steep, blasted (literally) trail 450 feet to this largest of the three lakes (*elevation: 4,500 feet*). Another faint path leads through a campsite

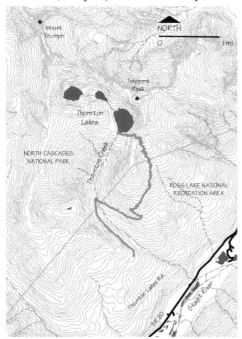

and along the west shore to the outlet of the middle lake. Ambitious hikers can explore the upper lakes or the high rocky ridge on their south rim. Or, for a view of the Triumph Glacier, climb the climbers path to a saddle northwest of the middle lake (dangerous beyond this point).

NORTH CASCADES—
93. Skagit River Loop

Distance: 1.8-mile loop   Time: Allow 1 hour
Elevation gain: 100 feet   Season: Almost year-round

When stopping at the North Cascades National Park Visitor Center on the way through Newhalem, take advantage of this fine little walk through pretty forest along the edge of the Skagit River. If this one is too easy, there are several short walks in the Newhalem area that can be strung together into a moderate day trip (*see Hikes #94 and 95; map. next page*). Watch for the sign to the visitor center just west of Newhalem near MP 120 of the North Cascades Hwy. There are walkways around the center, including a short, accessible boardwalk to the Sterling Munro Overlook—named for an accomplished aide to Senator Henry Jackson when the National Park was established in 1968. At the opposite end of the building, find the River Loop trail heading left and down a hillside on a gentle grade to level ground below. The path intersects a campground access on the right; left represents the end of the loop, so either head left or continue straight. A short distance downstream there is a good place to wander out on a river bar if the water isn't too high. Otherwise, the Skagit is normally too cold and swift for frolicking. The campground junction can also be reached by wheelchair from between the campground's A and B loops.

River Loop.

NORTH CASCADES—
94. **Lower Newhalem Creek** (Rock Shelter)

Distance: 0.4 - 0.8 mile round trip   Time: Allow 1 hour

Elevation gain: Minimal   Season: Almost year-round

This relatively new trail may be very short, but the protected Rock Shelter is definitely worth a look—a grotto of sorts that was occupied by Native Americans who were hunting and gathering in the upper Skagit watershed 1,400 years ago. A platform view and small exhibit inspire the imagination. Head east on the North Cascades Hwy. to MP 120, immediately before Newhalem and turn right. Cross the river on the narrow bridge, then turn left on a service road leading east to a bridge over Newhalem Creek. The small, signed trailhead is just ahead on the right. Or, for a more worthwhile hike, continue to the visitor center and walk the River Loop Trail (*Hike #93*) to the campground junction; turn right and follow this trail 0.3 mile through the campground to Newhalem Creek and the Rock Shelter Trail across the service road. One could also hike from the west end of the Trail of the Cedars (*Hike #95*) and go 0.3 mile past the powerhouse to reach the same spot. Once you're heading up, head right at the fork for the overlook (**0.2 mi**; wheelchair accessible with assistance), or left to a nice creekside view (**0.3 mi**).

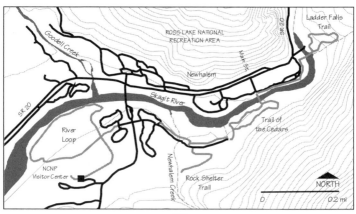

NORTH CASCADES—
95. Ladder Cr. Falls & Trail of the Cedars

Distance: 0.5 - 1.6 miles round trip   Time: Allow 1 - 2 hours
Elevation gain: 100 feet   Season: Almost year-round

For a small mountain town, Newhalem offers some exceptional short hikes, including the two saunters described here. They are easily combined into a single outing, or choose either for a quick leg-stretch on the drive through the North Cascades. Both are reached via suspension bridges over the Skagit River. For Ladder Falls, turn right (south) off SR 20 at the east end of Newhalem just before the big green bridge and park on the left across from Seattle City Light's Gorge Dam powerhouse. Walk south along the road a short distance to the suspension bridge over the river. Cross and wander 0.5 mile of obvious paths and stairs up through the falls area. The lovely falls were "enhanced" with a lighting and sound system many years ago to create a locally-famous evening stroll. The falls are still lit on sum-

mer evenings. The old gardens nearby are intriguing with their steps, paths, pools and odd surprises—thanks to the inspired work of Superintendent J. D. Ross. Mid-spring to early summer are the best months for flowers and waterfall viewing. The powerhouse may be open to visitors in summer from 8 am to 4 pm daily. A skinny tunnel leads from the gardens back to the suspension bridge.

Ladder Creek Falls.

After re-crossing the suspension bridge, one can continue west along the road about 0.3 mile to the next suspension bridge off the end of Main St. (one could also park along this street). Cross the river and head right for the 0.5-mile loop through an impressive grove of large cedars adjacent to the river. The Newhalem Creek power-house stands at the east end of the loop where a short spur signed "evacuation route" leads upslope several hundred feet—a reminder of the impending doom that threatens the community should there ever be a catastrophic failure of one of the dams upriver.

NORTH CASCADES—
96. Gorge Creek Falls

Distance: 0.5 - 1.0 miles round trip   Time: Allow 1 hour

Elevation gain: Minimal   Season: Almost year-round

The overlook at Gorge Creek Falls is a popular stop along the North Cascades Hwy. (SR 20), but few may be aware of the short loop trail that leads south to great views of Gorge Lake, the name-sake dam, and the Skagit River gorge. The route is paved and barrier-free for 0.2 mile then gravel for 0.4 mile to complete a 0.6-mile loop. Find the trailhead on the south side of SR 20 at MP 123.5.

A short ramp or steps near the left corner of the parking lot lead to the mostly level paved path. The steep-walled Skagit River gorge was a forbidding obstacle to early explorations. Intrepid prospec-

tors managed to build and navigate a diffi-cult path through the gorge in order to reach scant goldfields of the upper Skagit. Perhaps the Park Service will some day give serious consideration to rebuilding por-tions of the historic route from Newhalem to Ruby Creek. The Diablo Lake Trail (*Hike #99*) and Gorge Creek Falls Loop could serve as key links in a complete gorge trail. On the return, be sure to check out the ap-pealing, unnerving catwalk along the high-way bridge for the classic view of the falls.

NORTH CASCADES—
97. Stetattle Creek

Distance: 4 - 7 miles round trip   Time: Allow 2 - 4 hours
Elevation gain: 500 - 900 feet   Season: Almost year-round

A pretty waterfall and views of Pyramid and Colonial Peaks are the main attractions of this moderately easy trip. The trail doesn't receive a lot of use and disappears after a few miles, but is otherwise in good condition, and makes an enjoyable wilderness walk spring through fall. The valley is essentially untouched wilderness and was once a common route for mountaineers on their way into the Picket Range. The well marked trailhead is at the town of Diablo (*elevation: 900 feet; map, p. 206*). Turn left off the North Cascades Hwy. (SR 20) at MP 126 just before the Gorge Lake bridge, and in 0.7 mile park at the far end of the Stetattle Creek bridge.

The path begins in lawn, hugs the edge of the creek behind homes, then becomes more obvious in the woods. Short switchbacks are encountered in the first mile and several small streams are crossed before reaching Bucket Creek Falls (**2.0 mi**; *elevation: 1,400 feet*). Looking back down the valley from the opposite side of the creek, there are good views of Pyramid and Colonial Peaks across the Skagit gorge. Turn around here or continue several miles up valley, as time and interest allow. More streams are crossed (difficult during high runoff) and the tread becomes fainter at each crossing. About 1.5 miles beyond the falls, the huge rock walls of the northeast face of Davis Peak (the steepest mile-high wall in Washington) comes into view through the trees. The old trail becomes more obscured by brush and fallen trees, so rather than losing it, a turn-around may be in order. For a 5,100-foot grunt to gorgeous views and an old fire lookout, try the Sourdough Mountain Trail (*Hike #98*) nearby to the east.

NORTH CASCADES—
98. Sourdough Mountain

Distance: 10.4 - 21 miles round trip   Time: Allow 7 - 12 hours
Elevation gain: 5,100 - 5,500 feet   Season: Mid-July - October

The trudge up Sourdough Mountain is one of the most strenuous dayhikes in the North Cascades, though it is often done as an overnighter as well. Either way, the panoramic spectacle from the summit lookout makes every step worth the effort. There are actually two trails leading up to the summit, one from Diablo and the other from Ross Lake, called the Pierce Mountain Trail. The latter is not quite as steep but is about four miles longer, although you can cut off a mile by hitching a short boat ride to Ross Lake Resort (*see Hike #103*). To keep the logistics simple and avoid the extra distance, most dayhikers choose the Diablo start. A few have gone up one side and down the other, and a handful have followed the Diablo Lake Trail back to the start for a 21-mile marathon loop—not recom-

Sourdough Mountain, below the lookout.

mended for most mortals.

From the North Cascades Hwy. at MP 126, turn left and continue through the Diablo community, staying right at a fork in 0.9 mile to find the small parking area at 1.8 miles (*elevation: 900 feet; map, p. 206*). The trail begins behind a building (the Diablo community siwmming pool). There are usually a few places for water, but carry plenty on the lower stretch, especially in warmer weather or late in the season. About 0.5 mile above the start, a good view of the town and Diablo Lake offer a short hike option—and encouragement for the grander views above.

The trail immediately begins an unrelenting ascent of more than 3,000 feet of endless switchbacks, followed by another 1,100 feet of easier grades to a camp at Sourdough Creek (**3.8 mi**; *elevation: 5,000 feet*). Tank up on water here. The trail bends to the east a mile in meadows to a few more switchbacks, and finally, the wide open rocky ridge crest. The historic lookout is just ahead on a high point (**5.2 mi**; *elevation: 5,985 feet*). Originally built in 1917, it was reconstructed in 1933. The view includes Ross Lake and Jack Mountain to the northeast, Ruby Mountain to the southeast, Diablo Lake, Thunder Creek valley, and Pyramid and Colonial Peaks to the south, the Skagit gorge and Davis Peak to the southwest, McMillan Spires, the Picket Range, Mount Baker and Sourdough Ridge to the northwest, and Sourdough Lake and Big Beaver valley below to the north. Experienced hikers can also explore an intermittent boot track running northwesterly along the high ridge of Sourdough Mountain. The trail from the Ross Lake side leaves the West Bank Trail (*Hike #103*) about 3.8 miles from SR 20, and climbs. Trail may be a little vague and brushy in an old burn area. Continue up to the high ridge between Sourdough and Pierce Mountain (**4.0 mi**), and a few small campsites in a pretty location among rocky tarns and wide views. Then head up the ridge to the lookout (**5.1 mi**).

NORTH CASCADES—
99. Diablo Lake & Skagit Gorge

Distance: 5 - 11 miles round trip   Time: Allow 3 - 7 hours
Elevation gain: 800 - 1,900 feet   Season: May - Mid-November

With the North Cascades high country buried under meters of snow much of the year, good spring and fall hikes with a view can seem like a scarce commodity in our region. Fortunately, we have the Diablo Lake Trail running the north side of the Skagit River gorge to console us during those otherwise snowbound months of pre- and post-summer. While snow cover can be an issue at times (like anywhere else), the high point of the trail is only 2,000 feet above sea level—and south facing—which means little or no snow-pack and an early melt most years. Thus, count this one as an excellent three-season hike. Pleasant forest, good views and a scenic crossing of the river and gorge make it worth considering almost anytime, but beware of avalanche activity from above in spring and early summer; turn back if you're uncertain about the conditions. For best lighting, hike east to west in the morning. The hike makes a good through hike in which two parties exchange keys midway, or an extra car or bike is planted

Skagit Gorge below Ross Dam.

at one end. An in-and-out hike is a reasonable choice as well, beginning at either end of the route.

The east end of the trail is reached from the Ross Dam trailhead (*elevation: 2,100 feet*) on the north side of the North Cascades Hwy. (SR 20) near MP 134. The easiest access from the west is at Diablo Resort. From SR 20 MP 127.5 turn north onto Diablo Dam Rd. (gate may be closed late afternoon until morning). Continue across the dam, turn right and look for the signed trailhead 1.2 mile from the highway (*elevation: 1,200 feet; map, p. 206*). (Note that one can extend the hike another 1.1 miles to the town of Diablo below the dam. That trailhead is 0.4 mile past the Sourdough Mountain Trailhead (*see Hike #98*); take the narrow drive through a substation; angle right then left to find the Diablo Lake Trail just past the Diablo Incline; *elevation: 900 feet*. This trail is steep at first, then easy; at a road turn right. Walk to the dam and upper trailhead noted above.)

From Diablo Resort (the recommended start), the route is well marked and traverses up and around the North Cascade Institute's spanking new Environmental Learning Center. Cross a road, stay right at a junction, and continue on easy grades then a gradual climb to great views at 2,000 feet (**2.2 mi**). Enjoy this wide open stretch above the very steep north slope of the gorge, roughly the halfway point for a through hike (may be unsafe or impassable if snowy or icy). Pyramid and Colonial Peaks tower to the southwest; Jack Mountain rises to the northeast, Ruby Mountain to the southeast. Beyond, the trail passes under transmission lines and descends 700 feet to the river, passing a short view spur, then crosses the Skagit on a suspension bridge within sight of Ross Dam (**3.4 mi**). What a spectacularly wild canyon this must have been! Across the bridge, head right and follow the road through a tunnel, then steadily up and around switchbacks and over a rise to a fork (**4.5 mi**); stay right; left leads to the dam and the West Bank and Big Beaver Trails (*Hike #103*). From the fork, walk up a short distance to find the trail on the right (the road leads to the lakeshore and possible boat ride to Ross Lake Resort). Climb 0.8 mile to Happy Creek Falls and the Ross Dam Trailhead noted earlier, 800 feet above the river (**5.3 mi**). If starting here, simply reverse the route (head right after crossing the suspension bridge).

NORTH CASCADES—
100. Pyramid Lake

Distance: 4.2 miles round trip   Time: 3 - 5 hours
Elevation gain: 1,500 feet   Season: May - October

This attractive lake is at 2,600 feet elevation so the trail is free of snow much earlier and later in the year than many other areas of the Park. Although the scenery is not spectacular, the lake feels wild and remote. The trail is used by climbers as an approach to Pyramid and Colonial Peaks, but is also good for restless hikers looking for an early season conditioner. There are no comfortable campsites. The signed trailhead is located on the south side of SR 20 at Pyramid Creek, MP 126.8 (*elevation: 1,100 feet; map, p. 206*).

The path is steep at first to quickly gain a ridge crest then eases off, passing through a large stand of lodgepole pine. Soon, the creek draining the lake is crossed in an area of big cedars (**0.9 mi**). The trail follows the creek valley in a forest of more typical cedar and douglas fir. Plenty of berries line the path above later in summer. The trail cuts through a huge fallen fir tree just before the final steep climb to the lake (**2.1 mi**; *elevation: 2,600 feet*). A comfortable resting place is hard to find. For more ambitious types, an improved view of the lake and Pyramid Peak can be found by scrambling left over loose rock, or right along a rough boot track to a large split rock.

North Cascades—
101. Thunder Knob

Distance: 1.8 miles round trip   Time: Allow 2 - 3 hours
Elevation gain: 400 feet   Season: April - November

Thunder Knob is one of those rare trails in the North Cascades that has great views and is low enough in elevation to avoid most of the winter snowpack, a fine three-season-plus saunter. In 2001, the new trail replaced an old one, providing a good look at Diablo Lake and Colonial Peak. The path is packed gravel, generally in excellent condition, and may be accessible to the more athletic wheelchair hiker. From the North Cascades Hwy. (SR 20) at MP 130.3, turn north into Colonial Campground and find the well-signed trailhead at the north end of the loop next to site #21 (*elevation: 1,300 feet; map, p. 206*). If this small parking area is full, one can also park just outside the entrance to the campground and walk 0.3 mile along the loop road to the trailhead.

Hiker's rest at Thunder Knob.

The trail crosses Colonial Creek on a stout bridge, enters a peaceful douglas-fir forest, and makes a gentle ascent to switchbacks where a short steep section (ten percent grade) leads to lodgepole pine forest and a small saddle. Just beyond,, two benches offer fine lounging potential with an excellent view of Colonial Peak (**0.9 mi**). The path continues in forest, descends briefly to pass a small, pond then meets a fork. Explore the left fork for good views of Colonial Peak and well-named Pyramid Peak to the southwest, and to the northwest, the double rock fangs of McMillan Spires rising above the Stetattle Creek valley and the steep north wall of Davis Peak. The right fork leads to a good view of Jack Mountain, one of the few non-volcanic mountains of the North Cascades that exceed 9,000 feet in elevation (**1.8 mi**; *elevation: 1,700 feet*). Sourdough Mountain is across the lake to the north. Both views have benches.

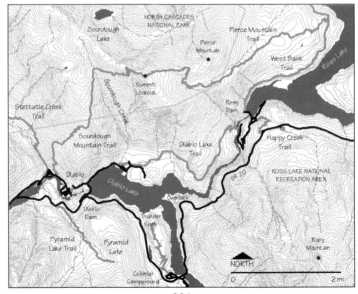

NORTH CASCADES—
102. Thunder Creek & 4th of July Pass

Distance: 2.2 - 11.7 miles round trip   Time: Allow 1 - 8 hours
Elevation gain: 100 - 2,400 feet   Season: April - November

Near Diablo Lake, the trail up this broad valley is an easy walk and leads to a number of popular destinations in the National Park. A nature trail and historic river crossing offer short, easy walks over an extended season, while Fourth of July Pass is a moderate climb up the southwest side of Ruby Mountain; at the pass, snow-pack may linger into June. Drive to the Colonial Creek Campground on the south side of SR 20 at Diablo Lake (MP 130.3). Campers will find the trailhead near the amphitheater. For others, the hike begins at a trailhead just above the big parking lot (*elevation: 1,200 feet*).

Shortly before a bridge crosses Thunder Creek, the 0.9-mile long Thunder Woods Nature Trail loops up and right through the forest (grades are moderately steep). Cross Thunder Creek on the main trail (**1.1 mi**); the rotted piling of an old bridge can still be seen—a reminder of the mining boom that occurred here more than a century ago. The trail passes a spur to Thunder Camp and climbs easily to a junction with the Fourth of July Pass Trail on the left (**2.1 mi**). The Pass is a moderate 2,300-foot climb in three miles. After the first mile the going gets easier, steepening again in the last mile. At Fourth of July Camp (**4.8 mi**), Colonial and Snowfield Peaks are visible

Trillium.

across the valley. Farther along the trail, Panther Potholes (ponds) are seen below on the right and a wet forested saddle is reached (**5.4 mi**; *elevation: 3,600 feet*). The Panther Creek Trail descends north-easterly 5.5 miles to SR 20 at the east end of Ruby Arm, a nine-mile drive from Colonial Campground.

On the Thunder Creek Trail, one can continue up-valley from the Fourth of July junction 2.7 miles to an opening with good mountain views. Extended backpack trips to Park Creek Pass or Easy Pass both offer high-end wilderness possibilities (overnight permit required). Old mining relics are still visible along the route.

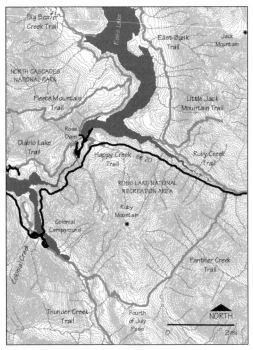

NORTH CASCADES—
103. West Bank & Big Beaver Creek

Distance: 7 - 17 miles round trip   Time: Allow 5 - 12 hours
Elevation gain: 1,000 feet   Season: April - November

Before emptying its snow and glacial meltwater into Ross Lake, Big Beaver Creek follows gravity down a major low-elevation valley of majestic old-growth forest. One of the largest groves of old-growth cedar trees anywhere in the Cascades is found here. The trail represents the east portion of a classic 40-mile trek from Hannegan Pass, but the lower stretch could be visited by strong hikers in a day—with a prearranged water taxi from the Ross Lake Resort (www.rosslakeresort.com). One can also reach Big Beaver by way of a seven-mile hike to Ross Dam and along the West Bank Trail—a long round trip for a day, however. Nevertheless, the West Bank Trail is also worth walking and makes a more moderate outing by itself. Several other possibilities are suggested below. All options begin at the Ross Dam Trailhead on the North Cascades Hwy. near MP 134 (*map, p. 206*).

On the way down to Ross Dam from the highway.

Descend the trail 800 feet to a road (**0.8 mi**) and turn right for the water taxi, or left, then right on the next road through a deep cut to cross the dam. The boat will take you to Ross Lake Resort not far to the north, or you can walk there by crossing the dam and hiking mostly easy, scenic trail in good condition. At this point catch the boat or keep walking. Beyond the resort, a spur leads down to a campground at Green Point, and soon a junction with the Pierce Mountain Trail is met (**3.8 mi**; *see Hike #99*). Finally, cross a steel bridge to find the Big Beaver Trail (**6.0 mi**), 0.2 mile from the boat landing. To explore the valley, head left. The best part of this leg is about three miles up, with large cedars near the trail for the subsequent two miles. Bears are occasionally seen. If you've arranged it, meet the boat at the landing for the return, leaving only the final mile to hike up to the Ross Dam Trailhead. Or reverse the route just described. Or, hire the boat both ways to skip the West Bank altogether. (Too many choices!)

NORTH CASCADES—
104. Happy Creek

Distance: 0.3 mile round trip   Time: Allow 1 hour

Elevation gain: Minimal   Season: April - November

In the 1990s, North Cascades National Park received funding from the Skagit Environmental Endowment Commission to develop this delightful boardwalk loop through the woods of Happy Creek near Ross Lake. The Commission was established in 1984 as part of a treaty between the U.S. and Canada that addressed impacts of the Ross Lake Dam and reservoir on lands that were, or might be, inundated in British Columbia. Seattle City Light who owns and operates the Ross, Diablo and Gorge Lake hydroelectric projects also agreed not to raise Ross Dam for at least 80 years. The Commission received several million dollars in funding from each side of the border and uses this endowment to fund environmental education, nature-based recreation, restoration, preservation, and scientific research within the upper watershed of the Skagit River. Happy Creek is one of the many projects funded to date.

Happy Creek in early winter.

Find the trailhead next to the North Cascades Hwy. (SR 20) at MP 134.4 (*elevation: 2,200 feet; map, p. 208*). In winter, when the gate is closed at the Ross Dam trailhead, the trail may still be within easy reach, just 0.5 mile beyond the gate. The walk is short (**0.3 mi**) and wheelchair accessible with gentle grades. Kids seem to enjoy this one also. The walkways are elevated above the ground, preserving the forest floor almost completely intact. Just being a few feet off the ground allows an interesting perspective into an ecosystem, subtly different from the usual ground-level view. Interpretive signs explain what nature has been up to. Happy Creek can also be combined with the steep hike down toward Ross Dam (*see Hike #99*).

NORTH CASCADES—
105. Little Jack Mountain

Distance: 11 - 17 miles round trip   Time: Allow 7 - 12 hours
Elevation gain: 4,000 - 5,500 feet   Season: Mid-June - October

All the high ground along this trail is south-facing, which allows the winter snowpack to recede quickly, sometimes by late May (no guarantee, of course). That makes this strenuous outing one of the best early summer hikes to the North Cascades' awesome alpine country. Wildflowers may be early too. The views are exceptional any time. Water is scarce by mid-summer, so bring plenty. The Little Jack Trail begins at a junction with the East Bank Trail at Ross Lake. Find the trailhead east of the lake on the north side of SR 20 near MP 138, about four miles beyond the Ross Dam Trailhead (*elevation: 1,800 feet; map, p. 208*). Hike down to the bridge across Ruby Creek (*see Hike #107*) and turn left. Follow the mostly easy grade to the Little Jack junction (**2.6 mi**). A spur drops left to the lake. The East Bank continues 28 miles along the lake to Canada. But turn right

Ross Lake and Ruby Arm from Little Jack Mountain Trail.

here and follow the trail up and east, turning dozens of moderately steep switchbacks on the climb to timberline. Views of neighboring peaks and Ross Lake glimmering below steadily improve on the ascent to a camp near the ridge crest (**7.5 mi**; *elevation: 6,400 feet*). If there's energy left, wander up the ridge another mile, plus 700 feet of vertical, for the grand vista (**8.5 mi**), including Jack and Crater Mountains to the north and east, Ruby Mountain and the Skagit gorge and lakes to the southwest, and the Picket Range to the west. A good boot track continues for several miles—this is a climbers approach to Jack Mountain, a long and serious climb requiring mountaineering skills and equipment.

NORTH CASCADES—
106. Crater Lake & Lookout

Distance: 11 - 15 miles round trip   Time: Allow 7 - 12 hours
Elevation gain: 4,000 - 5,400 feet   Season: Mid-July - October

This is a strenuous day trip also suited to a two or three-day overnighter for experienced backpackers. The high cirque of Crater Mountain guarding this tiny lake, plus excellent views of near and distant peaks, offer sufficient rewards for the effort it takes to get there. There is good camping near the lake. Below, water can be scarce after mid-summer. The trailhead is east of Ross Lake at the confluence of Granite and Canyon Creek, just east of MP 141.2 on the North Cascades Hwy. (SR #20; *elevation: 1,900 feet*). Follow the Canyon Creek Trail to the stout footbridge over Granite Creek and stay left (**0.1 mi**), passing a junction with the Canyon Creek Trail (to Chancellor), and reaching an old cabin and footlog over Canyon Creek (**0.2 mi**). Once across the latter, follow the Devils Park/Crater Mountain Trail northeast (upstream) through what seems like endless forest switchbacks, with occasional views and a few small stream crossings along the way. After a gain of 3,400 feet a junction at the subalpine meadows of McMillan Park is reached (**4.2 mi**). Stay left to reach Crater Lake (**5.0 mi**; *elevation: 5,800 feet*). A huge wall of rock surrounds the lake—generally snow-free by mid-July. For great views, take the old trail to the right up to a former lookout site (**7.0**

mi; *elevation: 7,054 feet*), overlooking Jerry Glacier, Jerry Lakes and Jack Mountain. Or, head leftward along the lake and 300 feet up to the crest of a low ridge to the southwest, passing several campsites. With sufficient time and energy one can hike nearly up to the west summit—the site of the original Crater Mountain fire lookout—about two miles and 1,500 feet above the lake. The trail ends at a series of dangerous cliffs (if snow-free and dry, experienced mountaineers can expect Class 2 and 3 rock climbing to the summit). At the McMillan Park junction, the Devils Park Trail is good for multi-day trips, including a 43-mile loop around Jack Mountain (described in other guides).

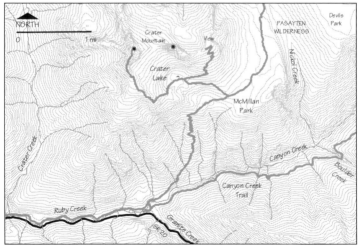

107. Ruby Creek & Canyon Creek

Distance: 2.6 - 11.8 miles round trip   Time: Allow 2 - 7 hours
Elevation gain: 200 - 800 feet   Season: May - November

W hen a walk in the woods is all you need to collect your thoughts, oxygenate, revitalize, or just break up the drive across the North Cascades, the Ruby Creek and Canyon Creek Trails (also called the "Chancellor Trail") are a good choice, particularly in crummy weather or early season when the high ground is still snowed in. With a bike shuttle, key swap or a patient driver, one can walk the scenic 2.6-mile Ruby Creek Trail from one trailhead to the next, or head up Canyon Creek as far as time allows. The Ruby Creek Trail is accessed from the East Bank Trailhead near Ross Lake, on the north side of SR 20 after MP 138 (*elevation: 1,800 feet*). Descend 100 feet to the creek, cross the bridge and turn right; left is the East Bank Trail to Ross Lake and Little Jack Mountain (*see Hike #105*). It's a pleasant stroll upstream to a skinny footbridge over Canyon Creek (**2.4 mi**); the

Footlog over Boulder Creek.

north-side trail continues up to McMillan Park and Crater Mountain (*see Hike #106*). But cross the log bridge to an old cabin and head right. At a nearby junction, the Canyon Creek Trail to Chancellor goes left. For the one-way Ruby Creek hike, continue straight to cross Granite Creek on a stout bridge and stroll rightward to the easterly parking lot (**2.6 mi**). This is the Canyon Creek Trailhead which is also on the north side of SR 20 at MP 141.2.

For the Canyon Creek hike, use the eastern trailhead and follow the wide path to the Granite Creek bridge. Cross and continue to the "Chancellor" junction (**0.2 mi**); turn right. The path climbs up a bank then ascends easy to moderate grades in deep forest. The trail does not get a lot of use by dayhikers and is more commonly experienced as one leg of a multi-day trek. As a day trip, the scattered ruins of the 1872 mining town of Chancellor may be a bit far to go, at 9 miles, but there are other more attainable destinations. After gaining about 500 feet in elevation, the path begins to descend and meets a spur on the left to "Rawley's Chasm" (**1.8 mi**). There once was an interesting bridge over an abyss not far down the spur, but it has collapsed and the path is no longer very interesting (exposed, not maintained and not recommended). Continue on the main trail with minor ups and downs, and pass a couple of small creeks, including one with a very nice waterfall in early season. Pass a good view of the canyon with Ruby Mountain in the distance. The trail descends to a skimpy footlog over Boulder Creek with another partial view just around the corner (**3.5 mi**); a good turn-around point. It's another two miles to Mill Creek and five more to Chancellor.

North Cascades—
108. PCT: Harts Pass to Grasshopper Pass

Distance: 6 - 11 miles round trip   Time: Allow 4 - 7 hours
Elevation gain: 500 - 1,000 feet   Season: Mid-July - October

This is an outstanding day hike on one of the finest segments of the Pacific Crest Trail (PCT) in the North Cascades. The trailhead is very high (*elevation: 6,500 feet*) and elevation gain is minimal. The PCT extends from Mexico to Canada and the route through the North Cascades of Washington State is superb. Longer trips are often made between Rainy Pass on SR 20 to Manning Park in British Columbia. Several guidebooks can be consulted to learn the details of such a trip. A few good campsites are available, though water sources are far apart by mid-summer; carry extra.

For a day hike, drive SR 20 over Washington Pass to Mazama, turning north at MP 186 (60 miles east of Newhalem). In 0.5 mile turn left and follow the signs 19 miles to Harts Pass (*elevation: 6,200 feet*). The gravel road is steep, narrow, winding and well used, especially on the weekends. It is usually in good condition, although some hair-raising curves about 12 miles from SR 20 require serious caution! About 0.1 mi *before* the pass, turn left to find the trailhead at the road end in 1.7 miles (past Meadows Campground). Due to

PCT near Grasshopper Pass.

high elevation, the road and trail are often snow covered into July.

Hike through trees then contour the open slopes up to a small saddle at the ridge crest for the first good views. Robinson Mountain dominates the scene to the northeast. The trail gently gains another 400 feet, climbing around a minor summit to another crest at 7,000 feet (**2.3 mi**). Continuing west, Tatie Peak is passed on the south and a saddle is reached just beyond. An easy rock scramble leads up from here to Tatie's 7,386-foot summit. On a clear day, the top of Mount Baker is visible far in the west.

The trail turns south, drops over a ridge, descends then climbs a bit to open meadows at Grasshopper Pass (**5.2 mi**). Azurite Peak and Mount Ballard tower high to the southwest and northwest across the South Fork of Slate Creek. The steep trail to Glacier Pass is visible below, but is not recommended as a day hike. The ridge crest to the south makes a nice saunter. This ridge system is the divide between the Skagit and Columbia River watersheds, it is the crest of the Cascade Range, and the line between Whatcom and Okanogan Counties.

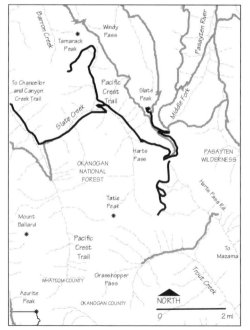

218

NORTH CASCADES—
109. PCT: **Slate Peak to Tamarack Peak**

Distance: 3.0 - 12.5 miles round trip   Time: Allow 2 - 6 hours
Elevation gain: 200 - 2,100 feet   Season: Mid-July - October

Comparable to the Pacific Crest Trail (PCT) south of Harts Pass (*Hike #108*), this stretch heading north is high and wild—and relatively easy walking for miles. One can walk for minutes, hours or days, if so inclined. The 40-mile stretch from Harts Pass to Canada represents the final leg of the 2,638-mile ultimate mountain trek from Mexico to Canada. For a taste of it, try the walk from either the pass or the trailhead below Slate Peak to Windy Pass or beyond. Tamarack Peak is more or less a "walk-up" for more experience hikers, but there is plenty to see from the main trail as well. From Harts Pass (*see Hike #108*), head up the road (right) 0.3 mile to an obvious trailhead on the left, or to cut 0.9 mile from the hike continue another short mile to the Windy Pass Trailhead on the left at a switchback

West Fork Pasayten River valley from the PCT.

(*elevation: 6,800 feet*). The road may still be blocked by snow into July. If dry, it's worth the short drive up to a gate below the summit of Slate Mountain—the highest point you can drive to in Washington, and where a short walk up the last bit of road leads to a lookout tower (*elevation: 7,440 feet; map, facing page*). This is the gorgeous crest of the Cascade Range.

From the switchback below, the trail follows gentle grades through a wonderland of flowery meadows and scattered subalpine timber, passing Benson Basin and Buffalo Pass with good views to the east. The trail has made a long gentle descent by the time you reach Windy Pass (**4.0 mi**; *elevation: 6,257 feet*),. The area's mining history becomes evident with the sight of old jeep tracks, diggings and a few buildings down in the trees. Some of these sites are actually privately owned, so best to leave them some space. Just ahead, Tamarack Peak's broad green slopes rise to 7,290 feet. The trail bends around the east side of the mountain, passing a bowl (camping) and climbing up to a rocky ridge crest with a great view of Foggy Pass and beyond. This is a good turn-around for a day hike. Experienced scramblers may be able to follow a boot track up this ridge to a thin, exposed ridge leading to the summit of Tamarack where it's possible to work down easy slopes through meadow and forest (easterly) to Windy Basin and the Pass, and the return to the trailhead.

Cascade Crest from Slate Peak Lookout.

NORTH CASCADES—
110. Hozomeen Lake & Willow Lake

Distance: 7.0 - 11.5 miles round trip   Time: Allow 4 - 8 hours
Elevation gain: 300 - 1,000 feet   Season: May - November

The remote north end of Ross Lake is seldom visited by Whatcom Countians. This is the northern segment of a trail that runs the entire length of Ross Lake, ending at Ruby Creek and SR 20, 31 miles distant. From Bellingham, access to this scenic blitz (save it for a sunny day) is by way of Hope, B.C., an hour and a half drive from Bellingham (via Sumas). Just before Hope and the bridge across Silverhope Creek, turn right on the Skagit-Silverhope Rd. to Ross Lake. Drive another 39 miles, crossing the border into North Cascades National Park.

There is a short interpretive trail worth visiting at the international boundary near the park entrance station. Find the well marked trailhead for Hozomeen and Willow Lakes in the campground area, often full on summer weekends (*elevation: 1600 feet*). This is the primary hike to be done from this end of Ross Lake and the trail is well maintained to both lakes. Note however, that

Hozomeen Lake is closed in early summer to protect nesting loons, when Willow Lake is the better destination.

The trail climbs through forest south of Hozomeen Creek, gaining nearly a thousand feet to a junction (**3.0 mi**). Hozomeen Lake is an easy walk left up the spur trail (**3.5 mi**; *elevation: 2,700 feet*). The views of the towering summits of Hozomeen Peak from the lakeshore are no less than spectacular. All three peaks had been climbed by 1951. From the junction it is another two miles and an easy 200-foot gain to a meadow at Willow Lake, tucked in a canyon due north of Desolation Peak. Beyond, the trail drops into the long crescent valley of Lightning Creek between Skagit and Desolation Peaks, the latter a famous Jack Kerouac lookout retreat.

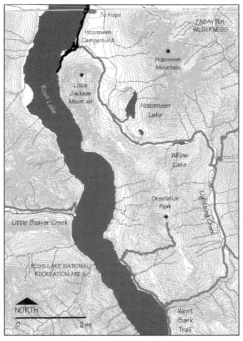

Other Hikes

We are fortunate in Whatcom County to have a great selection of trails in the North Cascades, the Chuckanuts, and in the city of Bellingham, while new trails are also happening in Blaine, Lynden, Everson and Ferndale. What's missing, however, are more public trails in the rural lowlands and foothills. While many unofficial trails do exist in these areas, they often cross private land which tends to limit their accessibility to the public. Listed below are a few trails that are generally open to the public, although some may be subject to landowner permission:

To enhance the regional trail system, just completing a few of the potential trails noted in the Introduction would go a long way toward filling in some of the major gaps, but we will need to secure funding and work out the details with landowners to get them developed. Trail user organizations and others can and do get involved in advocating for specific trails, as well as providing help with volunteer maintenance. If you want to help make a new trail happen, or prefer to roll up your sleeves and do a little grubbing on the trail, contact your local park department. Whatcom County Parks and Recreation offers an Adopt-a-Trail program, and the City of Bellingham runs a Greenways volunteer program, and both can help get you pointed in the right direction.

Here are some possibilities to consider...

Lummi Mountain

Two former routes 1,500 feet up the north and east sides of Lummi Mountain both crossed private lands and public access has become difficult. Hopefully a new public-friendly route will materialize eventually. If it does, views west into the San Juan Islands are fantastic. The entire south end of Lummi Island is unique in Whatcom County and has the potential for an excellent, albeit limited, wilderness trail system utilizing old road beds and some new trails. Sensitive wildlife habitat requires special care in locating any new trail.

Portage Island

Off the end of Lummi Peninsula and within the Lummi Nation, this undeveloped island is physically accessible to hikers at low tide and a stroll around the island on an old road grade offers good potential. However, access to the island requires prior permission from the Lummi Tribe. At one point, the island was supposed to become a public park and natural area as part of a settlement reached with Whatcom County many years ago. The tribe wants both natural and cultural resources protected.

Lummi River Dikes
This area is also within the Lummi Nation and access may be limited. From the Red River Road, miles of dikes stretch across the delta of the historic mouth of the Nooksack River. Bird life is a strong attraction, and winter walks are enjoyable. Permission may be required.

Ferndale Pioneer Park
The city's favorite park has been expanding recently to include ballfields, natural areas and a looped trail system. Access is off Ferndale Rd.

Chuckanut Mountain
A future trail network is planned to connect existing trails and park facilities in this urban wilderness south of Bellingham. Likely connections are: Larrabee, Arroyo and Fairhaven Parks, the Interurban Trail, the north Lost Lake and Chuckanut Ridge trails, Fragrance Lake, and Pine and Cedar Lakes. Many routes will follow old logging roads. A few will be designated hiker-only.

Other Areas in the Foothills
Forested foothills, including Lookout, Stewart, Sumas and Black Mountains, Van Zandt Dike and other high hills are etched with extensive logging roads, old and new, and a few horse, hiker and mountain bike trails, some of which are worth exploring. A few are described in this guide, but others could be hiked as well. State lands are generally open and most large timberland owners accommodate some degree of non-motorized recreational access, which generally precludes camping or fires. Permission may be required in some areas.

Federal Lands
There a few abandoned trails and remnants on National Forest and National Park lands which may offer some potential for the intrepid hiker, but these are probably best omitted from the guidebooks. Veteran hikers in the region may help you sleuth them out. Avoid brushing out old, overgrown trails on park or wilderness lands. Many old logging roads are walkable as well. A couple of old trails that are still routinely visited, though not frequently, include:

Silesia Creek

This old trail appears on many maps and leaves the pass east of Twin Lakes, descending into lovely old-growth forest in the valley bottom. The route once continued to Canada, but nature has totally reclaimed that portion (not passable). Most of the trail above Silesia Creek was recently brushed out, but it was still in generally poor condition in late 2002.

Swift Creek

This old trail extends from near the Mount Baker Hot Springs to the Lake Ann Trail below Austin Pass. Some areas are overgrown, hard to follow, and critical bridges are missing at Swift and Rainbow Creeks (2.0 and 0.5 miles from the south end, respectively). These crossings are dangerous much of the spring and summer and only marginally passable by late summer or fall at low water. If going, start at the bottom to see if the creeks are negotiable, otherwise it's a long slog back out to Austin Pass in the event you hiked all the way down the main valley and were forced to turn back.

Chilliwack River

Few folks from outside Canada ever visit Chilliwack Lake, a spectacular gem, eh, in a wild and rugged setting. The rough trail up the river that feeds the lake penetrates a classic ancient forest of giant cedar and fir, and leads to North Cascades National Park, less than 2 miles in (backcountry permit required for the border crossing). Unfortunately, the trail was seriously blocked by downed trees a few years ago, has not been maintained, and has become very difficult to follow. Should you decide to give it a try, here is the description from a previous edition of this guide:

From Bellingham, drive Mt. Baker Hwy. and SR 9 to the border crossing at Sumas. Continue north to the Trans-Canada Hwy. (#1) then east to Chilliwack. Take the Chilliwack-Sardis exit and go south to the Chilliwack River bridge; turn left before crossing. Follow this road to its end at the south end of Chilliwack Lake, two hours from Bellingham (stay right at Paleface and Depot Creeks). Walk the old road 200 yards to the trail on your left. The path enters a grove of mature cedar, then hardwoods, then bigger cedars (up to 10 feet across). Walk as far as you like, negotiating fallen logs, occasional brush, and footlogs over small streams (some may be difficult). Reach the border at 1.7 miles. Beyond, the trail passes several camps and gradually improves as it climbs to junctions with Copper Lake, Hannegan Pass and Whatcom Pass trails (all overnight trips). An exciting suspension bridge crosses Indian Creek seven miles up. Brush is worst mid-June to mid-September. And watch out for bears, eh.

Picture Lake

The wheelchair accessible path at Picture Lake is not a forgotten trail at all, but is a bit short for a full write-up. It is a beauteous subalpine stroll nonetheless. Find it next to the highway below the Mt. Baker Ski Area, just after the road becomes a one-way loop.

Heather Meadows

Just above the Mt. Baker Ski Area in summer is a fine little paradise for easy and moderate hikes, scenic picnic sites, a visitor center and more, including a 0.5-mile interpretive loop trail, wheelchair accessible and partly paved. Amble meadows to the lake shore and look out at a whole lot of scenery.

Artist Point (July-October)

Drive Mt. Baker Hwy 2.5 miles past the ski area to a parking lot at the road end (may be snowbound into July). Wander the easy trail atop Kulshan Ridge to Huntoon (Artist) Point a half-mile to the southeast. The 360-degree view from Mt. Baker to Mt. Shuksan is incomparable. The Rainbow and Park Glaciers of Mt. Baker gleam in the morning sun, while towering Mt. Shuksan and the ice cliffs of the Curtis and Hanging Glaciers loom to the east. Northward are Tomyhoi, the Border Peaks, Mt. Larrabee and Goat Mt. Baker Lake glistens far below while Glacier Peak and Mt. Rainier glow against a distant smoggy sky. Several other trailheads are located nearby (*see Hikes #70, #71 and #73*).

East Bank Trail (Ross Lake)

See Hikes #105 and #110 for directions to the south and north ends of this 31-mile trail up the east side of Ross Lake, from SR 20 to Canada. It is a classic walk, with plenty of easy stretches and modest ups and downs, including some elevation gain to get over Hidden Hand Pass near the south end, and around the east side of Desolation Peak near the north end. Boat access on the lake can be arranged for a possible drop-off and a walk back out, with or without spending a night or two in camp.

Panther Creek

This trail leaves south from SR 20 across the road from the Ruby Creek/ East Bank Trailhead and climbs to Fourth of July Pass (*Hike #102*). It is not often hiked due to an odd section near the start that takes you hundreds of feet up, then hundreds of feet back down for seemingly no reason at all, before continuing up again on a more gradual ascent next to the scenic creek.

East Creek

Beginning near the county line east of Ross Lake, the East Creek Trail starts out steep but in good shape for a few miles, then deteriorates near a junction at four miles. The main route bends south to Mebee Pass four miles beyond, with a link down the other side to the Pacific Crest Trail and the Methow River. From the four-mile junction, an old trail passes an old mining area and climbs steeply to a 6,400-foot crossing of the East Creek–Boulder divide, descending north to the Canyon Creek Trail near Mill Creek. Both trails can be rough, brushy and/or difficult to follow in places.

Skagit County

Several hikes in the Blanchard Mountain area are officially in Skagit County but are of much interest to Whatcom County residents and were therefore included in this guide. A new guide to other trails in Skagit County should be published later in 2003. That guide will provide descriptions for other areas in the lowlands and foothills, like Anderson Mountain and the Pacific Northwest Trail, as well as hikes on federal lands that are near the Whatcom-Skagit County line, such as Dock Butte, Blue Lake, Newhalem Creek, Cow Heaven, Diobsud Creek, and many others.

Parks

Public parks around the county are briefly noted here. Note that Washington State Parks began charging a daily parking fee of $5.00 per vehicle at the beginning of 2003. Cyclists and walk-ins do not have to pay the fee. If you are among the many who believe that free access to our parks and trails should be one of the basic rights we enjoy as taxpayers, then please contact the governor's office and your local state representative to insist that these fees be eliminated and that our public parks and trails be adequately funded. Interestingly, parks are one of the few government services that actually produce more tax revenue from visitors than what they cost to run. So if money's the issue, we should be expanding, not shrinking, our park system.

All city and county parks are free to enjoy by area residents, although the county does collect a nominal $4 fee (per vehicle) from out-of-county users. No parking or day-use fees are charged on federal lands, including North Cascades National Park; however, trail parking passes are required at most trailheads (*see p. 41*).

Bellingham Parks

CORNWALL PARK

This 65-acre park in maturing forest has a fitness trail, picnic and play areas, tennis courts, horseshoes, a rose garden and the babbling waters of Squalicum Creek. The park is located east of Meridian St. and north of Illinois St. Eventually, the Bay-To-Baker Trail may connect the park with Bug Lake and Sunset Pond to the east, and the proposed Little Squalicum Park to the west (*see Hike #16 for more*).

MARITIME HERITAGE PARK

This park, marine center and salmon hatchery has become the largest public greenspace and recreation site in the downtown area. Paved trails, viewpoints and a pedestrian bridge at lower Whatcom Falls provide access to Whatcom Creek (watch for spawning salmon in the fall). A "hill-climb" amphitheater and extensive native landscaping were added several years ago. Boardwalks and more trails have been proposed by the city to connect with the waterfront and Squalicum Harbor. The park is located between Prospect and West Holly (*see also Hikes #19 and #21*).

Zuanich Point Park

Zuanich is a Port of Bellingham facility on the outer lobe of Squalicum Harbor. Named for a long-time port commissioner, attractions include nicely maintained lawns, benches overlooking Bellingham Bay, a gazillion boats, a memorial to lost fishermen, the spendy-looking Squalicum Boathouse, and a paved walkway connecting with extensive bicycle and pedestrian facilities around the harbor. The park is a kite-flyers' favorite as well. From Roeder Avenue, head west on Coho Way and take a left at the stop sign (*see also Hike #8*).

Sehome Hill Arboretum

Every denizon's favorite, this 180-acre nature reserve is adjacent to the university and offers a viewing tower and six miles of foot trails with access points on all sides (*see Hike #23 for more*). "Sehome" comes from the name of a Clallam Tribal leader. The hill was logged off and burned in the 1870s, but by the 1920s the city had acquired much of the hill for a park. Scenic drives were constructed around the summit, though the views would soon be obscured by the reemerging forest. With the support of the university, the arboretum was established in the early 1970s and the roads were closed to traffic.

Boulevard Park

One of the most-utilized and appreciate parks in the city, Boulevard got its start as a site for heavy industry and has since been converted to a site of lawns, picnic and play areas, walkways, a pedestrian pier, and a viewing tower—which the city recently spoiled with an unsightly and view-obstructing cage (*see Hike #9*).

Marine Park

Facing Bellingham Bay off the end of Fairhaven's Harris Ave., Marine Park is a small but popular place whenever good weather beckons. Lounging, picnicking, kite-flying, and launching a kayak are among the favored activities at this Port of Bellingham facility (*see also Hike #10*).

Fairhaven Park

Just south of Fairhaven off Chuckanut Dr., this old park still charms with big lawns, picnic shelters, trails, bridges, a salmon stream (Padden Creek), as well as tennis and basketball courts, and a small wading pool (*see also Hike #25*).

Whatcom Falls Park

Whatcom Falls Park is 241-acre urban wilderness gem. Several beautiful waterfalls, a stone bridge, maturing forest, miles of hiking and biking trails, play and picnic areas, a kids fishing pond, and a state trout hatchery make this an attractive destination anytime. Annually, the hatchery rears millions of rainbow trout and Lake Whatcom kokanee (the latter are released as fry in area lakes). The bridge was built in 1939 by Roosevelt's Works Progress Administration from recycled Chuckanut sandstone harvested from a downtown building that had been destroyed by fire. The park is located near the intersection of Lakeway Dr. and Electric Ave. (*see also Hike #20*).

Lake Padden Park

The city's largest park (over 1,000 acres) includes a golf course, a lake nearly a mile long, over ten miles of horse, bike and hiking trails, ballfields, picnic areas, shelters, showers, boat launch (non-motorized) and more (*see Hikes #26 and #27 for several enjoyable treks around the lake*). The park is located on the south side of Samish Way about two miles southeast of its intersection with I-5 in Bellingham.

Arroyo Park

An urban wilderness park, Arroyo has some of the nicer woods around, plus great trails and a salmon stream (Chuckanut Creek). About 1.5 mile south of Fairhaven, at the edge of the Chuckanuts (*see Hike #28*).

Undeveloped Parks

Several undeveloped park sites in Bellingham may see improvements in coming years, including Little Squalicum (*see Hike #7*), Northridge (*Hike #18*), Salmon Park (*Hike #21*), and at least two unnamed parks: one north of Squalicum Pkwy. and another on Galbraith Mt. south of Lakeway Dr. (*Hike #42*).

Blaine Parks

Marine Park

A first-class waterfront park, Blaine's Marine Park occupies an extensive portion of the Semiahmoo Bay shoreline. There are trails, lawns, picnic shelters, wildlife viewing platforms, interpretive signs, an amphitheater, a totem pole, fishing dock, an intriguing orca sculpture, a diorama dedi-

cated to lost seafarers, and more. The park is located just west of the last
I-5 exit before Canada (*see Hike #3 for details*).

Lincoln Park

East of I-5 on the north side of H St., Lincoln Park is a refuge of undeveloped nature offering a 0.5-mile loop trail through a lovely conifer forest. Trails are easy to follow. Park near the sign across the street and just
beyond shoppersville.

Montfort & Skallman Parks

These small parks in Blaine may be of more interest to area residents.
Montfort is mostly wooded with short grassy paths and a good view of
Drayton Harbor. From Peace Portal Dr. turn on Hughes (opposite Sweet
Rd.), then left on Dodd one block. Skallman has a duck pond next to a
tiny oasis of cedar and fir trees, but in a commercial area next to the
airport. Find it hidden off Yew Ave. a long block south of Boblett St.

Lynden Parks

Lynden City Park

Lynden City Park's ten acres straddles Fishtrap Creek north of the downtown area off Depot Rd. and has the usual play and picnic areas, as well
as the city's principal trail corridor (*see Hike #14*). Fishtrap Creek gets
its name from the fact that, historically, Native Americans trapped an
abundance of salmon on the creek.

Berthusen Park

Managed by the City of Lynden, this 236-acre park and forest preserve
was donated to the city by Hans and Lida Berthusen in their will. Several paths through a 24-acre grove of old-growth douglas fir and cedar
offer a glimpse of the great forest that once covered much of the Whatcom
Basin. A city plan calls for a two-mile connecting trail from Lynden to
the park. There's a campground, play areas, horseshoes, a 1913 barn,
meeting hall, old farm equipment on display, and a cuddly carved black
bear peers out from a stump near the creek. Portions of the land are
leased to farms, nursery and a gun club. The Antique Tractor Association holds an Annual Threshing Bee here. Head north of Lynden on the
Guide Meridian, then left on the Badger Road a mile, turning left again
on Berthusen Road and right into the park (*see also Hike #37*).

Ferndale Parks

Pioneer Park

Beginning as a 25-acre historic park, Ferndale's famed Pioneer Park has been expanding recently with the addition of more land for ballfields, trails, play areas and an arboretum. A new parking lot is on Ferndale Rd., just south of the park. The central charm, however, is the eleven log cabins dating to 1873 that were relocated here from around the county many years ago to preserve a portion of the region's heritage. Tucked among big cedar trees, the park makes a fine stop for a picnic and stroll. A nearby dike could eventually become part of the Nooksack River Trail linking Ferndale to Hovander Park and beyond. From I-5, turn left off Main St. as you enter downtown Ferndale.

VanderYacht Park

VanderYacht is a 13-acre park on former farmland adjacent to the Nooksack River, quiet, with a 0.5-mile loop trail (*see Hike #15*).

Everson/Nooksack Parks

Riverside Memorial Park

A small riverfront park off the west end of Main Street in Everson, with ballfields, a cabin and an interesting historic interpretive trail. This could become an important access to the Nooksack River Trail some day, if adjacent landowners are willing to accommodate it (*see Hike #41*).

Nooksack City Park

A small community park with trees, lawn and play area. Located 0.5 mile north of South Pass Rd., on the east side of SR 9.

Sumas Parks

Sumas City Park

The city park in Sumas straddles Johnson Creek and offers a small respite from the hubbub of border traffic. The park is east of SR 9 a few block south of the Canadian border.

Newhalem Parks

Much of the company town of Newhalem, at the foot of the North Cascades, feels as though it could be one big park. Lawns, gardens, paths, picnic areas, historic sites and access to the Skagit River are dominant features. A pastoral, small-town ambience tugs at all the highway traffic and many do stop and look around. The towns sprang up with development of Seattle City Light's upper Skagit dams—Gorge, Diablo and Ross—from 1918 through the 1960s, and many workers still raise there families here. There is much history and beauty to be explored in this easterly outpost of Whatcom County, and a few short hikes to boot (*see Hikes #93, #94 and #95*).

Whatcom County Parks

Lighthouse Marine Park (Pt. Roberts)

Lighthouse is a 22-acre park on the tip of Point Roberts, a six square-mile peninsula that overlooks the Strait of Georgia and the Gulf Islands of British Columbia. You'll find boardwalks, creative covered picnic facilities, a view tower, boat ramps and campsites adjacent to a half-mile of sandy marine beach. Short beach walks are possible any time (*Hike #1*). Occasionally in spring grey whales may be seen migrating offshore, while orcas are more common in summer. In August plan to attend the annual arts and crafts festival at the park, a major summer event.

Semiahmoo Park (Blaine)

Whatcom County's 20-acre Semiahmoo Park is located on the narrow neck of a unique 1.3 mile long sandy spit. This unusual landform was naturally constructed by currents that bring sediments northward from high eroding bluffs to the south. At its narrowest point, opposing beaches are only yards apart, certainly an odd place for a road. At the turn of the century, a large fish cannery and company sailing port occupied the spit (some structures still exist). The interpretive facilities and historical library at the park illustrate those memories well. Canoe rentals are sometimes available for exploring the protected waters of Drayton Harbor and the Blaine Marina, and clam shovels may be available. Directions: Take I-5 exit 272 to Portal Way, then immediately turn left on Blaine Rd. Follow the signs to Semiahmoo Resort. (*See also Hike #2.*)

Tennant Lake/Hovander Homestead Park (Ferndale)

See Hikes #39 and #40 for information and directions to this important nature preserve and historic site on 346 acres. Interpretive facilities, a fragrant herb garden with labels in braille, view towers, boardwalk trail through a swampy lakeshore, a nicely preserved turn-of-the-century barn and farmhouse, and summer cultural events like the Scottish Highland Games and international folkdancing highlight these adjoining Whatcom County parks just south of Ferndale.

Samish Park (Bellingham Area)

Whatcom County's first major park, Samish occupies 39 acres, has a quarter-mile of lake front, and is great for swimming, canoe paddling and picnicking. Canoes and pedal boats are often rentable in summer. A quiet trail wanders the lakeshore to the west and another climbs north to an overlook (*Hike #34*). From I-5 exit 246, follow North Lake Samish Rd. to the park on the right.

Squires Lake Park (Alger)

This relatively new 80-acre park was a joint project of Whatcom and Skagit Counties and the Whatcom Land Trust (and an anonymous donor) in 1995. A looped trail system circles the lake and overlooks a beaver pond. (*See Hike #45 for details.*)

Silver Lake Park (Maple Falls)

This scenic 411-acre park is considered by some to be the finest county park. The steep forested slopes of Black Mountain rise above the opposite shore, while slightly rolling forest and lawns within the park offer good camping, picnicking, paddling, creative lounging, and aimless wandering on lonely forest paths and a boardwalk and bridge across a shallow bay. Several rustic and inviting cabins (rentable) are perched above the shoreline, but you'll likely need a reservation (www.co.whatcom.wa.us/parks/cabins.htm). The historic, beautifully crafted Gerdrum House stands against Red Mountain to the west. The park makes a great base camp for other hiking areas in the region north of Mt. Baker. Group picnic areas, children's play areas, a boat launch (under 10hp), horse stables and camps, fishing, swimming, showers, and paddling are also available. Drive 31 miles east of Bellingham on the Mt. Baker Hwy. (SR 542) to Maple Falls. Turn left on the Silver Lake Rd. Its about 3.5 miles to the park entrance (*see Hike #54*).

Washington State Parks

Peace Arch State Park (Blaine)
At the Blaine I-5 border crossing, Canadian and Washington State park agencies maintain extensive lawns and gardens converging on the Peace Arch. The Arch was built in 1914 with money raised by kids to commemorate the lasting friendship between the two countries. Take exit 274 and follow signs a short way to the northeast. Also visit Blaine Harbor west of I-5 and look for the new trail and viewing areas along the waterfront.

Birch Bay State Park (Blaine Area)
Fortunately, this park was established before the beach could be developed with a crowd of vacation cottages like those that line much of the bay to the north. A mile of sunny beaches and warmish water makes this a gem among marine parks. In summer, thousands of visitors fill the entire community, so early morning, weekday or off-season visits are recommended. Campsites, restrooms, and countless picnic tables and grills are available. The variety of bird life is amazing in winter and spring. (*See Hike #38 for directions.*)

Larrabee State Park (Bellingham Area)
Washington's first state park, Larrabee is one of the finest marine parks in the Northwest. The dramatic rocky shoreline borders a verdant forest of old and tall douglas fir, western red cedar, Pacific madrone and big cottonwoods. Picnic shelters and tables, boat launch, many campsites, two mountain lakes, scenic viewpoints, and at least twenty miles of hiking trails (and the potential for a lot more) make this a great place to visit many times over. Several paths give access to tide pools at low water. (*See Hikes #11, #12 and #13 for more.*) The park is about 5 miles south of Fairhaven on Chuckanut Drive (SR 11).

Federal Lands

North Cascades National Park Complex
The combined North Cascades National Park and Ross Lake and Lake Chelan National Recreation Areas comprise one of the largest (1.2 million acres) and most outstanding wilderness recreation areas anywhere in the U.S. Major campgrounds are located at Newhalem, Goodell Creek

and Colonial Creek. Fishing and boating are popular on the Ross and Diablo Lake reservoirs. Hundreds of miles of trails lead up through virgin forests and gorgeous meadows, along high scenic ridge tops overlooking glaciers, lakes and clouds. Some of the finest territory is very remote and can only be reached after a day or two backpacking. Still, many day trips are possible, with a number of them noted in this guide. Excellent maps and up-to-date trail information are available through the Marblemount Ranger Station, at Newhalem, and at Sedro Woolley Park headquarters. The Park is east of Marblemount north and south of the North Cascades Hwy. (SR 20).

National Wilderness Areas

Three outstanding wilderness areas occupy lands in Whatcom County, including the Mt. Baker and Noisy-Diobsud Wilderness Areas (132,000 acres total) west of North Cascades National Park, and the larger Pasayten Wilderness (530,000 acres) to the east. Major features close to Bellingham include Mount Baker and the Twin Sisters Range, The Border Peaks, Nooksack Ridge, and numerous lakes, streams and forests surrounding the icy landmark volcano. The Pasayten extends east of Ross Lake into Okanogan County and contains some of the most remote high country anywhere in the Northwest. Several hundred miles of hiker and horse trails penetrate these wildlands. There are no roads or development in these areas, although camping and boating facilities are available in nearby National Forest and National Recreation Areas. Further information may be obtained from Forest Service Ranger Stations in Sedro Woolley, Mazama and Winthrop.

Efforts to preserve the wilderness resources of the Mt. Baker region date back to the turn of the century, finally succeeding (partially) in 1984. Spectacular as it is, most of the area is rock and ice, or high elevation old-growth forest not suited to timber harvest, which helps to explain why environmentalists have been so determined to save what little is left of the lower elevation ancient forest. To learn more or to help save the rest, see www.wildwashington.org.

Viewpoints & Water Access

Point Roberts Peninsula

At the county park, there are good views of Canada's Gulf Islands across Georgia Strait. Many birds and occasionally orcas (summer) and grey whales (spring and fall) are seen. Residents have been working to develop a pedestrian pier off the end of Gulf Rd. Maple Beach at the northeast corner of the Point is another good spot. Experienced paddlers can launch a kayak at all three locations. Take binoculars. (*See also Hike #1*.)

Blaine Harbor (Blaine)

See Hike #3 for details about this first-class urban waterfront area in Blaine. Paths, overlooks, the boat harbor, boat ramp, and a public fishing dock at the west end of Marine Dr. offer nice views. The historic MV Plover docks here for the short run to Semiahmoo on summer weekends.

Semiahmoo Spit (Blaine)

From this spit near Blaine on a fair day, see Drayton Harbor, Semiahmoo Bay, Mt. Baker, the Olympics, and the city of White Rock, B. C. The foot ferry, MV Plover, offers wildlife watching on the short summer run to and from Blaine. An easy place for launching a kayak or canoe, small boats have also been rented here in summer. (*See also Hike #2*.)

Birch Bay

Although Birch Bay can get a little crowded on warm summer weekends, the extensive beach areas at the state park are well worth visiting on weekdays, or anytime between September and May. Take your binoculars for bird life. Hand-carried boats are easily launched at several locations. (*See Hike #38*.)

Cherry Point

This is one of the few good beaches in the county that are not within a park, so there are generally fewer folks around to share it with. The San Juan and Gulf Islands are visible, as are the terminal facilities of the nearby refinery and aluminum industries. Experienced paddlers can also launch here. Good for sunsets also. Find it off Gulf Rd. 0.5 mile south of Henry Rd. (*See Hike #5*.)

Lake Terrell

A beautiful 500-acre marshy lake, Lake Terrell makes up one-third of a 1,500-acre state game range, popular with fishermen, waterfowl and pheasant hunters. The range was established for the "production and harvest of wild game" in 1947, although the north half is closed to hunting. A small dam on the creek helped form the lake. Photographers, paddlers, and bird watchers equally enjoy its serene character. There are a few paths and two boat launches for small craft. For hunting season information, check www.wa.gov/wdfw/huntcorn.htm. From I-5 (exit 262), head west through downtown Ferndale and stay on the main road as it curves west out of town, becoming Mt. View Road. In 4 miles, turn right on Lake Terrell Rd. The lake is a half-mile north. Return to Mt. View Rd. and continue west a half-mile, curving right on Rainbow Rd. A good viewpoint is on the right (signed).

Tennant Lake (Ferndale)

The unique view tower, interpretive center and boardwalk on the lake shore make 80-acre Tennant Lake worth more than a visit for the view. The lake forms the heart of a 720-acre reserve jointly managed by Whatcom County Parks and the Washington Department of Fish and Wildlife. There are no boat launch facilities. (*See Hike #39.*)

Lummi Island

Lummi Island is a great place, as any islander will attest: it's scenic, there's little traffic (good for biking), roads are narrow, and the atmosphere is generally relaxed. Unfortunately, public access to some of the more interesting features is seriously lacking. The once-popular hike up Lummi Mountain has no public access. Access is iffy to Inati Bay and points south, including hundreds of acres of state land. Even most of the beaches are private. At the west end of Legoe Bay Rd., a privately-owned rocky knoll called Lovers Bluff was used informally by the public for many years. Unfortunately, the current owners have asked us all to keep out. This unique bluff easily deserves protection, perhaps as a pocket park for walk-in or bike-in visitors. Lummi Island has slowly lost many of its public-friendly places, sharply countering the traditions some of us once knew. For now, either lament the situation, or just go pedal a bike around the north end for a quiet ride with limited views. The islanders are still friendly folks. From Bellingham, head 14 miles out Marine Dr. and Lummi Shore Dr. (views of Bellingham and Mt. Baker), or from I-5 (exit 260), head west on Slater Rd. 3.7 miles, then south on Haxton Rd. about 6 miles to the Lummi Island ferry dock. Ferry crossings are every hour. Look to the right as you exit the ferry for a small overlook with a bench.

Little Squalicum Beach

This public beach is accessible by trail and from the new parking area adjacent to Mt. Baker Plywood (*see Hike #7*). The parking area is suitable for kayak launching.

Squalicum Harbor (Bellingham)

The harbor is the only area of the downtown waterfront that is reasonably accessible to the public, although it's heavily developed. The marina and Zuanich Point Park are suitable for launching small craft, or taking an easy stroll to watch boats motor in and out of port. (*See Hike #8*.)

Boulevard Park Tower (Bellingham)

Besides offering a fine view of Bellingham Bay, this tower supports a pedestrian bridge over the railroad mainline into Bellingham. Sailboats litter the bay in fair weather. Lummi Island and Lummi Peninsula form the opposite shores. Stroll along the pier at the park's south end. It's feasible to launch a hand-carried boat at the park as well. From downtown, follow State St. and the Boulevard south about 2 miles to Bayview Dr. Turn right at the park sign and drive down the hill to the parking lot. The tower is hard to miss (and can somebody please get rid of that awful cage!. *See Hike #9*).

Sehome Hill Tower (Bellingham)

Certainly the finest vantage point from which to view the city, this tower is located at the north end of the Sehome Hill Arboretum adjacent to Western Washington University (*see Hike #23*). Beyond the cityscape are Bellingham Bay, Georgia Strait, the San Juan and Gulf Islands, Whatcom County's lowland basin, B.C.'s Coast Range, and Mt. Baker and the Twin Sisters Range. Sunset is a good time to visit, although the park closes at dusk. From Samish Way, follow Bill McDonald Parkway and take the first right past the high school. Follow this narrow paved road 0.7 mile to the parking lot at the top. Short paths to the tower are well marked.

Clark Point (Bellingham)

A pleasant spot near the Edgemoor neighborhood overlooking Bellingham Bay—used to be a great place to watch a storm or a sunset, but the area is closed now, thanks to the greedy railroad nerds and their tacky signs and fences. On the bright side, a significant portion of this outstanding peninsula was protected from urban encroachment when the munificent Clark family gave up development rights to ensure its preservation. For many, many years one could access the shore of Chuckanut Bay from the end of Fieldston for a fine stroll at low tide, but that too is fenced off. Kayakers now have the best views at Clark Point.

Cyrus Gates Overlook

From the end of the Cleator Rd. (gravel) at Larrabee Park, the view of the San Juan Islands, Samish Bay, Bellingham, western Whatcom County and even Canada is exceptional. Drive four miles south of Fairhaven on Chuckanut Drive (SR 11) turning left on Cleator (or Highline) Road just before the park. The overlook is 3.2 miles up the narrow, mostly unpaved road. At the last road switchback (a hard right curve), a good viewpoint of Lost Lake and Mt. Baker is less than a 100 yards distant along an obvious path (*see Hike #32*).

Chuckanut Drive

This winding narrow highway (SR 11) is a popular ten-mile scenic drive overlooking Bellingham, Chuckanut and Samish Bays. There are numerous turnouts from Larrabee State Park and beyond. Follow the signs south from Fairhaven. Watch out for bicycles, falling rocks and wondrous sunsets. Other than at Larrabee State Park, there are no public facilities for boat access.

Lake Samish

See Samish Park and trail listings (*Hike #34*) for directions and details concerning this jewel of a lake west of I-5 a few miles south of Bellingham. Swimming, small boat access and dock facilities are available at the park. There is also public fishing access and boat ramp on the east side, midway down the lakeshore.

Lake Whatcom

This glacially carved, beautiful and somewhat over-developed 5,000-acre lake is one of the more dominant and striking landscape features of the region. Perhaps best enjoyed by way of the Lake Whatcom Trail (*Hike #46*), the lake has several public boat launch areas where a paddler or small day sailor can put in for an hour or a day. Because this is the region's primary drinking water source, motorized boats are strongly discouraged, especially those with standard two-stroke engines which are known to release large amounts of unburned fuel into the water. Bloedel-Donovan Park at the north end and a Washington Department of Fish and Wildlife boat ramp at the south end are the principal access points. A quieter, little used access by way of a trail can be found at Euclid Park, east of Euclid Ave., north of Lakeway Dr. The university owns and maintains access facilities for students, faculty and alumni at Lakewood, just north of Sudden Valley.

STIMPSON NATURE RESERVE
A 350-acre complex of state land and adjoining properties that were partly donated and partly purchased now provide one of the most significant nature reserves in the Lake Whatcom watershed, including a long-protected beaver pond (*see Hike #43*). A second 369-acre reserve and former estate of Leila June Olson was recently acquired by the city and county for similar watershed protection purposes and limited public enjoyment (*see Hike #44*).

TOAD LAKE
Renamed "Emerald" Lake by developers as a marketing ploy, locals seem still to prefer "Toad" as the more official moniker of this placid water body high on a hill. A public fishing access and small boat launch can be found off the end of Emerald Lake Way east of Britton Rd., a half-mile south of Mt. Baker Hwy.

SQUALICUM LAKE
A very small lake with lily pads and a skinny access lane south off Mt. Baker Hwy. near its intersection with Y Rd.

NOOKSACK RIVER
The mainstem of the Nooksack can be accessed for viewing and for small boats at several locations, including Hovander Homestead and a public boat ramp near Ferndale (*Hike #40*), at VanderYacht Park (*Hike #15*), at a fishing access south of the Guide Meridian bridge over the river (a tricky turn, avoid it when traffic is heavy), and beneath the Nugent's Corner bridge on Mt. Baker Hwy. The Lummi Tribe and Washington

Department of Fish and Wildlife manage lands closer to the mouth of the river. Recently, a major acquisition by the state of 600 acres along the east shore of the river from Slater Rd. to Marine Dr. almost doubled the size of the Tennant Lake Wildlife Area and will benefit hunters, hikers—and, of course, fish and wildlife (*see also Hikes #39 and #41*).

Wiser Lake

South of Lynden, the Guide Meridian passes through the middle of Wiser Lake—an environmental no-no that would be much harder to pull off today. To access the eastern part, watch for the small boat launch next to the highway at the north shore.

Fazon Lake

Another small lake with a public fishing access, just east of Everson-Goshen Rd., and north of E. Hemmi Rd.

Deming Homestead Eagle Park

In 2000, the Whatcom Land Trust received a major donation from the Deming area Rensick family of this original homestead that is now an eagle-watching park in winter and a pleasant picnic spot the rest of the year. Short trails and interpretive signs are also here. The park is south of Mt. Baker Hwy. at MP 15 on Truck Rd., 0.6 mile ahead. Views are good but there is no easy river access.

Kendall Fish Hatchery

This state fish hatchery south of Kendall welcomes visitors to see the rearing ponds and facilities where they have raised chinook, coho and chum salmon, steelhead, and rainbow and cutthroat trout for transplant to area lakes and streams. From Mt. Baker Hwy. at MP 21.1 take the Fish Hatchery Rd.

Silver Lake

See Silver Lake Park and Hike #54 for directions and details about this attractive lake and county park north of Maple Falls. Small boats can access the lake at the park or at a public fishing access near the north end, 1.4 miles north of the park entrance.

Wickersham/Twin Sisters Range

A popular stopping point for travelers on SR 9 offers the closest view of the Twin Sisters Range from a paved road. Head north from Wickersham to a highway turnout just north of MP 68. The rural ambiance of the broad South Fork Valley is capped by Mt. Baker just left of the North Twin Sister. The South Twin is flanked on the right by Skookum, Hayden, Little Sister and Cinderella Peaks.

South Fork Nooksack River

Recent acquisitions by Whatcom County Parks and the Whatcom Land Trust have secured park lands, an historic homestead and several miles of riverfront property along the South Fork Nooksack. River access is difficult and seasonally discouraged to help protect declining salmon runs. (*See Hike #48*.)

Middle Fork Nooksack Gorge

A nice view of an interesting gorge on the Middle Fork Nooksack River can be reached by way of a 30-minute round-trip hike to the City of Bellingham's diversion dam. Water is scooped into a large tunnel blasted through the mountain which empties into Mirror Lake, which in turn drains to Lake Whatcom to augment the city's water supply. The future of the diversion is uncertain, given the nuances of local water politics, water quality concerns in the lake, and the needs of imperiled salmon. Drive Mt. Baker Hwy to MP 16.8 and go right on Mosquito Lake Rd. In 4.6 miles, head left on Porter Creek Rd. (USFS Rd. #38); park in two-plus miles at a gated spur road next to a sign suggesting we take care of our watershed. Walk down the spur to a bridge for the view. Someday a spectacular two-mile trail could lead down the canyon from here to the Mosquito Lake Road bridge.

Canyon Lake

Whatcom County Parks and the Whatcom Land Trust have also secured much (2,300 acres) of the Canyon Lake watershed east of Deming, including a unique 600-acre stand of old-growth yellow cedar, with some trees nearly 1,000 years old. There are excellent trails here, but no boat access facilities. Fishing is allowed, but no motor boats (*see Hike #49 for more*).

Mount Baker Viewpoints

From Bellingham, this great 10,778-foot volcano is mostly obscured by foothills. Often only the top third or half (three to five thousand feet) are visible, making it appear much smaller and more distant than it actually is (25 miles). The illusion is broken by viewing the peak from a few miles north of Bellingham. Try Noon Road north of Hemmi Road where pastoral farms might interest photographers. Several vantage points exist along the Mt. Baker Hwy. (SR 542), near Deming and between Maple Falls and Glacier. Try the roadside attraction at MP 29.5 where an informative sign discloses that Captain Vancouver's Lieutenant Baker spotted the mountain in the spring of 1792.

What has long been the best view anywhere by car is at the end of the Glacier Creek Rd. #39. Turn right off Mt. Baker Hwy. (MP 34.3) just beyond the old ranger station. Mt. Baker and the Black Buttes (an ancient eroded volcanic cone) are visible at several points, but the best view is near the end of the road at 4,200 feet, 9.3 miles from the highway. Some minor, but strategic tree-pruning is needed to keep this classic view from being obstructed altogether. A scene from the movie, *Deer Hunter*, was filmed here in the late 1970s. It's spooky to see how much the Coleman Glacier has receded since that scene was staged. Nevertheless, the massive Roosevelt and Coleman Glaciers illustrate why this is considered the iciest of the Cascade volcanoes. Rock features include the Cockscomb on the left skyline and the Roman Nose, an S-shaped ridge extending up the right side of the volcano. Climbers and their tracks can often be seen beneath the Black Buttes (a.k.a. Colfax and Lincoln Peaks) leading to the saddle on the right skyline.

Another excellent view is from Artist Point at the end of the Mt. Baker Hwy. (see below). A good view from the southeast is near Baker Lake Dam, a mile east of Baker Lake Rd., about 13 miles north of SR 20. The Easton, Squak, Talum, Boulder and Park Glaciers appear as one solid mass of ice. In some years, mud flows (lahar) are visible on Boulder Glacier below the steaming crater. See Hikes #79 and #80 for access to the Easton Glacier, and Hike #72 for a good view of the Mazama, Rainbow and Park Glaciers. Many of the Mount Baker area hikes listed in this guide provide great views of the mountain as well.

Glacier Public Service Center

Formerly the Glacier Ranger Station, this historic service center provides displays, maps, books, trail passes, restrooms, friendly staff, and current information on trail and road conditions in the Mount Baker area. It's located on Mt. Baker Hwy. just east of Glacier at MP 33.8, and is generally open 8 am to 4:30 pm daily from Memorial Day to mid-November and weekends the rest of the year.

Boyd Creek Interpretive Trail

East of Glacier, this very short walk of about 0.1 mile, is really more of a viewpoint with an opportunity to learn about, and possibly observe, spawning salmon. Nevertheless, it's a wild place with a nice boardwalk, viewing platform and interpretive information—worth a visit. From mid-summer to fall, look for chinook and pink salmon, and from fall to mid-winter, coho. You might even see steelhead or sea-run cutthroat in the spring. The fish enter from the North Fork Nooksack River across the road.

Nooksack Falls

One of the largest and most impressive waterfalls in the county is found on the North Fork Nooksack River about seven miles east of Glacier. The viewpoint is perched on a high cliff where the thundering 170-foot falls disappear into mist, tempting some to scramble around the fence for a supposedly better view—DON'T! Because of the contour of the rock walls, the view is not any better anywhere else, and way too many young people have died trying. Fortunately, the view has improved considerably with some recent, careful pruning of vegetation. Across the gorge, Wells Creek rushes headlong into the river. There's a nice historical display and a memorial to those who've perished here, all of them young. Turn right off the Mt. Baker Hwy. at MP 40.6 on Wells Creek Rd. #33. Park in 0.6 mile immediately before the river bridge. On a clear day continue up this road about five miles for a good view of Mount Baker and the Mazama Glacier.

Picture Lake (year-round)

Follow Mt. Baker Hwy. to aptly named Picture Lake at MP 54, just before the ski area. Park at the west end. This view of Mt. Shuksan reflected in the water is said to be the most photographed scene in the North Cascades and the picture is hung on walls around the world. Lighting is best during the later part of the day. The Picture Lake loop trail is an easy subalpine garden walk on a paved path suitable for wheelchairs. The road is plowed to the ski area in winter when the views are even better.

Heather Meadows & Artist Point

(See the note on these gems under Other Hikes.)

Baker Lake

Many campgrounds, lake access and picnic areas are available at Baker Lake—plus good views of surrounding mountains. Mount Baker is visible from the Boulder Creek bridge, from the lake itself (by boat), and from near the dam. (*See also Hikes #77, #88, #89 and #91.*)

Goodell Creek

On the way across the North Cascades, a rare glimpse of the towering pinnacles of the southern Picket Range is found at the turnoff to Goodell Creek Campground, and from a short boardwalk path at the National Park Visitor Center west of Newhalem. There are no roads or maintained trails into the Pickets. Some of the most challenging alpine mountaineering anywhere in the Cascades is done in this remote region. Turn right off Hwy. 20 at MP 119.4 and immediately look to the north, or continue to the well-signed visitor center just ahead. Pinnacle Peak, also called the Chopping Block, is most prominent. See also Hike #93.

North Cascades Visitor Center

The North Cascades National Park Visitor Center just west of Newhalem is definitely worth checking out—nice exhibits to the sounds of nature. It's open every day from mid-April to mid-November, and weekends only the rest of the year (9 am - 4:30 pm; later in summer).

Gorge Creek Overlook

Beyond Newhalem, the North Cascades Hwy. enters the spectacular gorge of the Skagit River. A dramatic tributary, Gorge Creek, offers the first good place to get off the road for a few photographs. The signed parking lot is at MP 123.5. Test your fear of heights on a pedestrian catwalk over the gorge, gazing through your feet to the noisy water below. A sizeable waterfall in an old geologic fault intensifies the scene above. Hang on to the kids! The creek is dispensing meltwater from the snowfields high on Davis Peak. (*See also Hike #96.*) Access to Gorge Lake is just ahead near the town of Diablo.

Diablo Lake Overlook

This is a definite stopping point while traveling across the North Cascades Hwy. The geological interpretive exhibits are excellent: you will know exactly what Skagit Gneiss (like "nice") looks like when you leave. The views of Diablo Lake, (a Seattle City Light reservoir on the Skagit

River), Jack Mountain, and the Colonial Peaks, including Pyramid, Snowfield and Paul Bunyan's Stump, are impressive. In summer the lake turns brilliant green from rock flour carried by streams from the glaciers above. The large parking area is 1.6 mile beyond Colonial Creek Campground at MP 131.7. Access to the lake is off the Diablo Dam Rd. near Diablo Resort, and at Colonial Campground on Thunder Arm (*see Hike #102*).

Ross Dam

One cannot drive to Ross Dam itself and it's not easy to see from the road. The best view of the dam from the North Cascades Hwy. (SR 20) is at a small turn-out at MP133. A mile east at MP 134, an 0.8-mile trail leads steeply down from the highway, passing a waterfall on the way to a good view above the dam and reservoir; or keep walking (left then right) to the dam (*see Hike #99*). Originally called Ruby Dam, it was renamed for the illustrious Seattle City Light Superintendent, J. D. Ross.

Washington Pass

Another excellent viewpoint, this one is actually ten miles outside of Whatcom County, but it should not be missed during your trip across the North Cascades Hwy. From a high cliff near the crest of the Cascade Range, gaze up at the huge rock pinnacles of Liberty Bell Mountain and Early Winter Spires. On a sunny summer day, one can observe (with binoculars) climbers ascending the sheer rock faces. To the east, Silver Star Mountain and the Wine Spires shred the skyline. The turn-off is north from the pass (MP 162.4) and is well signed. Follow the short paved access road to a parking lot and restrooms. Two easy paths lead to the viewpoint; the lower one is wheelchair accessible.

Harts Pass & Slate Peak

Harts Pass and nearby Slate Peak are the highest points you can drive to in the North Cascades (the road is steep, narrow and little frightening in spots). This is still Whatcom County, 115 miles from Point Roberts, at the crest of the Cascade Range and the divide between the Skagit and Columbia River basins. The Pacific Crest Trail passes through the area (*see Hikes #108 and #109 for details and directions*). From the PCT Windy Pass Trailhead, the road continues another mile to a parking area. Walk the last half-mile or less to the summit lookout. The view is great but the summit is one big scar. The US Air Force carved the top 70 feet off the mountain in 1960 for a radar station that was later abandoned.

Campgrounds

Lynden
Berthusen Park, over 50 sites, south of Badger Rd. on Berthusen. Info: (360) 354-2424

Whatcom County Parks & Recreation
(360) 733-2900; www.co.whatcom.wa.us/parks/parklist/campsites.htm
Lighthouse Marine Park, 30 sites, Marine Dr. at Point Roberts (no reservations accepted)
Silver Lake Park, many sites, also rustic rentable cabins. On Silver Lake Rd., north of Maple Falls

Washington State Parks
(888) 226-7688, www.parks.wa.gov/reserve.asp
Larrabee State Park, 87 sites, close to saltwater, off Chuckanut Dr. five miles south of Bellingham
Birch Bay State Park, 167 sites, close to the bay, off Birch Bay Dr. southwest of Blaine
Rasar State Park, 49 sites, 14 miles east of Sedro Woolley
Rockport State Park, 62 sites, near Rockport on SR 20

Washington Department of Natural Resources
Hutchinson Creek, this site recently closed due to vandalism, but could reopen; off Mosquito Lake Rd. two miles east of Acme
Reil Harbor, Small, boat-access only campground mid-way along the east shore of Lummi Island

Mt. Baker-Snoqualmie National Forest
Some campgrounds on National Forest (and National Park) lands are open year-round; most are open at least from late May through early September. But many are not, due to a variety of factors. Call ahead in the off-season to be sure. Fees and facilities vary. (360) 856-5700, www.fs.fed.us/r6/mbs/recreation/activities/campgrounds/index.shtml

North Fork Nooksack River
Nice facilities are accessed from Mt. Baker Hwy. east of Glacier:

Douglas Fir, 28 sites on the river near Horseshoe Bend Trail (*Hike #55*)
Excelsior, 2 sites on the river (group camp only)
Silver Fir, 20 sites on the river just beyond Hannegan Pass Rd.

Baker Lake Area

A number of campgrounds are maintained along the lake, by way of Baker Lake Rd. off SR 20 north of Concrete:

Kulshan, 108 sites, with boat ramp near the lake's south end
Horseshoe Cove, 34 sites, with boat ramp near lake's south end
Bayview, group site only, 2 sites
Panorama Point, 15 sites, with boat ramp midway up the lake
Boulder Creek, 8 sites, minimal facilities, midway up the lake
Park Creek, 11 sites, minimal facilities, midway up the lake
Shannon Creek, 19 sites, with boat ramp near the north end of the lake

Marblemount Area
Marble Creek, 23 sites, minimal facilities, Cascade River Rd.
Mineral Park, 8 sites, minimal facilities, Cascade River Rd.

North Cascades National Park
Campgrounds in the NCNP are first-come, first-served (no reservations). (360) 856-5700, www.nps.gov/noca/pphtml/camping.html

Goodell Creek, 21 sites, open all year (free in the off-season, but no services); off North Cascades Hwy west of Newhalem
Newhalem Creek, 111 sites, near the National Park Visitor Center off North Cascades Hwy at Newhalem
Colonial Creek, 162 sites, North Cascades Hwy at Diablo Lake
Hozomeen, 122 sites, north end Ross Lake; access is from Hope, B.C.

Ross Lake
A number of sites with minimal facilities are available to boaters and hikers. Some are boat access only. Those with trail access are listed below (south to north). For more information on these and other boat-access sites, see www.nps.gov/noca/rola/rosslake.htm, or call

Green Point, 5 sites   **Big Beaver**, 7 sites
May Creek, 1 site   **Rainbow Point**, 3 sites
Lightning Creek, 6 sites   **Devils Junction**, 1 site
Lodgepole, 3 sites   **Cat Island**, 4 sites
Little Beaver, 5 sites

Hiking Organizations & Agencies

Organizations

Bellingham Mountaineers, P. O. Box 3187, Bellingham, WA 98227 www.bellinghammountaineers.org
Bellingham Mountain Rescue Council, P.O. Box 292, Bellingham, WA 98227
Mount Baker Hiking Club, P.O. Box 73, Bellingham, WA 98227, www.mountbakerclub.org
Nooksack Nordic Ski Club, P.O. Box 28793, Bellingham, WA 98228 www.nooksacknordicskiclub.org
North Cascades Audubon Society, P.O. Box 5805, Bellingham, WA 98227, www.northcascadesaudubon.org
North Cascades Conservation Council, P. O. Box 95980, University Station, Seattle, WA 98145, www.northcascades.org
North Cascades Institute, 810 State Route 20, Sedro Woolley, WA 98284, www.ncascades.org
Northwest Ecosystem Alliance, 1208 Bay #201, Bellingham, WA 98225, www.ecosystem.org
Pacific Northwest Trail Association, PO Box 1817, Mount Vernon, WA 98273, www.pnt.org
Sierra Club, Cascade Chapter: Mt. Baker Group, P.O. Box 1722, Bellingham, WA 98227, www.mtbakergroup.org
Skagit Alpine Club, P.O. Box 513, Mt. Vernon, WA 98273, www.skagitalpineclub.com
Washington Native Plant Society, www.wnps.org
Washington Trails Association, www.wta.org
Whatcom Association of Kayak Enthusiasts (WAKE), Bellingham, www.wakekayak.org
Whatcom Land Trust, Bellingham, www.whatcomlandtrust.org

Agencies

Bellingham Parks & Recreation, 3424 Meridian, Bellingham, WA 98225, (360) 676-6985, www.cob.org/parks
Mountain Pass Report, (800) 695-7623, www.wsdot.wa.gov/traffic/road/mnts/mntbas.htm

North Cascades National Park, Sedro Woolley, (360) 856-5700, www.nps.gov/noca, Marblemount Ranger Station, Marblemount, WA 98267, (360) 873-4590

Northwest Weather & Avalanche Center, www.nwac.noaa.gov

Northwest Forest Pass, www.fs.fed.us/r6/mbs/passes

U. S. Forest Service, Mt. Baker District, Sedro Woolley, (360) 856-5700, www.fs.fed.us/r6/mbs/contact/mbrd.shtml, Glacier Public Service Center, Glacier, (360) 599-2714

Washington Department of Fish & Wildlife, Olympia, www.wa.gov/wdfw

Washington DNR, NW Region, Sedro Woolley, (360) 562-6010, www.wa.gov/dnr

Washington State Parks, 7150 Cleanwater Lane, Olympia, WA 98504, (360) 562-0990, www.parks.wa.gov

Washington State Patrol, Bellingham, (360) 676-2076

Weather Forecast (NOAA), www.wrh.noaa.gov/Seattle

Whatcom County Parks, 3373 Mt. Baker Hwy, Bellingham, WA 98226, (360) 733-2900, www.co.whatcom.wa.us/parks

Whatcom County Sheriff, Bellingham, (360) 676-6650

ALL EMERGENCIES: CALL 911

Index

About the author...

A resident of Northwest Washington since 1967, Ken Wilcox is an avid explorer of the sprawling hills and mountains we call the North Cascades. When he isn't hiking trails and climbing mountains—habits that ought to last a lifetime—Ken works as a writer and consultant for environmental and recreation projects. He is author of *Hiking the San Juan Islands* (2001), *Hiking Snohomish County* (1998), and *Chile's Native Forests: A Conservation Legacy* (1996). He lives in Bellingham.